Traditional Country Cooking

from Herschberger's Country Bakery

Sweet Heart

© August 2007 Herschberger's Country Bakery

All rights reserved. No portion of this book may be reproduced by any means, electronic or mechanical, including photocopying, recording, or by any information storage retrieval system, without written permission of the copyright owner, except for the inclusion of brief quotations for a review.

For additional copies contact your local bookstore or

Herschberger's Country Bakery
Post Office Box 93
Jasper, NY 14855

Carlisle Printing
OF WALNUT CREEK Ltd.

2673 TR 421
Sugarcreek, OH 44681

Introduction

First we'd like to say a special "Thank you" to all those who may have helped in the preparation of this cookbook by the way of taking time and sharing their tasty traditional favorites with us. We hope everyone will have as much fun cooking, canning, and using helpful hints as we've had putting it together.

We have endeavored to put traditional favorites of family and friends in order to provide an outstanding book of tasty and delicious recipes that can be enjoyed by all. In this wonderful book, you'll find many recipes that use simple ingredients, you will normally have on hand anyway.

You'll also find a section on Health Advice and Home Remedies. Again, we thank everybody and hope you have many happy and tasty meals from the pages of Traditional Country Cooking.

Emanuel and Esther Herschberger

Contents

Equivalents

3 Tbsp.	1 Tbsp.	16 oz.	1 lb.
2 Tbsp.	1/8 c.	1 oz.	2 Tbsp. fat or liquid
4 Tbsp.	1/4 c.	2 c.	1 pt.
8 Tbsp.	1/2 c.	2 pt.	1 qt.
16 Tbsp.	1 c.	1 qt.	4 c.
5 Tbsp. + 1 tsp.	1/3 c.	5/8 c.	1/2 c. + 2 Tbsp.
12 Tbsp.	3/4 c.	7/8 c.	3/4 c. + 2 Tbsp.
4 oz.	1/2 c.	8-10 egg whites	1 c.
8 oz.	1 c.	12-14 egg yolks	1 c.

Substitutions

1 c. unwhipped cream	2 c. whipped cream
1 lb. shredded American cheese	4 lb.
1 c. sugar	1 1/3 c. brown sugar or 1 1/2 c. powdered sugar
1 tsp. baking powder	1/4 tsp. baking soda + 5/8 tsp. cream of tartar
1 Tbsp. cornstarch	2 Tbsp. flour or 1 1/2 Tbsp. quick cooking tapioca
1 c. cake flour	1 c. – 2 Tbsp. all-purpose flour
1 c. all-purpose flour	1 c. + 2 Tbsp. cake flour
1 sq. chocolate	3 Tbsp. cocoa and 1 Tbsp. fat
1 c. melted shortening	1 c. vegetable oil (may not be substituted for solid shortening)
1 c. milk	1/2 c. evaporated milk and 1/2 c. water
1 c. sour milk or buttermilk	1 Tbsp. lemon juice or vinegar and enough sweet milk to measure 1 c.
1 c. heavy cream	1/4 c. milk and 1/4 c. lard

If you find any mistakes in this book, they are there for a purpose. We try to offer something for everyone. Some people always look for mistakes, and we don't want to disappoint them.

Appetizers, Beverages and Dips
Sweet Heart

- One lemon yields about $\frac{1}{4}$ c. juice. One orange yields about $\frac{1}{3}$ c. juice. This is helpful in making fresh orange juice or lemonade.

- Don't let coffee water boil. It brings out the acid and causes a bitter flavor.

- Add a pinch of salt to drinks, coffee and teas. It will bring out the flavor wonderfully.

Frosted Grapes

Dip tiny bunches of **washed grapes** into **lemon juice**. Then sprinkle with **granulated sugar**. Dry on wire rack. A tasty garnish for that special fruit salad or other dishes.

—*Mrs. Danny (Edna) Borntrager, Wisconsin*

Cheese Ball [1]

16 oz. cream cheese
½ lb. cheddar cheese, thinly grated
1 Tbsp. chopped onion
4 tsp. Worcestershire sauce
1 Tbsp. lemon juice

Mix well. Form into ball and chill for 24 hours. Serve with crackers.

—*Mrs. John (Anna) Yoder, Michigan*

Cheese Ball [2]

16 oz. cream cheese
1 lb. Velveeta cheese
½ c. chopped onions
2 tsp. pimento
1 tsp. lemon juice
2 tsp. Worcestershire sauce
paprika

Mix all together and roll into a ball. Chill. Roll in nuts if you wish.

—*Mrs. Emanuel (Esther) Herschberger, Michigan*

Gambling is a way of getting nothing for something.

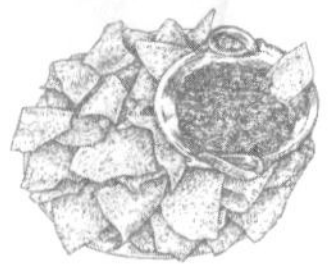

Party Punch

1 pkg. cherry Kool-Aid
1 pkg. strawberry Kool-Aid
1 (6 oz.) can frozen orange juice
1 (6 oz.) can frozen lemonade
1-2 c. sugar
3 qt. water
ice
7-Up

Mix all together. Makes 1 gallon.

—Ms. Emma J. Yoder, Michigan

Grape Juice

10 c. washed Concord grapes
12 c. water
3 c. sugar

Boil grapes and water together for 45 minutes. Strain and add sugar. Put in jars and coldpack for 15 minutes or may bring juice to a boil then put in jars and seal.

—Ms. Miriam D. Herschberger, Michigan

To Can Apple Juice

After juicing, let **apple juice** stand two days for riper flavor. Cold pack just to the boiling point. Remove from water to cool.

—Mrs. David (Naomi) Herschberger, Michigan

We probably wouldn't worry what people thought of us if we knew how seldom they do.

Rhubarb Drink

4 c. rhubarb
4 qt. water
2-3 c. sugar
1 c. pineapple juice
6 oz. orange juice

Boil rhubarb and water until rhubarb is soft. Drain and add sugar, pineapple juice and orange juice. Put in jars and cold pack. Heat just to boiling point. Or heat juice in kettle to boiling point. Pour in warmed jars and seal. **7-Up** may be added when ready to use.

—Mrs. David (Naomi) Herschberger, Michigan

Rhubarb Juice

6 qt. rhubarb, chunked
12 qt. water
3 c. sugar
2 pkg. strawberry Kool-Aid

Cook rhubarb and water until rhubarb is soft. Strain and add sugar and Kool-Aid. Delicious!

—Mrs. Elizabeth R. Borntreger, Wisconsin

Orange Vanilla Pops

1 pkg. orange Kool-Aid
2 c. water
¾ c. sugar
1 (3 oz.) pkg. instant vanilla pudding
2 c. milk

Combine Kool-Aid, water and sugar. Set aside. Mix pudding and milk. Stir in Kool-Aid mixture and blend thoroughly. Set outside and freeze.

—Mrs. Alvin (Susie) Yoder, Ohio

Ginger Juice

2 qt. water
1/4 c. lemon juice
1/4 c. vinegar
1 1/2 c. sugar or
maple syrup to taste
pinch salt
1/2-3/4 tsp. ginger

Stir all together with a wire whip. We like this if it's very warm outside or when putting up hay, etc.

—Mrs. David (Naomi) Herschberger, Wisconsin

Ginger Swichel

3 Tbsp. vinegar
1/4 tsp. ginger
1 c. sugar
enough water to make 2 qt.
ice if desired

This is a very good drink when the summer heat seems to beat you out, especially when making hay, etc.

—Mrs. Enos (Ada) Mast, New York

Root Beer

1 pt. lukewarm water
1/2 tsp. yeast
4 lb. sugar
1 bottle root beer extract
4 3/4 gal. lukewarm water

Mix 1 pt. lukewarm water and yeast. Let stand at room temperature for 5 minutes. Dissolve remaining ingredients and add to yeast mixture. Best to let stand at 80° for 2 days. Refrigerate and enjoy!

—Mrs. David (Naomi) Herschberger, Michigan

Hot Chocolate

9 c. dry milk
6 oz. coffee creamer
3 c. Nestle's Quik
3 c. powdered sugar

Mix all together. Store in an airtight container. Mix 3 Tbsp. mix to 1 c. hot water.

—Mrs. Simon (Malinda) Yoder, Ohio

Cappuccino Mix

¾ c. creamer
¾ c. powdered sugar
¼ c. instant coffee
⅔ c. dry milk
½ c. Nestle's Quik
¼ tsp. salt

Mix all together. Mix ¼ c. mix with 1 c. hot water. This is a good "get up and go" for those groggy mornings or anytime you need a boost. Try it! Serves 12 people.

—Mrs. Andrew (Ella) Mast, Ohio

Grape Wine

20 lb. grapes
10 lb. sugar
1½ gal. hot water

Wash grapes and put in crock with remaining ingredients. Let stand 4 days. Put through a cloth and pour in jugs. Do not seal. Let it work out on top and keep filled with water or wine. Put balloons on top for about 2 weeks. Put on caps and store in cellar.

—Mrs. David (Naomi) Herschberger, Michigan

Grape Juice to Can

2 c. grapes per qt.
1 c. sugar per qt.

Put grapes and sugar in a quart jar. Fill with water. Cold pack for 10 minutes. When opening jars to use, drain juice into pitcher.
Variation: Use 3 c. grapes per qt. and add ½ qt. water on opening.

—Mrs. David (Naomi) Herschberger, Michigan

Cruelty of Cooks

If you itemize the terms of cooks,
You'll find we quite deceive our looks
The things we do sound very cruel,
Like fighting a one-sided duel.

We beat the eggs, whip the cream,
Blow pudding up with hot steam,
We mash potatoes, slice the bread,
Tear apart the cabbage's head.

We chop the onion, grate the cheese,
Lemons and oranges get a squeeze,
We burn the sugar, gash the steak,
The celery's heart we often take.

We skin the tomato, peel the pear,
Scrape the carrots everywhere.
We scald the milk, freeze the salad,
Strain the tea that's really pallid.

We prick the unsuspecting pie,
And remove the baby potato's eye.
And then if that's not enough,
We smother chickens and other stuff.

Goodness knows what else we do,
I'm really quite abashed, aren't you?
We do all this and never cry
'Till we get onions in our eye.

Pancakes and Cereals

- Pancakes and waffles are better if you use sweet cream instead of milk, but you need to use about twice as much cream as you would milk. You may also use half cream and half milk.

- To make egg whites smoother, add a pinch of cream of tartar while beating. I do this for meringues and even for beaten egg whites in pies, cakes, pancakes, etc. It makes a smoother, creamier batter.

- A teaspoon of vinegar added to homemade syrup will keep it from becoming sugary.

Pancakes—Light and Fluffy

3 eggs, separated
1 c. milk
1 c. flour
pinch of salt
1 Tbsp. sugar
2 tsp. baking powder
2 Tbsp. butter, melted or vegetable oil

Beat together egg yolks and milk. Add dry ingredients and butter or oil. Fold beaten egg whites in last. Then fry in a hot pan.

—Mrs. Danny (Edna) Borntrager, Wisconsin

Favorite Pancakes

Pancake Mix:
10 c. flour
1 c. sugar
¾ c. baking powder
5 tsp. salt

To Use:
1 egg
2 Tbsp. vegetable oil
1 c. milk
1 c. pancake mix

Beat egg. Add oil and milk. Add mix last.

—Mrs. David (Barbara) Hershberger, Michigan

Formula for a long life—
Keep breathing.

Pancakes

1 c. flour
2 tsp. sugar
1 Tbsp. baking powder
½ tsp. salt
1 egg, beaten
1 c. milk
2 Tbsp. butter, melted
1 tsp. vanilla

In a large bowl, combine dry ingredients. In another bowl, combine remaining ingredients. Add to dry ingredients and stir until just combined. Preheat griddle; grease, using ¼ c. batter for each pancake. Bake 3 minutes; turn and bake other side. Makes about 8 pancakes.

—Mrs. Amos (Emma) Hershberger, Ohio

Flannel Pancakes

2 c. flour
4-6 tsp. baking powder
2 Tbsp. sugar
2 eggs, beaten
¼ c. vegetable oil, optional
½ tsp. salt
sweet milk to make a fairly thin batter

Just mix with a fork. Do not overbeat. Fry in butter on a hot skillet. Delicious served with maple syrup or chicken gravy. Pile them high, set on the table and see what happens.

—Mrs. John (Anna) Yoder, Michigan
—Ms. Rachel J. Hochstetler, Wisconsin

A couple were enjoying a dinner party at a a home of friends. Near the end of the meal, the wife slapped her husband's arm. "That's the third time you've gone for dessert," she said, "the hostess must think you're an absolute pig!" "I doubt that," the husband replied, "I've been telling her it's for you."

Pancakes

2 eggs, beaten
¼ c. salad oil
1 Tbsp. vinegar
2 c. milk
2 Tbsp. sugar
2 c. flour
1 tsp. soda
2 tsp. baking powder
1 tsp. salt

Butter milk or sour milk may be used.

—Mrs. Moses (Martha) Troyer, Wisconsin

Waffles [1]

2 eggs
1½-1¾ c. milk
1 tsp. vanilla, optional
2 c. flour
2 Tbsp. sugar
4 tsp. baking powder
1 tsp. salt
6-8 Tbsp. butter

Separate the eggs. Add milk and vanilla to the egg yolks. Beat in flour, sugar, salt and baking powder. Melt butter and add. Whip egg whites and fold in. Makes 6-8 waffles.

Variation: Make pancakes instead of waffles. We use about 3 Tbsp. less butter and put butter in the pan to fry them. Our favorite pancakes!

—Ms. Emma M. Hershberger, Wisconsin
—Mrs. Andy (Fannie) Slabaugh, Wisconsin

Waffles [2]

3 eggs
1½ c. buttermilk
1¾ c. flour
2 tsp. baking powder
1 tsp. baking soda
½ tsp. salt
½ c. shortening

Separate eggs. Add remaining ingredients to yolks, folding in beaten egg whites last. Variation: You may use sweet milk instead of buttermilk. Omit baking soda and increase baking powder to 4 tsp.

—Ms. Laura R. Borntreger, Wisconsin

Dutch Honey

1 c. brown sugar
1 c. white sugar
1 c. corn syrup
½ tsp. salt
2 c. cream

Bring to a boil, stirring often. Boil for 1 minute.

—Ms. Mary S. Herschberger, Michigan

Pancake Syrup

1¼ c. brown sugar
¾ c. white sugar
⅓ c. light corn syrup
1 c. cold water
1 tsp. vanilla
½ tsp. maple flavoring, optional

Bring everything except flavorings to a boil in a saucepan, stirring constantly. Simmer on low heat for 5 minutes. Remove from heat and add vanilla and maple flavoring if desired.

—Mrs. Andy (Fannie) Slabaugh, Wisconsin
—Mrs. Enos (Ada) Mast, New York

Granola Cereal [1]

6 c. rolled oats
4 c. crisp rice cereal
1 c. coconut
1 c. chocolate chips
2 pkg. graham crackers
1½ tsp. baking soda
1 c. brown sugar
½ c. butter
¾ c. vegetable oil

Mix together oats, crisp rice, coconut, chocolate chips, graham crackers, baking soda and brown sugar. Melt butter. Mix oil and butter with cereal mixture. Put in pans and toast until nice and brown.

—Mrs. Noah (Malinda) Raber, New York

Granola Cereal [2]

20 c. quick oats
1 c. wheat flour
4 c. brown sugar
½ c. butter, melted
1 c. sweet cream
¼ c. maple flavoring
½ pkg. or 1 box Cheerios, optional
½ pkg. or 1 box puffed wheat, optional

Mix everything except cereals thoroughly and toast, but not too hard. Cool. Add Cheerios and puffed wheat if you wish. Makes 13 qt.

—Mrs. Levi (Sadie) Yoder, Ohio

The little boy's parents told him he couldn't go to the picnic because he had been naughty. After a while, they forgave him and told he could go. He began to cry. They asked him what was wrong, and he told them. "It's too late. I already prayed for rain!"

Good Granola

1 c. sugar
12 c. oats
4 c. coconut
1 tsp. salt
2 pkg. graham crackers
1½ c. margarine
2 Tbsp. maple flavoring
1 Tbsp. baking soda
¾ c. chocolate chips
¾ c. butterscotch chips

Combine first 5 ingredients. Mix together margarine, flavoring and baking soda. Pour over first mixture and mix together. Immediately after toasting add chocolate and butterscotch chips, so they can melt a little on other cereal.

—Mrs. Andy (Anna) Hershberger, Ohio

Bran Muffin Cereal

1¼ c. butter
5 c. brown sugar
5 eggs, unbeaten
7½ c. bran
5 c. buttermilk
5 c. sifted pastry flour
5 tsp. baking soda
2½ tsp. salt

Bake like a cake. Crumble like grape nuts. Toast in oven. You may also add raisins if you wish. Very good!

—Mrs. Henry (Sarah) Mast, Ohio

Wheat Germ Crunchies

5 c. whole wheat flour
2 c. wheat germ
2½ c. oat bran
2 c. brown sugar or
maple syrup
4½ c. coconut
6½ c. oatmeal
2 tsp. salt
2 Tbsp. baking powder
4 tsp. cinnamon
4 eggs, beaten
2½ c. olive oil or canola oil
1 Tbsp. vanilla
1½ tsp. maple flavoring

Mix dry ingredients before adding wet ingredients. Bake quickly and crumble with hands as soon as it is cool enough to handle. Toast golden brown like granola. Makes 3 large cookie sheets.

—Mrs. Paul (Edna) Brenneman, Michigan

Grapenuts [1]

8 c. wheat flour
4 c. brown sugar
2 c. rolled oats
1 c. butter or vegetable oil
4 tsp. baking soda
2 eggs, beaten
1 Tbsp. vanilla or maple flavoring
enough sweet milk to make a stiff dough

Mix all together. Bake like a cake. Crumble and toast in warm oven. Makes 1 gallon.

—Mrs. John (Anna) Yoder, Michigan

Grapenuts [2]

8 lb. whole wheat flour
2 lb. brown sugar
1¼ Tbsp. salt
2 Tbsp. baking soda
6 c. buttermilk or sour milk
1½ c. butter, melted
2½ c. maple syrup
2 Tbsp. vanilla

Mix all dry ingredients in a bowl except baking soda. Dissolve soda in milk and add to mixture. Add butter, maple syrup and vanilla. The thickness varies with store bought or whole wheat flour. Add more milk if too thick or wheat flour if too thin. Put in pans and spread evenly with a spoon. Bake at 350° until done. Makes approx. 15 lb.

—Mrs. Levi (Mattie) Yoder, Michigan

Brown Sugar Grapenuts

3 c. graham flour
2 c. brown sugar
2 tsp. baking soda
1 c. oatmeal
1½ c. milk
½ c. vegetable oil
1 egg

Mix flour, sugar, baking soda and oatmeal together. Add milk, oil and egg; mix well. Bake in 9" x 13" cake pan. Grind. Toast about 40 minutes at 350°, stirring every 10 minutes.

—Mrs. Joseph (Martha) Miller, Ohio

The Farmer's Love Letter

My dear sweet potato, do you carrot all for me? With your radish heart and turnip nose my heart beets for you! My love for you is as strong as an onion. If we cantaloupe, lettuce marry, and we will be a happy pear!

Breads and Rolls

- To cut rolls use a bread knife coated with flour.
- Use lard to grease your bread pans, and the bread will slide out freely.
- Do you know how to tell that bread has been baked sufficiently? The loaves should be well colored on sides and bottom as well as on the top. Tap the bottom and sides with fingers. If there is a hollow sound, this proves that the bread is baked all the way through. As soon as you remove the bread from the pan, place your palm on bottom of loaf. If it is very hot, it's not done baking. If it doesn't burn you, it is done.
- For extra flavor in homemade bread use cooking oil instead of lard.
- For a soft, tender crust, brush loaves with butter or other shortening after removing them from the pan. Cover with a towel a few minutes to soften the crust.
- For best results with bread use warm, not hot water (115°).
- One good way to refresh stale homemade bread is to moisten the whole uncut loaf with water. Wrap completely in heavy-duty foil. Turn oven to 350° and place in oven for 30 minutes. It's like fresh again.
- Let baked bread set in pans for 10 minutes, and it will come out easily.
- When bread is baking, a small dish of water in the oven will help to keep the crust from getting too hard.

White Bread

3 Tbsp. yeast
1 Tbsp. white sugar
1 c. warm water
¾ c. white sugar
¼ c. brown sugar
1 Tbsp. salt
1¼ c. corn oil
1 qt. warm water
bread flour

Stir yeast, 1 Tbsp. white sugar and 1 c. warm water together in a small bowl. In a large bowl, stir together ¾ c. white sugar, brown sugar, salt, corn oil and 1 qt. warm water. Add yeast mixture and bread flour. Let rise for 15 minutes. Punch down and let rise another 15 minutes. Punch down and let rise until double or more. Put in 6 bread pans and let rise until double or more. Bake at 350° until brown. Makes 6 loaves.

—Mrs. Joseph (Martha) Miller, Ohio

Delicious White Bread

1 c. white sugar
1 Tbsp. salt
2 Tbsp. yeast
½ c. lard
2 qt. lukewarm water
4 c. self-rising flour
bread flour

Put sugar, salt, yeast and lard in a bowl. Add water. Let stand until yeast starts to rise, then add self-rising flour. Add bread flour as needed. Let stand and punch it down every 30 minutes – 3 times. The fourth time work it out and put in loaf pans. Let stand 30 minutes. Bake 45 minutes at 350°. Makes 6 loaves.

—Mrs. Menno (Anna) Hershberger, Kentucky

Cookbooks are the biggest sellers, and diet books are second. The moral of the story is, "Don't eat what you just learned to cook!"

Quick Bread

½ c. white sugar
½ c. brown sugar
⅓ c. flour
2 Tbsp. salt
1½ c. hot water
3 c. cold water
3 Tbsp. yeast
1¼ c. vegetable oil
12½ c. flour

Mix first 6 ingredients. Add yeast and let stand until bubbly. Add oil and flour. Work down every 15 minutes for the first hour. Work out and let set until ready to bake. Makes 5 loaves.

—Ms. Dora M. Herschberger, Ohio

My Favorite Wheat Bread

5 c. whole wheat flour
1 c. sugar
1 Tbsp. salt
¼ c. yeast
2 eggs, beaten
⅔ c. vegetable oil
5 c. very warm water
9 c. white flour

Combine whole wheat flour, sugar, salt and yeast and mix with a wooden spoon. Add eggs, oil and water and mix well. Add flour 3 c. at a time. Knead on floured board about 10 minutes, adding reserved flour as needed until dough is smooth. Let rise 20 minutes. Punch down and let rise approximately 1 hour. Punch down and shape into six 1½ lb. loaves. Place in greased bread pans and let rise about 1 hour. Bake at 300° for 25-30 minutes. Makes 6 loaves.

—Mrs. Danny (Edna) Borntrager, Wisconsin

Think of something to give
instead of something to get.

Honey Wheat Bread

1/4 c. dry yeast
5 c. lukewarm water
1 c. vegetable oil
1 c. honey
1 1/2 Tbsp. salt
5 eggs, beaten
12 c. whole wheat flour
6 c. white flour

Dissolve yeast in water. Add oil, honey, salt and eggs. Gradually add whole wheat flour. Work in white flour until elastic and not too sticky. You may need to use more or less flour. Let rise until double. Punch down and let rise again. Form into loaves and bake at 350° for 35-40 minutes. Makes 6-7 loaves.

—Mrs. David (Naomi) Herschberger, Michigan

Brown Bread

2 c. whole wheat flour
1 Tbsp. yeast
1/3 c. vegetable oil
2 tsp. salt
2 Tbsp. molasses
2 c. warm water
white bread flour

Mix whole wheat flour and yeast in a bowl. Add oil, salt, molasses and water. Add white flour slowly until dough is soft and elastic. Let rise for 30 minutes. Shape into 2 loaves. Let rise until double. Bake at 375° for 40-50 minutes.

—Mrs. Levi (Fannie) Mast, Ohio

Very Good Brown Bread

1/3 c. brown sugar
1/3 c. white sugar
3 Tbsp. flour
1 c. boiling water
2 c. cold water
2 Tbsp. yeast
pinch of salt
3/4 c. vegetable oil
2 c. whole wheat flour
6 c. bread flour

Stir brown sugar, white sugar, flour and boiling water together. Add cold water, yeast and salt. Let set until yeast starts to work. Add oil and flours and knead. Let rise for 1 hour, punching down every 15 minutes. Put in bread pans. Let rise. Bake at 325° for 35 minutes. Makes 4 loaves.

—Mrs. Simon (Malinda) Yoder, Ohio

Two-Hour Buns (Mom's Favorite)

1½ Tbsp. yeast
1 c. warm water
¼ c. sugar
1 egg
2 Tbsp. shortening
½ tsp. salt
3 c. bread flour

Beat yeast, warm water, sugar and egg until foamy. Add shortening, salt and flour. Knead together just enough to blend well. Let rise until double in shape. Shape into buns and let rise again. Bake at 400° for 15-20 minutes. Serves 12 people.

—Mrs. Dan (Anna) Raber, Ohio

Cornbread

1¼ c. flour
2 tsp. baking powder
1 tsp. salt
¾ tsp. baking soda
2 Tbsp. shortening
¼ c. sugar
2 eggs
1 c. cornmeal
1 c. sour milk or buttermilk
¼ c. cream

Sift together flour, baking powder, salt and baking soda. Cream shortening and sugar. Add eggs, cornmeal, flour and milk. Bake at 375°.

—Ms. Elizabeth R. Borntreger, Ohio

Very Good Gingerbread

½ c. butter
1 c. brown sugar
½ c. cane syrup
2 eggs
3 c. flour
½ tsp. ginger
2 tsp. baking powder
½ tsp. cinnamon
½ tsp. salt
1 c. sweet milk

Stir butter, sugar, syrup and eggs together. Sift dry ingredients together. Add alternately with milk. This is good warm with milk and fruit. Enjoy!

—Mrs. Eli (Emma) Yoder, Michigan

Zucchini Bread

3 eggs
2 c. sugar
1 c. vegetable oil
2 tsp. vanilla
2 c. peeled and grated zucchini
3 c. flour
1 tsp. salt
1 tsp. baking powder
½ tsp. cinnamon
approx. 1 c. nuts, optional

Beat eggs, sugar, oil and vanilla. Add zucchini, then add flour sifted with salt, baking powder and cinnamon. Add nuts. Bake at 350° in 2 greased and floured loaf pans for 1 hour or until done. If using glass pans, reduce oven temperature to 325°.

—Mrs. Tobie (Ada) Miller, Michigan

O weary mother, mixing dough
Don't you wish that food would grow?
Your eyes would like, I know to see
A cookie bush or a doughnut tree!

Banana Nut Bread

1½ c. white sugar
½ c. vegetable oil
2 eggs
½ tsp. salt
1 tsp. vanilla
1 c. mashed bananas
¼ c. water
1 tsp. baking soda
2 c. flour
2 tsp. cinnamon
nuts

Mix in order given. Put in bread pans and bake at 350°.

—Mrs. Samuel (Katie) Herschberger, Michigan

Banana Bread

½ c. shortening
1 c. sugar
2 eggs
2 bananas, mashed
¼ c. nuts, optional
2 c. flour
1 tsp. baking soda
1 tsp. salt

Cream shortening and sugar. Add eggs, bananas and nuts. Sift flour with baking soda and salt and add. Bake at 350° for 50-60 minutes. This is good to cool and freeze in foil.

—Mrs. David J. (Naomi) Herschberger, Michigan

Each time you turn the pages
Looking for something new to cook
Fondly remembers the persons
Who made possible this book.

Pumpkin Bread

8 eggs
6 c. sugar
2 c. vegetable oil
1 c. water
4 c. pumpkin
7 c. flour
4 tsp. baking soda
1 Tbsp. salt
2 tsp. cinnamon
2 tsp. nutmeg

Beat eggs. Add sugar, oil, water and pumpkin. Mix dry ingredients in well. Bake in a slow (325°) oven. Makes six 7" x 3½" x 2½" bread pans. This is a recipe we use at our local bakery. A good seller in the fall.

—Mrs. Andrew (Ella) Mast, Ohio

Zucchini Bread

3 eggs
2 c. white sugar
2 tsp. vanilla
1 c. vegetable oil
2 c. shredded, unpeeled zucchini
1 (8¼ oz.) can crushed pineapple, drained
3 c. flour
2 tsp. baking soda
1 tsp. salt
¼ tsp. baking powder
1½ tsp. cinnamon
1 c. walnuts
1 c. raisins

Beat eggs, sugar, vanilla and oil until thick. Stir in zucchini, pineapple, flour, soda, salt, baking powder and cinnamon. Add walnuts and raisins. Pour into 2 greased 3" x 5" loaf pans. Bake at 350° for 1 hour or until done. Cool for 10 minutes in pan, then turn onto wire rack to cool.

—Mrs. Jake (Anna) Herschberger, Michigan

Muffins

½ c. sugar
⅓ c. shortening
1 egg
1½ c. flour
1½ tsp. baking powder
½ tsp. salt
¼ tsp. nutmeg
½ c. milk

Topping:
6-8 Tbsp. butter, melted
½ c. sugar
1 tsp. cinnamon

Cream sugar, shortening and egg together. Sift dry ingredients together and add alternately with milk. Bake at 375° until golden brown. Immediately roll in melted butter, then in sugar and cinnamon mixture. Makes 8-12 muffins.

—Mrs. Uria (Sara) Miller, Michigan
—Mrs. Andy (Martha) Kauffman, Wisconsin

Southern Raised Biscuits

2 pkg. dry yeast
¼ c. warm water
2 c. buttermilk
5 c. flour
⅓ c. sugar
1 Tbsp. baking powder
1 tsp. baking soda
2 tsp. salt
1 c. shortening

Combine yeast and water until yeast dissolves. Add buttermilk and set aside. Combine dry ingredients in a large bowl. Cut in shortening. Add buttermilk mixture, mixing with a fork until dry ingredients are moistened. Knead dough lightly for a minute or two. Add flour as needed. Roll dough to ½" thickness and cut with biscuit cutter. Place on lightly greased baking sheet. Cover and let rise 1 hour. Bake at 450° for 10-12 minutes. Makes 2 doz. biscuits.
Note: Biscuits may be frozen. Bake 5 minutes and cool. Wrap in foil and freeze.

—Mrs. Moses (Amelia) Gingerich, Ohio

Southern Gal Biscuits

2 c. flour
4 tsp. baking powder
1 tsp. salt
2 Tbsp. sugar
½ c. shortening
1 egg
⅔ c. milk

Mix dry ingredients and shortening until crumbly. Stir in egg and milk. Drop on cookie sheet. Bake at 400° for 10-12 minutes.

—Mrs. Neil (Esther) Kauffman, Wisconsin

Biscuit Supreme

2 c. flour
2 tsp. sugar
4 tsp. baking powder
½ tsp. salt
½ tsp. cream of tartar
½ c. shortening
⅔-1 c. milk

Sift flour, sugar, baking powder, salt and cream of tartar together. Cut in shortening until mixture resembles crumbs. Add milk all at once and stir just until dough follows fork around bowl. Bake at 450° for 10-12 minutes. Makes 12-14 biscuits. Good with chicken broth gravy.

—Ms. Rachel A. Mast, Ohio
—Mrs. Andy (Martha) Kauffman, Wisconsin

Light and Tasty Biscuits

2 c. flour
2½ tsp. baking powder
½ tsp. salt
lard
¾ c. milk
melted butter

Mix flour, baking powder and salt. Cut in lard. Add milk. Knead like pie dough. Drop on greased cookie sheet and brush tops with melted butter. Bake at 475° for 12-15 minutes.

—Mrs. Mahlon (Sarah) Gingerich, Ohio

Baking Powder Biscuits

2 c. flour
1 tsp. salt
1 Tbsp. baking powder
5 Tbsp. shortening
1 c. water or millk

Mix flour, salt and baking powder in a bowl. Cut in shortening until mixture resembles pie crumbs. Add milk or water and stir only until flour is wet.

—Mrs. Andy (Fannie) Slabaugh, Wisconsin

Our Favorite Biscuits

2 c. white flour
1 c. whole wheat flour
5 tsp. baking powder
1 Tbsp. sugar
1 tsp. salt
2 eggs
⅓ c. lard or butter
¾ c. milk

Mix flours, baking powder, sugar and salt together. Add eggs, lard or butter and milk and mix all together. It will give a stiff dough but that is best. Drop by teaspoon on cookie sheet and bake at 300° for 25-30 minutes or until golden brown and crisp. Good with gravy.

—Ms. Elizabeth J. Herschberger, Michigan

Pizza Dough

1 c. warm water
1 Tbsp. yeast
1 tsp. sugar
1-1½ tsp. salt
2-4 Tbsp. vegetable oil
2½-3 c. flour

Dissolve yeast in warm water. Add remaining ingredients. Let rise for 20 minutes. This is plenty for 1 round pizza pan. Bake at 375°-400°.

—Ms. Barbara J. Yoder, New York
—Ms. Dora M. Herschberger, Ohio

Pizza Hut Crust

1 Tbsp. yeast
1½ Tbsp. white sugar
1 c. warm water
1½ Tbsp. corn oil
⅛ tsp. garlic powder
¼ tsp. oregano
½ tsp. salt

Mix yeast, sugar and water. Let stand for 5 minutes. Add remaining ingredients and mix. Put in a large pizza pan. Top with your favorite sauce and toppings. Bake at 450° until lightly browned. This is our favorite! Serves 10 people.

—Mrs. Dan (Anna) Raber, Ohio

Pizza Hut Pizza Dough

⅔ c. warm water
2 pkg. yeast
2 tsp. sugar
2 c. cold water
2 Tbsp. sugar
¼ tsp. garlic salt or powder
3 Tbsp. vegetable oil
1 Tbsp. (scant) salt
½ tsp. oregano
6½ c. flour

Mix warm water, yeast and 2 tsp. sugar. Let stand 5 minutes until bubbly. In another bowl, mix cold water, 2 Tbsp. sugar, garlic powder, oil, salt, oregano and 3 c. flour. Beat until smooth. Add yeast mixture. Add remaining flour. Work until elastic. Let rise until double. Press half of dough on a greased pan. Let rise 5-10 minutes. Repeat with other half. Add sauce. Bake at 400° for 10-15 minutes. Then add meats and cheese. Makes 2 pizza crusts.

—Ms. Laura R. Borntreger, Ohio

Jiffy Pizza Dough

2 c. flour
1 Tbsp. baking powder
1 tsp. salt
⅔ c. milk
⅓ c. vegetable oil

Combine flour, baking powder and salt. Add milk and oil. Press on pizza pan. Bake at 350° for 15-20 minutes.

—Mrs. Alvin (Susie) Yoder, Ohio

Pizza Crust

1 c. warm water
1 Tbsp. yeast
2 Tbsp. sugar
2 Tbsp. vegetable oil
2½ c. flour
1 tsp. salt

Combine first 3 ingedients. Let set until foamy. Add remaining ingredients. Mix well and let set for 5 minutes. Press into pizza pan. Bake at 350° for 8-10 minutes.

—Mrs. Atlee (Susan) Yoder, Ohio

Apple Rolls [1]

1½ c. flour
2 tsp. baking powder
½ tsp. salt
¼ c. butter
4-6 Tbsp. milk
2 Tbsp. butter, melted
4 med. apples, peeled and diced

Blend flour, baking powder, salt and butter. Add enough milk to make a soft dough. Roll out dough. Spread butter over dough and add apples. Roll up and slice 1½" thick and put in pan. Pour hot sauce over rolls. Bake at 350° for 35-40 minutes. Serve warm with milk.

Sauce:
1 c. brown sugar
1 c. hot water
½ tsp. cinnamon
2 Tbsp. butter

Combine all and bring to a boil.

—Mrs. Dannie (Lizzie) Yoder, Michigan

A good housekeeper does not spend time wondering where the dirt comes from but showing it where to go!

Apple Rolls [2]

2 c. flour
3 Tbsp. sugar
1 Tbsp. baking powder
¼ tsp. salt
3 Tbsp. lard
1 egg
½ c. milk
melted butter
cinnamon
peeled, chopped apples

Mix together flour, sugar, baking powder and salt. Cut in lard until mixture is fine crumbs. Mix egg and milk and add just enough to crumbs to moisten. Roll out ¼" thick. Brush dough with melted butter and sprinkle with cinnamon. Spread with chopped apples. Roll up, cut and put in pan. Cover with syrup and bake.

Syrup:
1 c. brown sugar
¾ c. water
a few drops maple flavoring

Combine and bring to a boil.

—Mrs. Jacob (Sadie) Hershberger, Wisconsin

Pineapple Sweet Rolls

2 Tbsp. yeast
¼ c. warm water
2 c. milk
1 c. sugar
¼ tsp. salt
½ c. shortening
2 eggs, beaten
7 c. flour
pineapple filling

Dissolve yeast in warm water. Heat milk to scalding. Remove from heat and add sugar, salt and shortening. Stir well. Cool to lukewarm. Add yeast mixture, eggs, and flour, kneading well. Let rise 1½ hours in a warm place. Roll out and spread with filling. Put in roll pans and let rise for 1 hour. Bake at 400° for 12-15 minutes. Very good!

—Ms. Rachel J. Hochstetler, Wisconsin

Sarah's Rhubarb Rolls

2 c. flour
1 tsp. salt
2 tsp. baking powder
3 Tbsp. lard
7/8 c. milk
softened butter
white sugar
finely chopped rhubarb
dash of nutmeg

Sauce:
1 c. sugar
1 Tbsp. (heaping) flour
1/4 tsp. salt
1 c. hot water
small lump butter

Sift flour, salt and baking powder together. Cut in lard. Add milk and mix well. Roll out 1/4" thick. Spread thickly with softened butter, sugar and rhubarb. Sprinkle with nutmeg. Roll up as you would cinnamon rolls and cut into 1½"-2" slices. Mix together remaining ingredients and boil for 3 minutes to make a sweet sauce. Place dough slices in pans and pour sauce over them. Bake at 350° until brown.
Variation: Apples may be used instead of rhubarb.

—Mrs. Mahlon (Sarah) Gingerich, Ohio

A mother came home from shopping and found her freshly baked pie dug crudely out from the center. A gooey spoon lay in the sink and crumbs were scattered over the kitchen counter and floor. She called her son into the kitchen. "Peter," she said sternly, "you promised me you wouldn't touch that pie before dinner." Peter hung his head. "And I promised you I'd spank you if you did," she continued. Peter brightened. "Now that I've broken my promise, it's okay with me if you break yours too!"

Orange Rolls

2 eggs
¼ c. sugar
½ c. sour cream
1 tsp. salt
¼ c. lukewarm water
1 Tbsp. yeast
6 Tbsp. butter, melted
3½ c. flour
¾ c. white sugar
2 Tbsp. orange rind

Beat eggs in a bowl. Add sugar, sour cream, salt and water. Then add yeast and butter. Add flour and knead well. Let dough rise until double. Roll out like pie dough. Mix ¾ c. sugar and orange rind and sprinkle onto dough. Cut into wedges. Roll up starting at the wide end. Bake. Put glaze over top while still hot.

Glaze:
¾ c. white sugar
½ c. cream
2 Tbsp. orange juice
¼ c. butter
clear jel
several Tbsp. orange Jell-O

Cook first 4 ingredients for 3 minutes. Add clear jel to thicken and Jell-O for flavoring.

—Mrs. Mahlon (Sara) Gingerich, Ohio

Pumpkin Log Rolls

3 eggs
1 c. white sugar
¾ c. cooked pumpkin
1 tsp. lemon juice
¾ c. flour
½ tsp. cinnamon
⅛ tsp. ginger
¼ tsp. nutmeg
¼ tsp. salt
¼ tsp. baking soda
¼ tsp. baking powder

Beat eggs until light and lemon colored. Gradually add white sugar, beating for 5 minutes. Continue beating and add pumpkin and lemon juice. Stir in dry ingredients. Pour in a greased and floured pan. Bake, then sift powdered sugar on a towel. Put cake on top of it. Roll up like a jelly roll. When cool, unroll and spread with icing. Roll up again and slice.

Icing:
3 oz. cream cheese
¼ c. butter
1 c. powdered sugar
½ tsp. vanilla

Combine and mix well.

—Mrs. David (Barbara) Hershberger, Michigan

Short Order Cook

When Daddy cooks, he doesn't read
The cookbooks Mother seems to need.
He doesn't fool with pies or cakes;
He never roasts or broils or bakes.
He doesn't use the rolling pin,
Or measure level spoonsful in.
He doesn't need to watch the clock;
He doesn't fill the cookie crock.
We watch him with admiring eyes
While Daddy fries and fries and fries!

Pumpkin Roll

3 eggs
2/3 c. pumpkin
1 tsp. lemon juice, optional
1 c. sugar
3/4 c. flour
1 tsp. baking soda
1/2 tsp. salt
2 tsp. pumpkin pie spice or 1/2 tsp. cinnamon
crushed walnuts

Beat eggs for 5 minutes. Add pumpkin and lemon juice if desired. Add dry ingredients. Pour into a sprayed jelly-roll pan and sprinkle with crushed walnuts. Bake at 350° for 12 minutes. After baking, loosen from pan and turn onto towel with powdered sugar. Roll up and cool. Unroll and spread with filling. Roll up again and slice. Very good. Serves 10-12 people.

Filling:
8 oz. cream cheese
1/4 c. butter
1/2 tsp. vanilla
1 c. powdered sugar

Mix well.

—Ms. Rachel A. Mast, Ohio
—Mrs. Albert (Lizzie) Miller, New York

Jelly Roll

4 eggs, separated
3/4 c. white sugar
3/4 c. bread flour
1 tsp. baking powder
1/4 tsp. salt
1 tsp. vanilla

Beat egg yolks well. Add sugar, flour, baking powder, salt and vanilla. Add well beaten egg whites last. Bake at 400° for 13 minutes.

Filling:
6 Tbsp. flour
1 c. hot water
3/4 c. brown sugar
1 Tbsp. butter
vanilla or maple flavoring

Combine flour, water and brown sugar. Heat until thick, stirring constantly. Remove from heat and add butter and vanilla or maple flavoring.

—Mrs. Amos (Emma) Hershberger, Ohio

Rolls

1 c. butter
1 qt. milk
2 Tbsp. yeast
1 c. lukewarm water
4 eggs
1 c. sugar
2 tsp. salt
flour

Melt butter, then add milk. Heat to lukewarm. Dissolve yeast in water. Beat eggs. Add sugar and salt. Add milk, yeast and enough flour to make a soft dough.

—Mrs. John (Esther) Brock, Iowa

Soft Rolls

2 c. quick oats
½ c. butter
1⅓ c. brown sugar
2 tsp. salt
4 c. boiling water
¼ c. yeast
2 Tbsp. white sugar
⅔ c. warm water
10 c. bread flour
softened butter
brown sugar
cinnamon
nuts

In a large bowl, combine oats, butter, brown sugar and salt. Pour boiling water over this mixture. Mix yeast, white sugar and warm water together. When oats mixture is lukewarm, add yeast mixture. Mix well. Add bread flour, 1 c. at a time. Let rise once, then work out and spread with softened butter, brown sugar, cinnamon and nuts. Roll up, cut and let rise. Bake at 325°.

Icing:
¾ c. butter
¾ c. Rich's Topping
1½ c. brown sugar
4 c. powdered sugar

Melt butter. Add sugar and milk. Bring to a boil. Cool partly. Add powdered sugar.

—Mrs. Edna J. Yoder, Ohio

Cinnamon Rolls [1]

1 c. boiling water
½ c. sugar
½ tsp. salt
½ c. shortening
1 c. milk
2 eggs, beaten
7 c. flour, divided
2 Tbsp. yeast
melted butter
1½ c. brown sugar
1 Tbsp. cinnamon
nuts, optional
raisins, optional

Pour boiling water over sugar, salt and shortening. Stir until shortening is dissolved, then add milk, eggs and a few cups of flour. Stir well. Add yeast, then add the remaining flour gradually. Knead lightly, working in just enough flour to handle the dough. Let rise until double in bulk. Punch down and let rise again, then roll out and spread with melted butter. Mix brown sugar and cinnamon together. Spread on top along with nuts or raisins if desired. Roll up and cut in ½" slices. Let rise and bake in 350° oven until light brown. Frost with 2-4-6 frosting.

—Mrs. Monroe (Mary) Hershberger, Wisconsin

Cinnamon Rolls [2]

2 c. milk, scalded
2 Tbsp. yeast
½ c. white sugar
2 c. bread flour
2 tsp. salt
4 eggs, beaten
½ c. butter, melted
3 c. bread flour
½ c. brown sugar
2 tsp. cinnamon

Scald milk and cool to lukewarm. Add yeast, sugar and 2 c. flour. When cool add salt, eggs, butter and 3 c. flour. Mix well and let rise once. Roll out and spread with brown sugar and cinnamon. Bake at 425° for 8-10 minutes. Frost with caramel frosting. Serves 14 people.

—Mrs. Henry (Emma) Raber, Ohio

Cinnamon Rolls [3]

¼ c. yeast
2 Tbsp. lukewarm water
1 c. sugar
4 tsp. salt
4 eggs, beaten
1 c. butter
4 c. lukewarm milk
flour

Dissolve yeast in 2 Tbsp. lukewarm water. Mix sugar, salt, eggs and butter separately in a bowl. Stir in milk and yeast. Add flour. Use butter to finish up and also to work out. Let rise 45 minutes.

—Mrs. Eli (Sarah) Mast, New York

Cinnamon Rolls [4]

2 Tbsp. yeast
⅔ c. white sugar
1½ c. warm water
1 c. vegetable oil
½ c. potato flakes
6 eggs, well beaten
1½ tsp. salt
7 c. (scant) bread flour
cinnamon

Dissolve yeast and sugar in water. Mix oil, potato flakes, eggs and salt. Add yeast and beat well. Add bread flour. Let rise, then roll out. Sprinkle with cinnamon, roll up and cut. Let rise until double in size. Bake at 350° until very light brown.

—Mrs. Mosie (Lizzie) Mast, New York

People may doubt what you say, but they will always believe what you do.

Cinnamon Rolls [5]

2 pkg. yeast
1 Tbsp. white sugar
½ c. lukewarm water
½ c. butter
2 c. milk, scalded
⅔ c. white sugar
3 or 4 eggs, beaten
1 c. cold water
1 Tbsp. salt
1 Tbsp. vanilla
flour
butter
brown sugar
cinnamon
crushed pineapple, optional

Dissolve yeast and 1 Tbsp. white sugar in water. Melt butter in milk. Add sugar, eggs, cold water, salt and vanilla. When cooled, mix in yeast mixture. Stir. Add flour until mixture is as thick as you can stir with a spoon. Cover and let rise to double in size. Roll out and spread with butter, brown sugar and cinnamon or crushed pineapple if you wish. Roll up and cut. Put in pans and let rise again until double. Bake at 375° and frost when done.

—*Mrs. Clara J. Herschberger, Wisconsin*

Cinnamon Rolls [6]

2 pkg. yeast
2 Tbsp. sugar
1 c. warm water
2 c. milk
6 Tbsp. butter
1 tsp. salt
3 eggs, beaten
½ c. sugar
8 c. bread flour
margarine
brown sugar
cinnamon

Dissolve yeast and 2 Tbsp. sugar in warm water. Scald milk and melt butter in it. Cool to lukewarm. Add salt, eggs, ½ c. sugar and yeast mixture and mix. Knead in bread flour. Let rise. Punch down, then roll out the dough on a greased surface to ½" thick. Spread margarine on surface of dough. Spread with a thin layer of brown sugar. Sprinkle cinnamon on top. Roll up and cut. Put in greased pans and let rise. Bake at 350° until golden brown. Do not overbake. Frost with your favorite icing.

—*Ms. Rachel D. Mast, New York*

Cinnamon Rolls [7]

1 c. scalded milk
½ c. white sugar
1½ tsp. salt
½ c. shortening
2 Tbsp. yeast
1 c. lukewarm water
2 eggs, beaten
7 c. flour
cinnamon
melted butter
brown sugar

Pour scalded milk over sugar, salt and shortening. Dissolve yeast in warm water, then add yeast and eggs to milk mixture. Beat well. Add flour gradually, beating well. Knead lightly, working in just enough flour so the dough can be handled. Let dough rise until double in size. Roll dough out into an oblong ¼" thick on a floured surface. Brush with butter and sprinkle with brown sugar and cinnamon. Roll up and cut into 1" thick slices. Let rise about 1 hour. Bake in a moderate oven (350°-375°).

Frosting:
1 c. butter
½ c. milk
2 c. brown sugar
powdered sugar

Melt butter, brown sugar and milk. Boil for 2 minutes. Remove from heat and add powdered sugar until desired consistency.

—Mrs. Reuben (Irene) Brock, Wisconsin

Best Cinnamon Rolls

2 Tbsp. yeast
2½ c. warm water
1 yellow or white cake mix
4 c. flour, divided
3 eggs
⅓ c.vegetable oil
1 tsp. salt

Dissolve yeast in warm water for 3 minutes. Add cake mix, 1 c. flour, eggs, oil and salt. Beat with beater until bubbles appear. Slowly add remaining flour. Stir with spoon, making a soft dough. Let rise until double in size. Roll out to about ¼" thick. Spread with butter, sugar and cinnamon. Bake at 350° for 20-30 minutes. Makes about 3 cake pans full.

Topping:
½ c. butter, melted
2 Tbsp. cinnamon
¾ c. brown sugar

—Mrs. John (Esther) Miller

Overnight Rolls

½ c. water
2 Tbsp. sugar
2 Tbsp. yeast
4 c. warm water
1 c. vegetable oil
1⅔ c. sugar
1 Tbsp. salt
2 eggs
14 c. or more flour

Start at 6 P.M. or earlier. Mix ½ c. water, 2 Tbsp. sugar and yeast. Let stand 10 minutes, then add remaining ingredients. Beat as long as possible. Let set for 2 hours. Punch down and let set again for 2 hours. Roll out and sprinkle with butter, brown sugar and cinnamon and put in pans. Bake the next morning or make in the morning and bake in the evening. These stay soft quite a while. Bake at 375° for 12-15 minutes. Makes 6-8 doz.

—Mrs. Samuel (Malinda) Mast, Pennsylvania
—Mrs. Harvey (Katieann) Raber, New York

Cherry Rolls

2 c. milk, scalded
½ c. butter
⅓ c. sugar
1 Tbsp. salt
2 Tbsp. dry yeast
¼ c. lukewarm water
2 eggs, well beaten
6 c. flour
butter
cherry pie filling

Scald milk and cool to lukewarm. Melt ½ c. butter in warm milk. Add sugar and salt. Dissolve yeast in lukewarm water. Add eggs and flour. Stir in milk mixture. Let rise until double in bulk. Roll out and spread with butter. Top with cherry pie filling and roll up and slice. Bake at 350° for 20 minutes.

—Mrs. David (Naomi) Herschberger, Michigan

Maple Twist Rolls

1 Tbsp. yeast
¼ c. lukewarm water
¾ c. milk
¼ c. butter
1 egg
1 tsp. maple flavoring
½ tsp. salt
3 Tbsp. sugar
3 c. flour

Filling:
½ c. brown sugar
1 tsp. cinnamon
1 Tbsp. butter
½ tsp. maple flavoring
⅓ c. nuts

Glaze:
1 c. powdered sugar
1-2 tsp. milk

Dissolve yeast in water. Heat milk and butter until scalding. Cool and add yeast. Beat egg, maple flavoring, salt and sugar. Add flour. Cover and let rise 1 hour. Divide into 2 equal parts. Roll out 1 part and put into greased pizza pan. Combine filling ingredients and put on top. Roll out second part of dough and lay over filling. Use a greased pizza cutter and slice toward middle leaving 2" in the middle not cut. Continue cutting toward the middle, making 10-12 slices. Twist each slice twice. Let rise and bake at 350° for 20 minutes. Combine glaze ingredients and drizzle over top. Serves 10-12 people.

—Mrs. Andy (Anna) Herschberger, Ohio

Cake Roll

4 eggs, separated
1 c. sugar, divided
1 c. sifted flour
¼ tsp. salt
2 tsp. baking powder

Beat egg whites until frothy. Gradually add ⅔ c. sugar and beat until stiff. Beat egg yolks and the remaining ⅓ c. sugar until light. Fold yolks, then dry ingredients into egg whites. Spread evenly on dusted sheet. Bake at 375° for 12 minutes. When done, immediately turn out on a moistened and floured towel and roll up. When cool, unroll and spread with desired filling. This cake roll is simple and nearly always perfect.

—Mrs. Amos (Ella) Beechy, Ohio

Caramel-Pecan Cinnamon Rolls

1/4 c. shortening
1/2 c. sugar
1 pkg. dry yeast
1 tsp. salt
5-6 c. flour
2 eggs
1 1/2 c. scalded milk

Mix rolls and let rise 1 hour.

Topping:
1 1/2 c. brown sugar
6 Tbsp. butter
1/4 c. corn syrup
vanilla
pecans

Melt brown sugar, butter, corn syrup and vanilla together. Spread in the bottom of two 9" x 13" pans and sprinkle with pecans. Place rolls on top and bake at 425° for 15-20 minutes. Turn pan upside down on sheets and remove from pan.

—*Mrs. David (Naomi) Herschberger, Michigan*

Sticky Rolls

2 qt. warm milk
2 c. sugar
2 c. warm water
2 c. butter, melted
2 tsp. salt
8 eggs, beaten
1/2 c. yeast
30 c. flour

Mix together all warm ingredients. Then add the rest. Mix well but not too stiff. Let rise 1 hour. Roll out and sprinkle with **cinnamon** and **brown sugar**. Shape into a roll, cut and set in syrup. Bake rolls in this syrup. After baking, turn rolls upside down on a pan and sprinkle with nuts.

Syrup:
1/3 c. butter
2 1/2 c. brown sugar
2 c. water
1 drop corn syrup
nuts, optional

Bring to a boil.

—*Mrs. John (Elizabeth) Mast, New York*

Syrup for Sticky Rolls

½ c. butter
1 c. brown sugar
1 tsp. vanilla
3 Tbsp. clear jel
¾-1 c. light corn syrup
2½ c. warm water

Cook together and pour over rolls and bake.

—Mrs. Harvey (Katieann) Raber, New York
—Ms. Lizzieann E. Mast, Michigan

Pineapple Turnovers

1 pkg. dry yeast
¼ c. warm water
½ c. milk
½ c. butter
¼ c. sugar
½ tsp. salt
1 egg, beaten
2¾-3¼ c. bread flour, sifted

Sprinkle yeast in warm water. Scald milk. Stir in butter, sugar and salt. Cool to lukewarm. Add egg and yeast mixture. Stir in flour, just enough to roll out. Fill with pineapple pie filling or your favorite filling. Cover and let rise until double in size. Roll out and let stand about 10 minutes. Bake.

—Mrs. Andrew (Emma) Yoder, Ohio

Let the words I speak be soft and tender, for tomorrow I may have to eat them.

Cream Sticks [1]

2 Tbsp. yeast
1 c. lukewarm water
1 c. milk
2 c. butter
⅔ c. sugar
2 eggs
½ tsp. salt
1 tsp. vanilla
at least 6 c. unsifted flour

Dissolve yeast in warm water. Scald milk, then put butter in hot milk to melt. Put sugar in milk and butter mixture. When cool enough add yeast, well beaten eggs, salt and vanilla. Add flour. Put in a warm place until double in bulk. Roll out and cut in pieces 1½" long and 3½" wide. Let rise again. Deep fat fry. Cut tops off cream sticks and fill with filling. Makes 70 cream sticks.

Filling:
3 tsp. (rounded) four
1 c. milk
1 c. shsortening
1 c. sugar
1 tsp. vanilla

Cook flour and milk until thick. Let cool. Cream shortening and sugar until creamy. Add flour and milk mixture. When cold, add vanilla. Mix well.

—Ms. Lavina D. Herschberger, Michigan

Cream Sticks [2]

1⅓ Tbsp. yeast
3 c. warm water
3 lb. doughnut mix
½ c. bread flour
2 Tbsp. white sugar

Dissolve yeast in warm water. Add remaining ingredients. Mix well, roll out, cut and deep fat fry. Fill with filling and frost with icing.

Filling:
3 c. powdered sugar
1½ c. shortening
3 egg whites
1 tsp. vanilla

Cream powdered sugar and shortening. Beat well. Beat in egg whites and vanilla. Whip until fluffy. Do not add water.

Icing:
1 c. brown sugar
½ c. butter
¼ c. milk
1¾-2 c. powdered sugar

Cook brown sugar and butter for 2 minutes, stirring constantly. Add milk and heat until it boils. Add powdered sugar. If icing is too stiff, add more milk.

—Ms. Lydia A. Mast, New York

Filled Doughnuts

5 Tbsp. dry yeast
3½ c. warm water
1¾ c. milk
¾ c. margarine
1 c. shortening
6 eggs, beaten
1¾ c. sugar
3 Tbsp. salt
20 c. flour

Dissolve yeast in water. Scald milk and melt margarine and shortening in it. Cool to lukewarm. Add yeast, eggs and remaining ingredients. Use your own judgement on the flour. Use more or less but should not be too stiff. Roll out, cut and deep fat fry. Let cool after frying and cut open and fill with frosting. Coat with doughnut or powdered sugar.

Filling:
¼ c. milk
1 Tbsp. flour
¾ c. shortening
2 tsp. vanilla
3 c. powdered sugar, divided
2 egg whites, beaten
8 oz. cream cheese, optional

Cook milk and flour together until thick. Let cool. Add shortening, vanilla and 1 c. powdered sugar. Beat together. Add beaten egg whites and 2 or more cups powdered sugar.

—Mrs. David (Naomi) Herschberger, Michigan

Even though the tongue weighs practically nothing, it's surprising how few persons are able to hold it.

Raised Potato Doughnuts

1 qt. milk, scalded
1 c. lard
1 c. sugar
1 c. cooked, mashed potatoes
2 tsp. salt
6 eggs
3 Tbsp. dry yeast
12 c. flour

In the scalded and cooled milk, put your lard, sugar, mashed potatoes, salt, eggs and yeast. Stir in the flour and let rise for 1 hour. Knead down and roll out to ¼" thick. Cut and let rise until double. Fry in hot lard or oil. Dip in glaze.

Glaze:
3 lb. powdered sugar
1 c. boiling water
2 pkg. gelatin
1 tsp. vanilla

Combine and mix well.

—Mrs. Jake (Anna) Herschberger, Michigan

Doughnuts

1 c. yeast
16 c. warm water
56 c. doughnut mix

Dissolve yeast in warm water. Add mix and stir well. Roll out, cut and deep fat fry. Makes 10 doz. doughnuts.

Glaze:
3¼ c. vanilla
3 Tbsp. + 1 tsp. salt
21 c. water
50 lb. powdered sugar

Combine and mix well.

—Ms. Cassie H. Mast, Michigan

Happiness Cake

1 c. good thoughts
1 c. kind deeds
1 c. consideration for others
2 c. sacrifice
2 c. well-beaten faults
3 c. forgiveness
4 c. prayer and faith

Add tears of joy, sorrow and sympathy. Flavor with love and kindly service. Fold in prayer and faith. Pour all this into daily life. Bake well with the heat of human kindness. Serve with a smile anytime.

Sunshine Pie

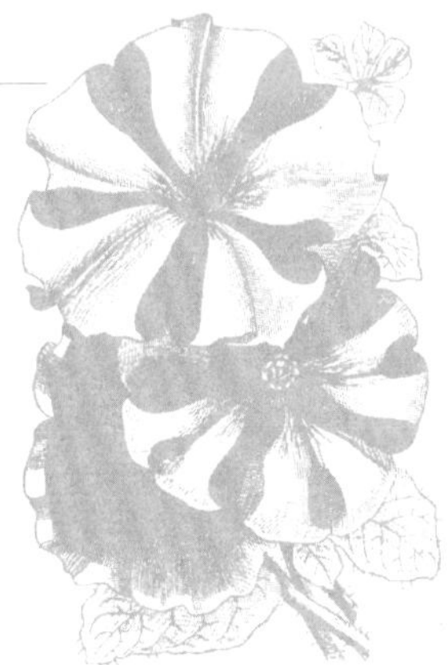

A lb. of patience you must find.
Mixed well with loving words so kind.
Drop in 2 lb. of helpful deeds,
And thoughts of other people's needs.
A pack of smiles to make the crust,
Then stir and bake it well you must.
Now I ask that you may try
The recipe of this Sunshine Pie.

Cakes and Frostings

- To take out baking soda taste in baked foods add a little vinegar.
- Put cornstarch in wedding cake frosting to help prevent sliding when in damp weather. This keeps it more firm.
- For better cake mixes, add ¾ c. flour, ½ c. white sugar and 1 tsp. baking powder plus the ingredients on the box. A little more oil and water can be added if batter seems too dry.
- When making a cake mix, add 1 Tbsp. cooking oil. This brings out more of the flavor and will make the cake moister.
- Egg whites will beat up better if left to warm at room temperature.
- To cut a fresh cake, use a thin sharp knife dipped in water.
- To test if a cake is done, stick a toothpick in the cake. If the batter clings to the toothpick, it isn't done.
- A cake is done when it springs back lightly when you touch it with your fingers.
- A different but good frosting is to mash a small boiled hot potato. Add vanilla and enough powdered sugar to have it spread nicely.
- There is no need to grease cake pans. Just swish water over pan and pour out, put batter in, and it will come out nicely.
- To keep icings moist and to prevent cracking, add a pinch of baking soda to the eggs before beating. Beat in the usual way and pour the hot syrup over the beaten eggs. It will be soft and creamy.
- If eggs are not beaten well or ingredients well mixed, a coarse-grained cake will result.

Glory Cake

9 eggs, separated
1½ c. sugar, divided
2 tsp. vanilla
¾ c. cake flour
2 tsp. cinnamon
1 tsp. salt
2 c. nuts

Beat egg whites. Gradually add ¾ c. sugar. Continue beating until very stiff. Do not underbeat. Combine egg yolks, vanilla and ¾ c. sugar in a small bowl. Beat until thick and lemon colored. Stir in cake flour, cinnamon and salt. Fold batter gently but thoroughly into egg whites using a wire whip. Fold in nuts. Pour in angel food cake pan and bake at 350° for 55 minutes.

–Mrs. Mahlon (Sarah) Gingerich, Ohio

Mother's Best Angel Food Cake

2 c. egg whites
1 tsp. vanilla
¼ tsp. almond extract, optional
½ tsp. salt
2 tsp. cream of tartar
2-2½ c. sugar, divided
1½ c. flour
Jell-O, optional

Beat egg whites, flavoring, salt and cream of tartar. Add 1-1½ c. sugar, 2 Tbsp. at a time and beat until stiff. Sift flour and 1 c. sugar together and fold in. Bake 50-60 minutes in a moderate oven. Can add any flavor Jell-O if desired.

–Ms. Esther S. Herschberger, Michigan
–Mrs. Jacob (Sadie) Hershberger, Wisconsin

Most smiles start with
another smile.

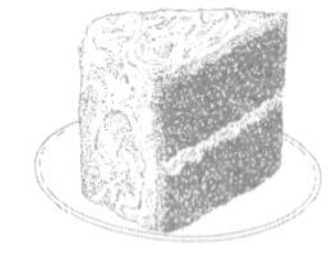

Never-Fail Angel Food Cake

2 c. egg whites
2 tsp. cream of tartar
1 c. sugar
1 c. flour
1 c. powdered sugar
1 tsp. salt
2 tsp. cornstarch
¼ tsp. baking powder
1-2 tsp. Jell-O, optional

Combine egg whites and cream of tartar. Beat until frothy. Add sugar a little at a time. In a small bowl, sift flour, powdered sugar, salt, cornstarch, baking powder and Jell-O together 3 times. Fold in and bake like usual angel food cake.

—*Mrs. Danny (Edna) Borntrager, Wisconsin*

Quick Cocoa Cake

3 c. flour
2 c. brown sugar
5 Tbsp. cocoa
2 tsp. baking soda
2 tsp. baking powder
1 tsp. salt
1¾ c. warm water
1¼ c. vegetable oil
4 eggs

Put all together in a mixing bowl and beat well with beater. Bake in a large cake pan at 350° for 45 minutes. This is my favorite cake—quick and simple.

—*Mrs. Henry (Emma) Raber, Ohio*

We cannot shine if we have not taken time to fill our lamps.

Jiffy Chocolate Feather Cake

3 c. flour
2 c. sugar
2 tsp. baking soda
2 tsp. baking powder
1 tsp. salt
½ c. unsweetened cocoa
1 c. vegetable oil
1 c. milk
1 c. prepared coffee
2 eggs
1 tsp. vanilla

Mix dry ingredients together first. Add vegetable oil, milk and coffee. Stir well. Add eggs and vanilla and beat until smooth. Pour in a 9" x 13" pan. Bake at 350° until done. Frost with Never-Fail Fudge Frosting.

—Ms. Emma M. Hershberger, Wisconsin

Happy Valley Chocolate Cake

3 c. flour
2 c. sugar
2 tsp. baking soda
1 tsp. salt
6 Tbsp. cocoa
⅓ c. shortening
2 c. cold water
2 tsp. vinegar
2 tsp. vanilla

Beat well until smooth. Bake in 9" x 13" greased loaf pan. Bake at 350° for 45 minutes.

—Mrs. Aden (Mary) Mast, New York

Funny Cake

3 c. flour
2 c. sugar
6 Tbsp. cococa
2 tsp. baking soda
¾ c. vegetable oil
2 Tbsp. vanilla
2 Tbsp. vinegar
2 c. water

Mix flour, sugar, cocoa and baking soda. Then add vegetable oil, vanilla, vinegar and water. Mix all together and bake at 350° until done. Our children memorized this.

—Mrs. John (Esther) Brock, Iowa

Wacky Cake

3 c. flour
2 c. sugar
⅔ c. cocoa
1 tsp. salt
2 tsp. baking soda
¾ c. vegetable oil
1 Tbsp. vinegar
2 tsp. vanilla
2 c. cold water

Mix in pan you are baking in. Mix until well blended. Bake at 350° for 45-50 minutes.

—Mrs. Eli (Anna) Mast, Wisconsin

Delicious Chocolate Cake

2 c. sugar
2 eggs
½ c. butter
2½ c. flour
½ c. cocoa
1 c. milk
2 tsp. baking soda
1 c. hot water

Mix sugar, eggs and butter. Add flour, cocoa and milk. Dissolve soda in hot water and add to batter. Mix well and bake.

—Ms. Elizabeth J. Yoder, Ohio

Moist Chocolate Cake

¾ c. butter and lard mixed
1 c. brown sugar
1 c. white sugar
3 egg yolks
½ c. cocoa
1 tsp. vanilla
½ tsp. salt
1½ tsp. baking powder
1½ tsp. baking soda
3 c. flour
1½ c. cold water

Combine butter and lard with sugars. Add egg yolks, one at a time. Stir well. Add dry ingredients alternately with water, adding stiffly beaten egg whites last. Bake in a 9" x 12" cake pan at 350° for 45 minutes or until a toothpick comes out clean. Our favorite chocolate cake—very moist.

—Mrs. Andrew (Ella) Mast, Ohio

Chocolate Cake

3 c. flour
2 c. sugar
2 Tbsp. cocoa
2 tsp. baking soda
2 eggs
⅔ c. vegetable oil
2 c. water or milk

Combine dry ingredients and make a well in them. Add eggs, vegetable oil and water or milk. Mix well. Pour in 9" x 13" pan. Bake at 350° for 25 minutes or until done.

—Mrs. Uria (Sara) Miller, Michigan

Cats have kittens;
Fish have little fishes.
So why can't sinks have little sinks,
Instead of dirty dishes!

Hot Fudge Cake

5 Tbsp. butter
1 c. sugar
¾ c. milk
2 tsp. baking powder
2 tsp. vanilla
pinch of salt
2 c. flour
1½ c. brown sugar
2 Tbsp. cocoa
1½ c. boiling water

Mix butter and sugar. Add milk, baking powder, vanilla, salt and flour. Mix well, then put in a greased cake pan. Mix brown sugar, cocoa and boiling water together. Pour over batter in pan. Bake at 350° for 50 minutes. Delicious with ice cream!

—Ms. Mary S. Herschberger, Michigan

Hot Fudge Sundae Cake

1 c. flour
¾ c. sugar
2 Tbsp. cocoa
2 tsp. baking powder
¼ tsp. salt
½ c. milk
2 Tbsp. vegetable oil
1 tsp. vanilla
1 c. nuts
1 c. brown sugar
¼ c. cocoa
1¾ c. hot water

Combine first 5 ingredients in an ungreased 9" x 9" pan. Mix in milk, oil and vanilla until smooth. Add nuts. Spread evenly in pan. Sprinkle with brown sugar, then ¼ c. cocoa. Do not mix. Pour hot water on top of this. Bake at 350° for 40 minutes. Let stand 15 minutes. Top with ice cream and sauce.

Hot Fudge Sauce:
3 Tbsp. butter
1 c. sifted powdered sugar
1 tsp. vanilla
3 Tbsp. cocoa
1 c. evaporated milk

Melt butter in a saucepan over medium heat. Add powdered sugar and cocoa alternately with the milk. Beat until smooth. Bring to a boil over medium heat, stirring constantly. Cook for 2 minutes. Add vanilla. Serve hot over ice cream.

—Ms. Anna T. Mast, New York

Chocolate Zucchini Cake

½ c. butter, softened
½ c. vegetable oil
1¾ c. sugar
2 eggs
¼ c. cocoa
½ c. sour milk
1 tsp. vanilla
2½ c. flour
½ tsp. baking powder
1 tsp. baking soda
½ tsp. salt
2 c. unpeeled, finely grated zucchini
chocolate chips

Mix in order given, sprinkling chocolate chips on top. Bake at 325° for 45 minutes. Cut into squares when cool and serve as brownies.

—Mrs. Enos (Ada) Mast, New York

Better Salad Dressing Cake

2¼ c. sugar
¾ c. cocoa
1½ c. hot water
1 c. salad dressing
1½ tsp. vanilla
1 Tbsp. baking soda
3 c. flour
2 eggs

Mix in order given. Bake at 350° until toothpick inserted comes out clean.

—Mrs. Enos (Ada) Mast, New York

Some people are like buttons—
popping off at the wrong time!

Very Good Chocolate Cake [1]

2 c. flour
1 c. white sugar
1 c. brown sugar
2 tsp. baking soda
2 tsp. baking powder
3 Tbsp. cocoa
½ c. vegetable oil
2 c. hot water
1 tsp. salt

Mix in order given. Bake until done.

Frosting:
1 c. brown sugar
½ c. butter
¼ c. milk or cream
2 c. powdered sugar
1 tsp. vanilla

Boil sugar and butter together for 2 minutes. Add milk. Remove from heat. Cool to lukewarm and add powdered sugar and vanilla.

—*Mrs. Eli (Rachel) Mast, New York*

Very Good Chocolate Cake [2]

½ c. shortening
1 c. white sugar
1 c. brown sugar
2 eggs
pinch salt
2 c. boiling water
½ c. cocoa
2 tsp. soda
2 tsp. baking powder
2 c. flour

Mix in order given. Batter will be thin. Bake at 350° for 38 minutes.

—*Mrs. Samuel (Malinda) Mast, Pennsylvania*

Turtle Cake

1 chocolate cake mix
14 oz. caramels
¾ c. butter
1 can sweetened condensed milk
1 c. chocolate chips
1 c. nuts

Mix cake mix according to package directions. Melt together caramels, butter and milk. Put half of cake mix in pan. Bake until done. Sprinkle chocolate chips and nuts over hot cake. Top with caramel sauce and remainder of cake mix and bake until done.

—*Ms. Amanda J. Mast, New York*

Best Ever Chocolate Cake

2 c. flour
1½ c. sugar
3 Tbsp. cocoa
2 tsp. baking soda
1 tsp. baking powder
½ c. instant chocolate pudding
½ c. vegetable oil
2 eggs
1 c. milk
1 tsp. vanilla
1 c. hot water

Mix dry ingredients together. Add all else except water and mix. Add water last. Beat just until lumpy. Bake at 350° for 30 minutes or until done. Serves 14 people.

—*Mrs. Allee (Susan) Yoder, Ohio*

Don't begin the day with a sigh, or you may end it with a downpour.

Easy Chocolate Cake

3 eggs
3 c. sugar
¾ c. shortening
3 Tbsp. cocoa
1 Tbsp. baking soda
¾ tsp. baking powder
½ tsp. salt
3 c. flour
¾ c. sour milk
1 Tbsp. vanilla
1½ c. boiling water

Combine eggs, sugar and shortening. Mix well. Add dry ingredients alternately with sour milk and mix well. Add vanilla and boiling water. Bake in a hot oven for 35-45 minutes.

—Mrs. Levi (Esther) Troyer, Ohio

Moist Chocolate Cake

6 c. flour
4 c. sugar
½ c. cocoa
4 tsp. baking soda
2 tsp. salt
1⅓ c. vegetable oil
4 tsp. vinegar
4 tsp. vanilla
4 c. cold water

Mix dry ingredients. Add remaining ingredients. Bake at 350° for 30-40 minutes or until done.

—Ms. Fannie L. Raber, Ohio

The best gift you can give to others is being a good example.

Extra-Moist Chocolate Cake

2½ c. flour
1¼ c. sugar
1 tsp. baking powder
¼ c. cocoa
¼ tsp. salt
2 eggs
1 c. vegetable oil
1 c. buttermilk or sour milk
1 tsp. vanilla
2 tsp. baking soda
1 c. hot water

Combine flour, sugar, baking powder, cocoa and salt. Add eggs, oil, milk and vanilla. Stir well. Dissolve soda in hot water and add to mixture. Pour into a 9" x 13" x 2" cake pan and bake at 350° until done.

Topping:
¼ c. sugar
⅓ c. milk
12 lg. or 120 sm. marshmallows
2 c. coconut

Heat together first 3 ingredients until melted. Cool and add coconut. Pour over hot cake.

Frosting:
2 Tbsp. milk
⅓ c. sugar
¼ c. butter
8 oz. chocolate chips
1 Tbsp. corn syrup

Melt together and pour over cake. Top with **almonds** or **nuts**.

—Mrs. Samuel (Naomi) Miller, Wisconsin

Our Favorite Chocolate Cake

1¾ c. flour
2 c. sugar
¾ c. cocoa
1½ tsp. baking powder
1½ tsp. baking soda
1 tsp. salt
2 eggs
1 c. milk
½ c. vegetable oil
2 tsp. vanilla
1 c. boiling water

Combine flour, sugar, cocoa, baking powder, baking soda and salt in a large bowl. Add eggs, milk, oil and vanilla and beat. Stir in boiling water. Batter will be thin. Bake at 350° for 30-35 minutes.

—Ms. Rachel M. Coblentz, Clarissa Minnesota

Texas Sheet Cake

1 c. butter
1 c. water
4 tsp. cocoa
2 c. flour
2 c. sugar
½ tsp. salt
2 eggs, beaten
1 tsp. baking soda
½ c. sour cream

Mix butter, water and cocoa in a saucepan and bring to a boil. Put flour, sugar and salt into a bowl. Pour hot cocoa mixture over and mix. Mix eggs, baking soda and sour cream and add to flour-cocoa mixture. Beat well. Bake in a jelly-roll pan at 350° for 15-18 minutes. Frost while still warm.

Frosting:
½ c. butter
¼ c. cocoa
⅓ c. milk
vanilla
powdered sugar

Bring butter, cocoa and milk to a boil. Add vanilla and powdered sugar until spreading consistency.

—Ms. Elmina C. Kauffman, Wisconsin

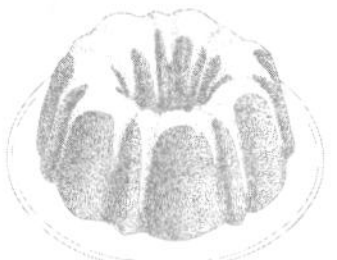

Peanut Butter Chocolate Cake

2 c. all-purpose flour
2 c. sugar
¾ c. cocoa
2 tsp. baking powder
1 tsp. baking soda
½ tsp. salt
2 eggs
1 c. strong coffee, cooled
1 c. milk
½ c. vegetable oil
2 tsp. vanilla

Sift all dry ingredients together. Add eggs and liquids. Stir until batter is smooth. Batter will be thin. Bake at 350° for 35 minutes or until done. This very moist dark cake may be made ahead of time, because it actually becomes more moist the second day.

Chocolate Cream Cheese Frosting:

3 oz. cream cheese
¼ c. butter, softened
2 c. powdered sugar
⅓ c. baking cocoa
3 Tbsp. milk
½ tsp. vanilla
dash salt

Cream the first 2 ingredients together until smooth. Add remaining ingredients and mix well.

Peanut Butter Frosting:

3 oz. cream cheese
¼ c. creamy peanut butter
2 c. powdered sugar
2 Tbsp. milk
½ tsp. vanilla
chocolate chips, optional

Cream the first 2 ingredients together until smooth. Add remaining ingredients and mix well.

—Mrs. Andy (Ada) Mast, New York
—Mrs. Perry (Elizabeth) Weaver, Ohio

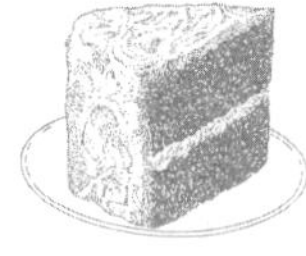

Chocolate Crest White Cake

2¼ c. sifted flour
1½ c. sugar
½ tsp. salt
1 Tbsp. baking powder
½ c. shortening
1 c. milk
1½ tsp. vanilla
¼ tsp. almond flavoring
4 egg whites, unbeaten

Sift flour, sugar, salt and baking powder together 3 times. Add shortening, milk and flavorings and stir well. Add egg whites and beat very well. Bake in a moderate oven. Can be baked in a loaf or layer pans.

—Ms. Sarah B. Brock, Iowa

Ice Water White Cake

½ c. shortening
2 c. sugar
3½ c. cake flour
¾ tsp. salt
1 Tbsp. baking powder
1½ c. ice water
4 egg whites
flavoring to taste

Cream shortening. Add sugar gradually and beat until fluffy. Sift flour. Add salt and baking powder. Add sifted dry ingredients alternately with ice water. Beat after each addition. Fold in stiffly beaten egg whites last. Bake at 350° for 30 minutes. Must be ice water or the cake will not be nice. This is a very good cake!

—Ms. Lydia A. Mast, New York

White Mountain Cake

2 c. sugar
1 c. milk
1 c. heavy cream
3 c. flour
1 Tbsp. baking powder
2 eggs
vanilla
salt

Don't stir until everything is in. Makes a large cake.

—Mrs. Ephraim (Amanda) Mast, Michigan

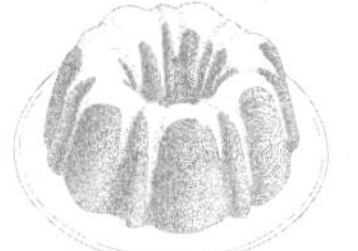

Delicious White Nut Cake

2 c. sugar
½ c. shortening
1 c. milk
3 c. cake flour
1 Tbsp. baking powder
1 tsp. vanilla
6 egg whites, stiffly beaten
½ tsp. salt, optional
approx. ½ c. finely chopped nuts, optional

Cream sugar and shortening. Add milk and dry ingredients alternately. Then add vanilla. Add stiffly beaten egg whites last.

—Mrs. Levi (Susan) Mast, New York
—Ms. Edna A. Slabaugh, Wisconsin

Yellow Love Light Chiffon Cake

2¼ c. flour
1 Tbsp. baking powder
1½ c. sugar, divided
1 tsp. salt, optional
⅓-½ c. vegetable oil
2 or 3 eggs, separated
1 c. water or milk
1 tsp. lemon or vanilla flavoring
1 c. nuts, optional

Sift flour, baking powder, 1 c. sugar and salt together. Add oil, egg yolks, water and flavoring in that order and beat well. Beat egg whites and remaining ½ c. sugar together. Mix in with other ingredients. Add nuts if desired. Bake at 350° for 40-50 minutes.

—Mrs. John (Susan) Miller, New York
—Mrs. Simon (Malinda) Yoder, Ohio

Failure is not defeat unless you stop trying.

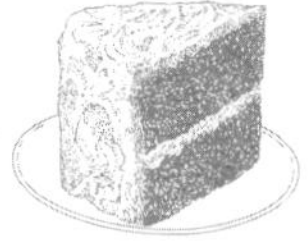

Golden Butter Cake

2/3 c. butter, softened
1 3/4 c. sugar
2 eggs
1 1/2 tsp. vanilla
3 c. cake flour
2 1/2 tsp. baking powder
1 tsp. salt
1 1/4 c. milk

Beat butter, sugar, eggs and vanilla until smooth. Stir dry ingredients together. Mix alternately with milk.

—Ms. Saloma E. Mast, New York

Easy Yellow Cake

2 c. flour
1 1/2 c. sugar
2 tsp. baking powder
1/2 tsp. salt
1/2 c. shortening
2 eggs
1 tsp. vanilla
1/2 tsp. almond flavoring, optional
1 c. milk

Mix together flour, sugar, baking powder and salt. Add shortening, eggs and flavorings and mix. Slowly stir in milk. Beat 300 strokes by hand. Bake at 325°. Variation: For chocolate cake add 1/4 c. cocoa to dry ingredients.

—Mrs. Jonas (Anna) Miller, Michigan

Lazy Daisy Shortcake

4 eggs
2 c. sugar
1 tsp. vanilla
2 c. flour
2 tsp. baking powder
1 c. hot milk
3 Tbsp. butter, melted
1/4 tsp. salt

In a large bowl, beat eggs until lemon colored. Slowly beat in sugar and vanilla. Stir in flour and baking powder. Slowly beat in hot milk, melted butter and salt. Bake at 350° for 35-40 minutes.

—Mrs. Amos (Ella) Beechy, Ohio

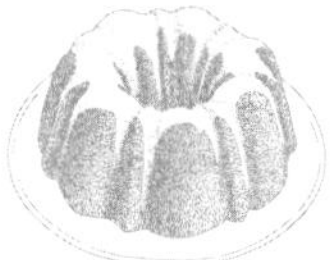

Delicious Shortcake

½ c. white sugar
6 Tbsp. butter
1 egg, optional
2 tsp. baking powder
¾ tsp. salt
1 tsp. vanilla
½ c. milk
2 c. flour
1½ Tbsp. butter, melted

Topping:
¼ c. sugar
1 Tbsp. flour
½ tsp. cinnamon

Combine first 8 ingredients in order given and put in pan. Drizzle with melted butter. Mix topping ingredients and sprinkle on top. Bake in a 8" x 8" greased cake pan at 375° for 25-30 minutes. Serve warm with milk and top with strawberries or peaches. Very good!

—Mrs. Mahlon (Mary) Miller, Michigan
—Mrs. Albert (Lizzie) Miller, New York

Cherry Coffee Cake

2 c. all-purpose flour
⅓ c. sugar
½ tsp. salt
2 tsp. baking powder
⅓ c. butter
2 eggs
¾ c. milk
1 (21 oz.) can cherry pie filling

Combine flour, sugar, salt, baking powder and cut in butter to make crumbs. Add eggs and milk to moisten. Dough will be lumpy. Pour batter in 9" x 13" x 2" pan. Top with cherries and spread with crumbs. Bake at 350° for 1 hour. Serve hot or cold with milk or cream.

Crumbs:
½ c. all-purpose flour
¾ c. brown sugar
1 c. quick oats
1 tsp. cinnamon
⅛ tsp. nutmeg
3 Tbsp. butter

Combine flour, sugar, oats, cinnamon and nutmeg. Cut in butter to make crumbs.

—Mrs. Paul (Edna) Brenneman, Michigan

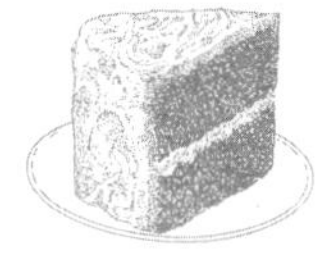

Cherry Filled Coffee Cake

1 c. margarine
1½ c. sugar
4 eggs
1 tsp. vanilla
3 c. flour
1½ tsp. baking powder
½ tsp. salt
1 can cherry pie filling

Cream margarine and sugar. Add eggs one at a time and beat well. Add vanilla, flour, baking powder and salt. Spread ⅔ of dough in a greased pan. Cover with pie filling and spoon remainder of batter on top. Glaze while still warm.

Glaze:
1½ c. powdered sugar
½ tsp. vanilla
2 tsp. butter
milk

Combine first 3 ingredients. Add milk to make a thin glaze. Drizzle over cake.

—Mrs. Edna F. Yoder, Ohio

God often digs wells of joy
with spades of sorrow.

Cream-Filled Coffee Cake

1 pkg. yeast
½ c. warm water
1 c. milk
½ c. butter
½ c. sugar
2 eggs, beaten
1 tsp. salt
3½-4 c. flour

Soak yeast in warm water. Heat milk and butter until a film forms. Pour over sugar and eggs. Add salt. Add soaked yeast when lukewarm and add flour. Let rise once. Put in three 9" cake pans. Sprinkle with topping and let set for 30 minutes. Bake at 375°. Cool. Split each layer in center to make 2 layers and spread filling in between.

Topping:
⅓ c. brown sugar
⅓ c. flour
3 Tbsp. butter, melted
1 tsp. cinnamon

Mix together.

Filling:
2 egg whites, beaten
1 c. shortening
2 c. powdered sugar
marshmallow creme

Combine and mix well.

—Mrs. Merle (Emma) Coblentz, Ohio

Seven days without prayer
makes one weak.

Delicious Coffee Cake

½ c. sugar
1 egg
¼ c. shortening
½ tsp. salt
½ c. milk
1½ c. flour
1½ tsp. baking powder

Mix in order given and put in cake pan. Sprinkle with topping and cut through a few times with a fork. Bake at 300° for 30 minutes.

Topping:
2 Tbsp. butter, melted
2 tsp. cinnamon
½ c. brown sugar

Mix in a small bowl.

—Mrs. Jake (Anna) Herschberger, Michigan

Filled Coffee Cake

¾ c. sugar
¼ c. lard
1 tsp. vanilla
1 egg, unbeaten
½ c. milk
2 tsp. baking powder
½ tsp. salt
1½ c. all-purpose flour

Combine sugar and lard and beat until smooth. Add vanilla, egg, milk, baking powder, salt and flour. Pour in pan and top with crumbs. Bake at 350° for 30 minutes. A double batch makes one 9" x 13" pan.

Crumbs for Topping:
½ c. brown sugar
¼ c. flour
½ tsp. cinnamon
½ tsp. nutmeg
¼ c. nuts
2 Tbsp. butter, softened

Mix together until crumbly.

—Ms. Rachel J. Hochstetler, Wisconsin

Cream Cheese Coffee Cake

1 c. butter, softened
1 c. sugar
2 eggs
2 c. flour
2 tsp. baking powder
½ tsp. salt
2 tsp. vanilla

Cream the butter and sugar. Add eggs and beat well. Mix flour, baking powder and salt. Add to creamed mixture. Add vanilla. Spread half of dough in bottom of a greased 9" x 13" cake pan. Spread with cream cheese filling and spoon remaining batter on top. Sprinkle with topping. Bake at 350° for 45 minutes. When done, drizzle top with glaze.

Filling:
16 oz. cream cheese
¼ tsp. vanilla
½ c. sugar
1 egg yolk
1 tsp. vanilla

Cream together cream cheese, vanilla, sugar and egg yolk.

Topping:
1 tsp. cinnamon
¼ c. sugar
½ c. flour
¼ c. butter, softened

Mix until crumbly.

Glaze:
½ c. powdered sugar
1 Tbsp. milk
vanilla

Combine and mix well.

—Mrs. Chris (Ella) Borntreger, Wisconsin

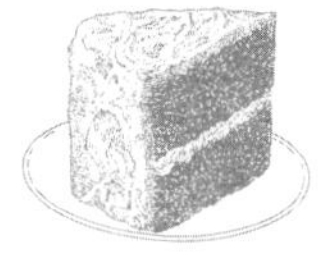

Apple Cake

4 c. chopped apples
½ c. vegetable oil
2 c. flour
1 c. nuts
2 eggs
½ tsp. salt
1 tsp. vanilla
1 tsp. baking soda
½ tsp. cinnamon
2 c. sugar

Combine and mix well. Bake.

—Mrs. Levi (Barbara) Mast, Pennsylvania

Blushing Apple Cake

1¼ c. flour
2 Tbsp. sugar
1 tsp. baking powder
½ tsp. salt
½ c. butter
1 egg
1 Tbsp. milk
1¼ qt. sliced apples
⅓ c. cherry Jell-O

Combine flour, sugar, baking powder, salt, butter, egg and milk. Press in pan. Put apple slices over dough in pan. Sprinkle with Jell-O. Cover with crumbs. Bake at 350° for about 55 minutes.

Crumbs:
1 c. flour
1 c. sugar
½ c. butter

Mix together until crumbly.

—Mrs. Levi (Esther) Nisley, Ohio

Carrot Cake [1]

3 c. flour
2 c. sugar
½ tsp. salt
1 tsp. baking powder
1 tsp. baking soda
1 tsp. cinnamon
¾ c. vegetable oil
3 eggs
½ c. milk
1 tsp. vanilla
2 c. grated carrots

Cream Cheese Frosting:
4 oz. cream cheese, softened
¼ c. butter
½ tsp. vanilla
2¼ c. powdered sugar
2 tsp. milk

Combine dry ingredients and mix well. Then add oil, beaten eggs, milk and vanilla and mix. Fold in carrots. Bake at 350° for 45 minutes or until done. Frost with cream cheese frosting. **Nuts** may be sprinkled on top.

—Mrs. Dannie (Lizzie) Yoder, Michigan

Carrot Cake [2]

2 c. brown sugar
2 c. flour
1 Tbsp. baking powder
1 tsp. salt
1 tsp. cinnamon
1 c. vegetable oil
4 eggs
3 c. finely grated carrots
½ c. nuts

Mix together sugar, flour, baking powder, salt, cinnamon and vegetable oil. Add eggs 1 at a time, beating well after each addition. Fold in carrots and nuts. Pour in 9" x 13" loaf pan and bake.

—Mrs. David (Naomi) Hershberger, Michigan

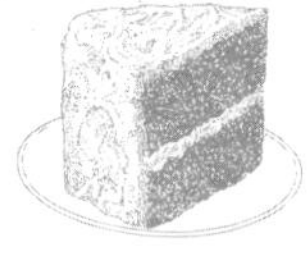

Banana Cake

2½ c. flour
1⅔ c. sugar
1¼ tsp. baking powder
1¼ tsp. baking soda
1 tsp. salt
⅔ c. shortening, softened
⅓ c. buttermilk or sour milk
1¼ c. (3) mashed ripe bananas
3 eggs

Sift first 5 ingredients together. Add remaining ingredients. Bake at 350°-400° for 30 minutes or until knife inserted comes out clean.

—Mrs. David (Naomi) Herschberger, Michigan

Rolled Oats Cake

1¼-1½ c. boiling water
1 c. quick oats
½ c. butter
1 c. white sugar
1 c. brown sugar
2 eggs, well beaten
1⅓-1½ c. flour
1 tsp. baking soda
1 tsp. baking powder, optional
½ tsp. salt
1 tsp. cinnamon

Combine boiling water and quick oats. Let stand for 20 minutes. Mix remaining ingredients. Add oatmeal mixture last and beat well. Bake in a loaf pan at 350° for 30-35 minutes. Spread topping on hot cake and pop back in oven to lightly brown top.

Topping:
1 c. brown sugar
¼ c. butter
½ c. cream
1 c. coconut
nuts

Bring sugar, butter and cream to a boil. Remove from heat and add coconut and nuts.

—Mrs. Mosie (Lizzie) Mast, New York
—Mrs. Noah (Edna) Brenneman, Michigan

Orange Cream Cheesecake

Crust:
2 c. graham cracker crumbs
½ c. margaringe or butter
1 tsp. cinnamon

Combine graham cracker crumbs, cinnamon, and butter. Press into the bottom of a greased 10" spring form pan.

Filling:
1 (3 oz.) pkg. orange jello
3 (8 oz.) cream cheese
1¼ c. sugar
5 oz. evaporated milk
1 tsp. lemon juice
⅓ c. orange juice concentrate
1 tsp. vanilla
1 (8 oz.) carton Cool Whip

Prepare Jell-O according to package instructions. Set ½ c. aside at room temperature. Chill remaining gelatin until slightly thickened. Meanwhile, beat cream cheese and sugar together. Gradually add milk and lemon juice. Add orange juice concentrate, vanilla, and room temperature Jell-O. Fold in Cool Whip. Pour over prepared crust.

Topping:
2 c. Cool Whip
¼ c. sugar

In a mixing bowl, beat Cool Whip and sugar. Beat in refrigerated Jell-O. (mixture will be thin) Chill for 30 minutes. Gently spoon over filling. (pan will be full) Chill 8 hours or overnight. We use whipping cream instead of Cool Whip. Delicious!

—Miss Phoebe T. Herschberger, Wisconsin

Take time to laugh; it is the music of the soul.

Cream Puff Cake

1 c. water
½ c. butter
1 c. flour
4 eggs
1 sm. container whipped topping

Heat water and butter until it comes to a boil. Add flour and mix until it forms a ball. Let cool. When cool, add eggs one at a time. Spread on a 9" x 13" glass pan. Spread mixture on bottom and a little up sides. Bake at 400° for 30-35 minutes. Let cool. Pour filling over crust and cover with whipped topping.

Filling:
4 c. milk
3 pkg. instant vanilla pudding
8 oz. cream cheese, softened

Beat milk and pudding until thick. Add cream cheese.

—Mrs. Noah (Malinda) Raber, New York

Dump Cake

1 can cherry pie filling
1 can crushed pineapple, undrained
1 box dry yellow cake mix
½ c. butter, chopped
1 c. chopped nuts, optional

Layer ingredients in a 9" x 13" loaf pan as listed. Bake at 350° for 30-40 minutes. Delicious with ice cream. This is an easy cake for children, since you just dump everything in the pan.

—Mrs. Alvin (Susie) Yoder, Ohio

Green Tomato Cake

2¼ c. sugar
1 c. shortening, melted
3 eggs
2 tsp. vanilla
3 c. all-purpose flour
1 tsp. salt
1 tsp. baking soda
1 tsp. cinnamon
½ tsp. freshly grated nutmeg
1 c. chopped walnuts
1 c. raisins
2½ c. diced green tomatoes
1 sm. can angel flake coconut

Preheat the oven to 350°. In a mixing bowl, cream the sugar, shortening, eggs and vanilla until smooth. Add the flour, salt, soda and spices and stir to blend. Stir in the nuts, raisins and tomatoes. Grease a 9" x 13" pan. Pour the batter into the pan and sprinkle the coconut on top. Bake for 1 hour. Serves 15-20 people.

—Mrs. Amos (Emma) Hershberger, Ohio

Tomato Soup Cake

2 eggs
½ c. shortening
1 c. sugar
1 c. tomato soup or 1½ c. milk
1 tsp. baking soda
2 tsp. baking powder
1 tsp. cloves
1 tsp. nutmeg
1 tsp. cinnamon
2 c. flour
½ c. raisins
1 c. nuts

Mix eggs, shortening and sugar. Add soup and baking soda. Add dry ingredients. Bake at 350° for 1 hour. Yum!

—Mrs. Atlee (Edna) Yoder, Wisconsin

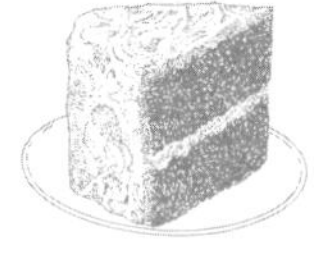

Spice Cake

2 c. sugar
1 c. butter
2 eggs
2 tsp. lemon extract
1½ c. buttermilk
3½ c. flour
1 tsp. allspice
¼ tsp. cloves
2 tsp. cinnamon
2 tsp. baking soda

Mix in order given. My mother got this recipe from her aunt Anna Keim, and we have used it many times.

—Mrs. Rudy (Ella) Borntreger, Wisconsin

Sunday Spice Cake

2½ c. sifted flour
⅔ c. shortening
1¼ c. sugar
1 tsp. salt
1 tsp. cinnamon
½ tsp. cloves
½ tsp. nutmeg
½ tsp. allspice
⅓ c. molasses
⅔ c. milk
2½ tsp. baking powder
½ tsp. baking soda
3 eggs
½ c. milk

Beat first 10 ingredients vigorously for 2 minutes. Stir in remaining ingredients and mix thoroughly. Bake in a moderate oven for 35 minutes.

—Ms. Lizzieann E. Mast, Michigan

Marble Cake

2 c. + 2 Tbsp. cake flour
3½ tsp. baking powder
1½ c. sugar
1 tsp. salt
½ c. shortening
1 tsp. vanilla
1 c. milk
4 lg. egg whites, beaten
1 Tbsp. cocoa
¼ tsp. baking soda
2 Tbsp. warm water

Mix flour, baking powder, sugar and salt. Add shortening, vanilla and milk. Add beaten egg whites. Pour ⅔ of the batter into a cake pan. Add cocoa, baking soda and water to remaining ingredients. Pour over white batter in stripes to marbleize. Bake at 350°.

—Mrs. Henry (Sarah) Yoder, Michigan

You are none the holier for being praised, and none the worse for being blamed.

Prince of Wales Cake

½ c. lard
1 c. sugar
1 egg
½ c. maple syrup
tsp. baking soda
1 c. sour milk
2 c. flour
1 tsp. cinnamon
1 tsp. cloves
1 tsp. nutmeg
raisins, optional
nuts, optional

Combine lard and sugar. Add egg. Beat well. Add maple syrup. Add dry ingredients alternately with milk, adding raisins and nuts last if desired. Ice with Seven-Minute Caramel Frosting.

Seven-Minute Caramel Frosting:

2 egg whites, unbeaten
1½ c. brown sugar
⅓ c. water
dash salt
1 tsp. vanilla

Combine egg whites, sugar, salt and water in top of double boiler. Beat for 7 minutes until thoroughly mixed and cook over rapidly boiling water, beating constantly with rotary beater until it stands up in stiff peaks. Remove from boiling water and add vanilla. Ready to spread on cake.

—Mrs. John (Edna) Herschberger, Wisconsin

The best way to do good to
ourselves is to do good to others.

Raspberry Angel Food Cake

2 c. egg whites, beaten
½ c. almond extract
2 tsp. cream of tarter
1 tsp. vanilla
½ tsp. salt
1¼ c. sugar, plus 1 c.

Add 1¼ c. sugar 2 Tbsp. at a time and beat until stiff. Sift flour and 1 c. sugar and fold in. For fruit flavor: (raspberry, cherry, orange, lemon, etc.) fold in 2 rounded Tbsp. dry Jell-O powder and swirl for a marbled effect. Bake 50 to 60 minutes in a tube pan in moderate oven. Yeild: one cake.

Crumb Cake

½ c. lard
2 c. brown sugar
1 egg
1 tsp. baking soda dissolved in
1½ c. sour milk
3 c. flour

Mix in order given. Top with crumbs. Bake.

Crumbs:
¾ c. flour
1 c. brown sugar
1 tsp. margarine
¾ tsp. cinnamon

Combine and mix well.

—Mrs. Simon (Clara) Miller, Michigan

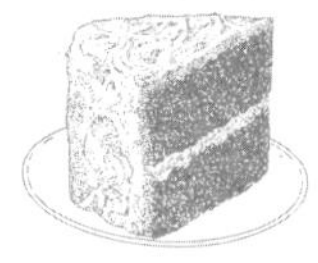

Cherry Crumb Cake

1 c. sugar
2 c. flour
2 tsp. baking powder
½ tsp. salt
½ c. butter
1 egg, beaten
cherry pie filling (other kinds may also be used)

Mix sugar, flour, baking powder and salt. Cut in butter and egg. Mix with crumbs. Put half of crumbs in bottom of pan. Spread pie filling on crumbs and top with remaining crumbs. Bake in a moderate oven for 30 minutes. Serve with ice cream. Enjoy! Serves 6-8 people.

—Mrs. Andy (Barbara) Schwartz, Michigan

Maple Pecan Chiffon Cake

2¼ c. cake flour or 2 c. all-purpose flour
¾ c. white sugar
¾ c. brown sugar
1 Tbsp. baking powder
1 tsp. salt
½ c. vegetable oil
5 egg yolks (with cake flour) or 7 egg yolks (with all-purpose flour)
¾ c. cold water
2 tsp. maple flavoring
1 c. egg whites (7 or 8 eggs)
½ tsp. cream of tartar
1 c. very finely chopped pecans

Heat oven to 325°. Stir together flour, sugars, baking powder and salt. Make a well and add oil, egg yolks, water and maple flavoring in order. Stir until smooth. Measure egg whites and cream of tartar into large mixing bowl. Beat until whites form very stiff peaks. Gradually pour egg yolk mixture over beaten whites, gently folding just until blended. Gently fold in the chopped pecans. Pour into an ungreased tube pan. Bake about 75 minutes or until done.

—Ms. Amelia A. Stabaugh, Wisconsin

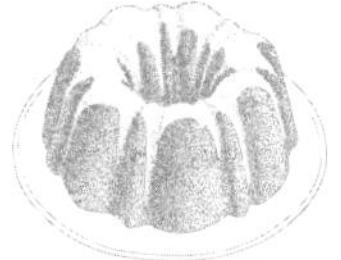

Hickory Nut Cake

3 eggs, separated
1 ½ c. sugar, divided
2 ¼ c. sifted flour
1 Tbsp. baking powder
1 tsp. salt
⅓ c. vegetable oil
1 c. water
1 tsp. vanilla or maple flavoring
¾ c. nuts

Beat egg whites until frothy. Add ½ c. sugar. Beat until stiff and glossy. In another bowl, sift remaining 1 c. sugar, flour, baking powder and salt. Add oil, water, egg yolks and flavoring. Beat until smooth. Fold in meringue. Add nuts. Bake in a 9" x 13" pan at 350° for 25 minutes. Frost.

—Ms. Emma M. Hershberger, Wisconsin
—Ms. Clara J. Herschberger, Wisconsin

Applesauce Cake

1 c. sugar
½ c. shortening
1 egg
1 c. applesauce
2 c. sifted flour
1 tsp. baking soda
1 tsp. baking powder
1 tsp. cinnamon
½ tsp. allspice
½ tsp. nutmeg
¼ tsp. cloves
¾ c. nuts

Cream sugar and shortening together. Add egg and beat well. Add applesauce. Sift dry ingredients together and add. Add nuts. Place in a greased 8" pan and bake at 350° for 50-60 minutes. Good with powdered sugar frosting.

—Mrs. Tobie (Ada) Miller, Wisconsin

Pone Cake

1 c. graham flour
½ c. cornmeal
¾ c. brown sugar
½ c. white flour
½ c. rolled oats
½ c. butter, melted
2 tsp. baking powder
1 tsp. baking soda
1 c. buttermilk
1 egg

Mix in order given and stir well. Bake at 300°-350°. Serve with milk and fruit. This is a good supper cake for a family.

—Mrs. Andrew (Edna) Miller, New York

Self-Filled Cupcakes

1 pkg. chocolate cake mix or your favorite chocolate cake
8 oz. cream cheese, softened
⅓ c. sugar
1 egg
dash of salt
6 oz. or 1 c. chocolate chips

Mix cake mix according to package directions or mix your favorite chocolate cake. Fill cupcake papers ⅔ full of cake batter. Combine cream cheese and sugar and beat well. Beat in egg and salt. Stir in chocolate chips. Drop 1 tsp. into each cupcake. Bake at 350° for 15-20 minutes. Variation: Increase sugar to ½ c. and use 12 oz. chocolate chips. Put ¾ Tbsp. filling into each cupcake.

—Mrs. Moses (Amelia) Gingerich, Ohio

White Mountain Frosting

½ c. sugar
¼ c. light corn syrup
2 Tbsp. water
2 egg whites (¼ c.)
1 tsp. vanilla

Combine sugar, corn syrup and water in a small saucepan. Cover and heat to a rolling boil over medium heat. Remove cover and boil rapidly, without stirring, to 242° on a candy thermometer or until a small amount of mixture dropped into very cold water forms a firm ball. As mixture boils, beat egg whites until stiff peaks form. Pour hot syrup very slowly in a thin stream into the beaten egg whites, beating constantly on medium speed. Beat on high speed until stiff peaks form. Add vanilla during last minute of beating. Fills and frosts two 8" or 9" layers or frosts a 9" x 13" cake.

Variation: Pink Mountain Frosting: Substitute maraschino cherry juice for the water.

Satiny Beige Frosting: Substitute brown sugar for the white sugar and decrease vanilla to ½ tsp.

—Ms. Amelia A. Slaubaugh, Wisconsin

Frosting for Wedding Cake

½ c. water
1 c. white sugar
1 tsp. salt
4 egg whites
2 c. shortening
10½ c. powdered sugar
4 tsp. vanilla

Boil water, white sugar and salt together for 1 minute. Beat egg whites, then add to boiled mixture while still hot. Stir and add shortening, powdered sugar and vanilla. Beat very well.

—Mrs. Jonas (Anna) Miller, Michigan

7-Minute Frosting

2 egg whites, unbeaten
1 c. white sugar
2 tsp. light corn syrup
5 tsp. water
1 tsp. vanilla

Combine egg whites, sugar and corn syrup in top of double boiler, beating with an egg beater until well mixed. Place over rapidly boiling water, beating constantly for 7 minutes. Remove from heat. Add vanilla. Beat until thick enough to spread.

—Ms. Lydia A. Mast, New York

Coconut Frosting

1 c. sugar
½ c. butter
1 c. cream
3 egg yolks, slightly beaten
1½ c. coconut
1 tsp. vanilla
1 c. nuts

In a 2-qt. saucepan, cook sugar, butter, cream and egg yollks over medium heat for 15 minutes or until thick. Add coconut, vanilla and nuts. Delicious on chocolate cake.

—Mrs. Uria (Sara) Miller, Michigan

Brown Sugar Frosting

¼ c. butter
½ c. brown sugar
1 tsp. vanilla
powdered sugar
warm water

Brown butter in a pan. Add brown sugar, vanilla and some water. Cook until sugar is dissolved. Remove from heat and add powdered sugar and more warm water if necessary.

—Mrs. Levi (Esther) Nisley, Ohio

A Love Cake for Mother

1 can of obedience
several lb. affection
1 pt. neatness
some holiday, birthday and everyday surprises
1 can of running errands (Willing brand)
1 box powdered "get up when I should"
1 bottle of "keep sunny all day long"
1 can pure thoughtfulness

Mix well. Bake in a hearty warma oven and serve to Mother every day. She ought to have it in big slices.

—Mrs. Andy (Barbara) Schwartz, Ohio

Friendships Cake

1 c. greetings
1-2 c. smiles
2 lg. handshakes
2-3 c. love
1 tsp. sympathy
2 c. hospitality

Cream greetings and smiles together, then add handshakes, beaten separately. Add love and slowly sift in sympathy and hospitality. Fold in very carefully. Serve to your family and friends.

—Mrs. Cassie H. Mast, Ohio

Recipe for Life

4 c. prayer daily
1 c. good thoughts
3 c. forgiveness
1 c. kind deeds
2 c. well-beaten faults
1 c. consideration for others

Bake with the heat of human kindness. Serve with a smile.

—Mrs. Cassie H. Mast, Ohio

The Garden Argument

The tomato said, with a face rosy red,
"I'm the queen of the whole garden bed.
So tart and delicious most everyone wishes
On my juicy meat to be fed."

Said the onion so strong, "You couldn't go wrong
To partake of my elements rare
With such a sweet savor I give a rich flavor
So all who might wish me may share."

Said the carrot so yellow, "I'm a popular fellow
At present I'm having my day.
My elements mild are so good for a child
They make him grow rosy and gay."

The cabbage head from the same garden bed
Said, "I'm bursting to have my say.
So crisp and so white with flavor just right,
I'm fit for a king any day."

The corn pricked his ears and
said, "Listen my dears,
I have heard every word you said
For I'm so tall, I look down on you all;
I'm the king of the whole garden bed."

The celery said, "Look! Here comes the cook.
We'll let her wise judgment decide
Which one she may choose, the rest of us lose."
"Fair enough, we agree," they all cried.

The cook came along with a smile and a song,
The vegetables she eyed as a group.
She cut and she sliced with her sharp paring knife,
And they all went into the soup.

Cookies and Bars
Sweet Heart

- Place a marshmallow on each cupcake just a little before removing from oven. It will melt to a nice frosting.
- For nice whoopie pies, use half pastry flour and half Thesco flour.
- When rolling out cookie dough, sprinkle board with powdered sugar instead of flour. Too much flour makes the dough heavy.
- A slice of bread added to a container of cookies will keep them soft.
- When a recipe asks for baking soda, dissolve it in a small amount of vinegar then it won't have that soda taste.
- A simple way to decorate your sugar cookies is to use an empty thread spool and press it into the dough for a pretty flower design.
- Mix ½ lb. baking soda and ½ lb. cream of tartar. Keep in an air-tight container in a dry place. You will have a better baking powder than you can buy.
- Measure shortening before molasses in a measuring cup, and it won't stick to the cup.
- An apple cut in half and placed in a cookie jar, cake box or bread box will keep your baked goods fresh and moist.

Monster Cookies

1 c. white sugar
1 c. brown sugar
¾ c. butter
4 eggs
1 lb. peanut butter
½ tsp. salt
2½ tsp. baking soda
1 tsp. corn syrup
4 c. oatmeal
½ c. flour
1 c. M&M's
1 c. chocolate chips

Cream sugars and butter. Add eggs 1 at a time, then add remaining ingredients. Bake at 350° for 8-10 minutes.

—Ms. Mattie J. Yoder, Ohio

Oatmeal Cookies

2 c. brown sugar
1 c. butter
2 eggs
2 tsp. vanilla
1½ c. flour
1 tsp. baking soda
1 tsp. baking powder
¼ tsp. salt
3 c. quick oatmeal
1 c. chocolate chips
½ c. coconut
¼ c. nuts

Beat sugar, butter, eggs and vanilla together. Sift the next 4 ingredients together and add to first mixture. Stir in oatmeal, chocolate chips, coconut and nuts. Refrigerate a few hours or overnight. Roll each ball in powdered sugar. Place on cookie sheet and bake at 350° for 10 minutes. They will be soft if lightly baked.

—Mrs. Mahlon (Mary) Miller, Michigan

Outrageous Oatmeal Cookies

1½ c. white sugar
1 c. brown sugar
1½ c. butter, softened
1½ c. peanut butter
1½ tsp. vanilla
3 eggs
3 c. flour
1 Tbsp. baking soda
¾ tsp. salt
1½ c. oatmeal
18 oz. chocolate or butterscotch chips

Mix in order given. Bake at 350° for 10-15 minutes or until golden brown.

—Mrs. Enos (Ada) Mast, New York

Oatmeal Scotch Chippers

1¼ c. shortening or butter
1½ c. brown sugar
1 c. white sugar
3 eggs
1¼ c. crunchy peanut butter
4½ c. oats
2 tsp. baking soda
1 c. chocolate chips
1 c. chopped nuts
1 c. butterscotch chips

Combine shortening and sugar. Add eggs and peanut butter then remaining ingredients. Drop on cookie sheet and bake.

—Mrs. Levi (Barbara) Mast, Pennsylvania

A clear conscience is a soft pillow.

Little Debbies

4 c. brown sugar
2 c. margarine
6 eggs
6 c. oatmeal
3½-5 c. flour
2½ tsp. baking soda
1½ tsp. salt
1 Tbsp. cinnamon
1 Tbsp. vanilla

Cream together sugar and margarine. Beat in eggs. Add remaining ingredients. Bake at 350°-375°.

Filling:
2 c. powdered sugar
1 c. shortening
2 tsp. vanilla
2 egg whites, beaten

Mix powdered sugar, shortening and vanilla together. Fold in beaten egg whites.
Emma makes a double batch of filling.

—Mrs. Levi (Susan) Mast, New York
—Mrs. Andrew (Emma) Yoder, Ohio

Oatmeal Cookies

5 lb. brown sugar
2½ lb. lard
7 eggs
2 oz. baking soda
1 qt. sour milk
2 lb. oatmeal
6 lb. flour
1 Tbsp. nutmeg
2 lb. raisins

Cream sugar and lard together. Add eggs. Dissolve baking soda in sour milk and add. Mix in oatmeal, flour and nutmeg next. Last add raisins. We sometimes use chocolate chips instead of raisins.

—Ms. Mary S. Herschberger

Oatmeal Whoopie Pies

4 c. brown sugar
1 c. margarine
4 eggs
4 tsp. baking soda
6 Tbsp. boiling water
½ c. buttermilk
2 tsp. salt
4½ c. flour
4 c. oatmeal
2 tsp. cinnamon
2 tsp. baking powder

Cream sugar and margarine together. Add eggs. Dissolve baking soda in boiling water and add. Stir in buttermilk. Mix salt, flour, oatmeal, cinnamon and baking powder. Add to batter. Bake at 400°. These should turn out soft and chewy. Spread filling between 2 cookies.

Filling:
2 egg whites
4 c. (or more) powdered sugar, divided
2 Tbsp. vanilla
1 c. shortening, softened
¼ c. milk

Beat egg whites until stiff. Add 2 c. powdered sugar. Beat in vanilla. In another bowl, cream shortening, adding a little of the egg white mixture at a time. Add milk and remaining powdered sugar alternately. Beat well.

—Mrs. Joseph (Martha) Miller, Ohio

Oatmeal Crisps

1 c. shortening
1 c. brown sugar
1 c. white sugar
2 eggs, beaten
1 tsp. vanilla
1 tsp. salt
1 tsp. baking soda
1½ c. flour
3 c. oatmeal
½ c. chopped walnuts
peanut butter, chocolate chips, butterscotch chips, optional

Cream shortening and sugars. Add eggs and vanilla and beat well. Add sifted dry ingredients, oatmeal and nuts. Add chips if desired. Form in long rolls and chill. Slice 1¼". Bake at 350° for 10 minutes. Makes 5 doz.

—Mrs. John (Elizabeth) Mast, New York

Oatmeal Raisin Cookies

1 c. shortening
1 c. white sugar
1 c. brown sugar
2 eggs
1 tsp. vanilla
3 c. rolled oats
1½ c. all-purpose flour
1 tsp. baking soda
1 tsp. salt
½ c. chopped walnuts
½ c. golden raisins

In a large mixing bowl, cream shortening and sugars. Beat in eggs and vanilla. Combine the oats, flour, baking soda and salt. Gradually add to creamed mixture. Add nuts and raisins. Drop by tablespoonsful 2" apart onto ungreased baking sheets. Bake at 375° for 10-12 minutes or until golden brown. Remove to wire racks to cool. Makes 5 doz.

—Mrs. Daniel (Gertie) Mast, New York

Chewy Oatmeal Cookies

3 c. brown sugar
1½ c. butter
4 eggs, beaten
1½ tsp. baking soda
2 tsp. vanilla
3 c. flour
4 c. oatmeal

Cream sugar and butter. Add beaten eggs and stir well. Add remaining ingredients. Drop by teaspoon onto cookie sheet. This is our family's favorite!

Frosting:
2 c. powdered sugar
2 egg whites, beaten
½ c. shortening
1 Tbsp. vanilla

Combine and mix well.

—Mrs. Albert (Emma) Lutzman, Ohio

Oatmeal Chip Cookies

1 c. shortening
2 c. sugar
2 Tbsp. molasses
2 eggs
2 c. flour
2 c. rolled oats
2 tsp. baking soda
2 tsp. cinnamon
1 tsp. salt
1 c. chocolate chips
2 tsp. vanilla

Mix shortening and sugar. Add molasses and eggs. Mix flour, rolled oats, baking soda, cinnamon and salt together. Add to mixture. Add chocolate chips and vanilla.

—Mrs. Noah (Malinda) Raber, New York

Oatmeal Spice Cookies

1 c. white sugar
1 c. brown sugar
1 c. shortening
2 eggs
1 c. sour cream
1 tsp. baking soda
2¾ c. flour
1 tsp. baking powder
1 tsp. salt
1 tsp. cinnamon
½ tsp. cloves
3 c. quick oats
1 c. chopped nuts
1½ c. dates or raisins

Cream sugars, shortening and eggs thoroughly. Add sour cream and baking soda, then flour, baking powder, salt, cinnamon and cloves. Last add oatmeal, nuts and dates or raisins. Drop by teaspoon on ungreased cookie sheets and bake in a hot oven.

—Mrs. Uria (Sara) Miller, Michigan

Chewy Chocolate Chip Oatmeal Cookies

4 c. butter, softened
5 c. brown sugar
2 c. white sugar
8 eggs
½ c. milk
vanilla
7 c. flour
4 tsp. baking soda
pinch of salt
10 c. quick oats
4 c. chocolate chips

Beat butter and sugars together until creamy. Add eggs, milk and vanilla and beat well. Combine flour, baking soda and salt and add. Mix well. Stir in oats and chocolate chips. Bake at 375°. This is a family favorite!

—Mrs. Rudy (Ella) Bontreger, Wisconsin

Perfectly Chocolate Chocolate Chip Cookies

2¼ c. flour
⅓ c. cocoa
1 tsp. baking soda
1 tsp. baking powder
½ tsp. salt
1 c. margarine, softened
¾ c. white sugar
¾ c. brown sugar
1 tsp. vanilla
½ tsp. maple flavoring
2 eggs
2 c. chocolate chips
1 c. chopped nuts, optional

Heat oven to 375°. Stir flour, cocoa, baking soda, baking powder and salt together. Set aside. Cream margarine, sugars and flavorings until creamy. Add eggs and beat well. Stir in dry ingredients, chocolate chips and nuts if desired. Drop on ungreased cookie sheet. Bake 8-10 minutes or until set.

—Mrs. Monroe (Mary) Hershberger, Wisconsin

Chocolate Chip Cookies [1]

2 c. brown sugar
1 c. white sugar
2 c. butter
6 eggs
1 Tbsp. vanilla
2 tsp. salt
4 tsp. baking soda
4 tsp. baking powder
3 c. regular flour
4 c. pastry flour
chocolate chips

Cream sugars and butter. Mix in eggs and vanilla well. Stir in dry ingredients and chocolate chips. Bake until done.

—Mrs. Eli (Anna) Mast, New York

Chocolate Chip Cookies [2]

2¼ c. brown sugar
1 Tbsp. vanilla
1½ c. corn oil
3 eggs, beaten
3¾ c. flour
1½ tsp. baking soda
½ tsp. salt
1 c. chocolate chips
nuts, optional

Cream sugar, vanilla, corn oil and beaten eggs together. Add flour, baking soda, salt and chocolate chips. Bake at 400°.
Note: Always use corn oil and bread flour.

—Mrs. Levi (Susan) Mast, New York

The happiest times we ever spend are those we share with a special friend.

Soft Batch Chocolate Chip Cookies

- 3/4 c. brown sugar
- 1/4 c. white sugar
- 1 c. butter, softened
- 1 pkg. (1/2 c.) instant vanilla pudding
- 2 eggs
- vanilla
- 2 1/4 c. flour
- pinch of salt
- 1 tsp. baking soda
- 2 c. chocolate chips
- 1 c. oatmeal, optional

Combine sugars, butter, pudding, eggs and vanilla. Beat until smooth. Add flour, salt, baking soda and chocolate chips. Batter will be stiff. Bake at 350° until lightly browned. Makes 4 1/2-5 doz.

—Mrs. Albert (Laura) Borntreger, Wisconsin
—Ms. Rachel A. Mast, Ohio
—Mrs. Henry (Edna) Hershberger, Ohio

Soft Chocolate Chip Cookies [1]

- 2 c. brown sugar
- 1 c. butter
- 2 eggs
- 1 c. milk
- 1 tsp. vanilla
- 2 tsp. baking soda
- 2 tsp. cream of tartar
- 4 c. flour
- 1 c. chocolate chips

Cream together sugar and butter. Add eggs. Beat well. Add remaining ingredients. Bake.

—Mrs. Tobie (Ada) Miller, Michigan

Soft Chocolate Chip Cookies [2]

1 c. butter, melted
2 c. brown sugar
2 eggs
1 tsp. vanilla
4 c. flour
1 tsp. salt
1 tsp. baking soda
½ c. sour milk
1 c. mini chocolate chips

Cream butter and sugar together. Add eggs and mix well. Add vanilla. Mix flour, salt and baking soda together. Add alternately with sour milk, mixing well after each addition. Add chocolate chips last. Drop on greased cookie sheets. Bake at 375° for 10 minutes or until done.

—Ms. Fannie L. Raber, Ohio

Blue Bonnet Chocolate Chip Cookies

10 c. all-purpose flour
4 tsp. baking soda
3 c. margarine, melted
6 c. brown sugar
4 eggs
3 Tbsp. + 2 tsp. vanilla
2-4 c. semi-sweet chocolate chips

Preheat oven to 350°. Combine flour and baking soda and set aside. In a large bowl, combine melted margarine and brown sugar. Mix well. Stir in eggs, vanilla and chocolate chips. Drop by teaspoonsful onto a cookie sheet, leaving about 2½" between each one. Bake at 350° for 9-12 minutes or until edges harden and centers are still soft.

—Mrs. Daniel (Katie) Mast, Wisconsin
—Mrs. Alvin (Susie) Yoder, Ohio

Delicious Chocolate Chip Cookies

½ c. shortening
1½ c. brown sugar
2 eggs
½ tsp. baking powder
1 tsp. baking soda
½ tsp. salt
2½ c. sifted flour
1 c. sour cream
1 tsp. vanilla
⅔ c. chocolate chips

Cream shortening, sugar and eggs. Add baking powder, baking soda and salt to sifted flour. Then add dry ingredients alternately with sour cream. Add vanilla and chocolate chips. Drop with a spoon and bake at 375° until light brown.

—Mrs. Harvey (Lisbet) Mast, Pennsylvania

Best Ever Chocolate Chip Cookies

2 c. shortening
4 c. brown sugar
4 eggs
8 c. (or less) flour
4 tsp. soda
3 Tbsp. + 1 tsp. baking powder
2 tsp. vanilla
2 tsp. salt
5 c. chocolate chips

Cream together shortening and sugar. Add eggs and mix well. Add remaining ingredients. Bake. Do not overbake.

—Mrs. Samuel (Edna) Mast, Pennsylvania

There is no garden so complete,
But roses make the place more sweet.
There is no life so rich and rare,
But one more friend can enter there.

Chocolate Chips Pudding Cookies

1½ c. butter, softened
1 c. brown sugar
½ c. white sugar
3 eggs
6 oz. instant vanilla pudding mix
1½ tsp. vanilla
3½ c. flour
1½ tsp. baking soda
2 c. chocolate chips
1 c. chopped nuts

Cream butter and sugars. Beat in eggs gradually. Beat until smooth and creamy. Add pudding mix and vanilla. Mix flour with baking soda. Add flour mixture, then stir in chocolate chips and nuts. Bake on a greased cookie sheet at 375° for 8-10 minutes. Press down with a spoon and water. Very good!

—Mrs. David (Lisbet) Mast, Wisconsin

Zucchini Cookies

¾ c. margarine
¾ c. sugar
1 egg
2 c. flour
1 tsp. baking powder
¼ tsp. salt
1 tsp. vanilla
1 c. shredded zucchini
½ c. chocolate chips

Cream margarine, sugar and egg. Add dry ingredients and vanilla. Add zucchini and chocolate chips last. Bake at 350° for 15 minutes. Cool before icing.

—Mrs. David (Naomi) Herschberger, Michigan

Thanksgiving begins in the heart.

Double Treats

2 c. flour
2 tsp. baking soda
½ tsp. salt
1 c. shortening
1 c. white sugar
1 c. brown sugar
2 eggs
1 tsp. vanilla
1 c. peanut butter
6 oz. chocolate chips
1 c. chopped peanuts, optional

Sift flour, baking soda and salt together. Beat shortening, sugars, eggs, vanilla and peanut butter together. Add dry ingredients. Stir in chocolate chips and peanuts. Shape into small balls and smash down a little. Place on an ungreased pan. Bake.

—Mrs. Levi (Esther) Troyer, Ohio

Moist White Cookies [1]

4 c. brown sugar
2 c. butter
4 eggs
2 c. sour milk
2 tsp. baking soda
4 tsp. baking powder
1 tsp. salt
3 Tbsp. + 1 tsp. vanilla
8 c. bread flour

Combine in order given. Bake at 400°. I use these for chips, flavoring and raisin filled cookies.

—Mrs. Eli (Sarah) Mast, New York

Moist White Cookies [2]

4 c. brown sugar
4 c. white sugar
2 c. lard
2 c. butter
8 eggs
16 c. all-purpose flour
4 tsp. baking powder
1 tsp. salt
4 c. sour milk
¼ c. baking soda
3 Tbsp. + 1 tsp. vanilla

Mix in order given. Roll out cookies about ½" thick. Sprinkle with sugar. The cookies will roll out easier if the dough is chilled overnight or several hours. The cookies will be softer if the milk is thick. Makes 11½ doz.

—Mrs. Henry (Sarah) Mast, Ohio
—Mrs. Noah (Susie) Gingerich, Ohio
—Ms. Mary L. Hershberger, Ohio

Molasses Cookies [1]

2¼ c. brown sugar
1½ c. white sugar
2¼ c. shortening
3 eggs
2 Tbsp. baking soda dissolved in ¾ c. buttermilk
¾ c. blackstrap molasses
1½ tsp. cinnamon
¾ tsp. salt
1½ tsp. baking powder
9 c. flour

Mix in order given. This will be a stiff dough. Chill for 1 hour. Shape in balls and roll in white sugar. Bake at 350° for 10-15 minutes. Fill with your favorite filling between 2 cookies.

—Mrs. Joseph (Martha) Miller, Ohio

Molasses Cookies [2]

3 c. shortening, melted
4 c. sugar
1 c. molasses
4 eggs
8 tsp. baking soda
8 c. flour
1 tsp. cloves
2 tsp. cinnamon
2 tsp. salt

Melt shortening. Add sugar, molasses, eggs and salt; mix. Add flour, cloves, cinnamon and salt. Form into balls and roll in sugar. Place on a greased cookie sheet. Do not press down nor overbake.

—Ms. Saloma S. Mast, New York

Molasses Cookies [3]

4 c. brown sugar
2 c. butter
4 eggs
1 c. blackstrap molasses
1 lb. ground raisins
2 tsp. vanilla
2 c. cold water
5 tsp. baking soda
5 tsp. baking powder
2 tsp. cinnamon
10 c. flour

Cream sugar and butter. Add eggs then molasses, raisins, vanilla and water. Sift dry ingredients and add gradually. Drop by spoonsful on a cookie sheet and bake.

—Mrs. Lewis (Elizabeth) Yoder, New York

Joy is not the absence of trouble
but the presence of God.

Cane Molasses Cookies

4 c. brown sugar
2 c. lard
2 c. cane molasses
4 eggs, unbeaten
2 tsp. vanilla
13 c. flour
3 Tbsp. + 1 tsp. baking soda
1 tsp. cinnamon
1 tsp. nutmeg
1 tsp. cloves
1 tsp. allspice
1 tsp. salt
1 c. cold water
1 lb. chopped raisins, optional

Cream sugar and lard in a big bowl. Add the cane molasses and mix well. Add eggs and vanilla; beat well. Mix flour and spices together. Add flour, soda and water alternately to dough, mixing well after each addition. Begin and end with flour. Stir in the raisins if desired. Drop by teaspoon onto cookie sheets and bake.

—Mrs. Andy (Fannie) Slabaugh, Wisconsin

In Giving
The more you give, the more you get.
The more you laugh, the less you fret.
The more you do unselfishly,
The more you live abundantly.
The more of everything you share,
The more you'll always have to spare.
The more you love, the more you'll find
That life is good and friends are kind.
For only what we give away
Enriches us from day to day.

Molasses Cream Cookies

2½ c. white sugar
2½ c. brown sugar
3 c. shortening
8 tsp. baking soda dissolved in
1 c. sour cream or milk
1 c. molasses
1 tsp. salt
4 eggs
4 tsp. cinnamon
2 tsp. baking powder
10 c. flour

Mix all together. Drop on cookie sheet and flatten with sugar. Bake at 350°. Spread filling between 2 cookies.

Mattie's Filling:
3 egg whites, beaten
3 c. powdered sugar
1 c. shortening
1 tsp. vanilla

Combine and mix well.

Rachel's Filling:
6 c. powdered sugar
1 tsp. salt
3 egg whites
6 Tbsp. water
¾ c. white sugar
1½ c. shortening

Mix powdered sugar, salt and egg whites together. Boil water and white sugar for 1 minute. Add to first mixture. Cream in vanilla and shortening.

—Mrs. Amos (Mattie) Garber, Ohio
—Mrs. Eli (Rachel) Mast, New York

Sandwich Molasses Cookies

2 c. butter
4 c. brown sugar
½ c. sour cream
¼ c. baking molasses
¼ c. blackstrap molasses
4 eggs
1 tsp. salt
½ tsp. ginger
4 tsp. cinnamon
4 tsp. baking soda
4 tsp. baking powder
1½ tsp. ground cloves
8 c. flour

Mix in order given. Refrigerate dough overnight. Bake at 350° until golden brown. Spread filling between cookies once cooled.

Filling:
2 egg whites, stiffly beaten
2 tsp. vanilla
3 c. powdered sugar, divided
1½ c. shortening

Beat egg whites and add vanilla and 2 c. powdered sugar. Beat well, then add shortening and 1 c. powdered sugar or more until the right consistency.

—Mrs. Melvin (Emma) Herschberger, Ohio

Disappearing Molasses Cookies

3 c. shortening, melted
4 c. sugar
5 eggs
1 c. molasses
2 tsp. salt
1 tsp. cinnamon
8½ c. flour
2 Tbsp. + 2 tsp. baking soda
sugar

Melt shorting. Add sugar, eggs, molasses, salt and cinnamon. Add flour and baking soda. Form into balls. Roll in sugar. Place on cookie sheet. Do not press down. Bake at 350°.

—Mrs. Henry (Sarah) Mast, Ohio

Sorghum Cookies [1]

5 c. white sugar
3 c. butter
4 eggs
1 c. baking molasses
8 tsp. baking soda dissolved in
  1 c. sour milk
12 c. Flaky Crust flour
2 tsp. cinnamon
1 tsp. salt

Cream together sugar and butter. Add eggs and mix well. Add remaining ingredients. Chill dough. Drop on cookie sheet and press down with a sugared glass. Bake at 325°-350°.

Filling:
3 egg whites, beaten
2 Tbsp. flour
1 c. shortening
1 tsp. vanilla
1 tsp. cream of tartar
4 c. powdered sugar
2 c. marshmallow creme
dash of salt

Combine and mix well.

—Mrs. Perry (Elizabeth) Weaver, Ohio

Sorghum Cookies [2]

1 c. butter, softened
1 c. shortening
3 c. brown sugar
5 eggs
1 c. sorghum
8 c. all-purpose flour
4½ tsp. baking soda
1 Tbsp. ginger
1 Tbsp. cinnamon
2 tsp. cloves
1 tsp. salt

Mix butter, shortening, sugar, eggs and sorghum together. Beat well. Add dry ingredients. Bake at 375°. These are very good and chewy.

—Mrs. Menno (Anna) Hershberger, Kentucky

Swedish Spice Cookies

3 c. butter
5 c. white sugar
5 eggs
1 1/4 c. molasses
2 tsp. salt
2 tsp. cinnamon
2 tsp. vanilla
8-10 c. flour
3 Tbsp. + 1 tsp. baking soda

Heat oven to 375°. Have ungreased baking sheets ready. Mix butter and sugar together. Add eggs and mix well. Add molasses, salt, cinnamon and vanilla. Mix well, then add flour and baking soda. Roll into balls or just take a spoonful of dough and dip or roll in sugar. Put on baking sheet and bake at 375°. If you want a soft, chewy cookie, do not press down, but if you prefer a crisp cookie, press down before baking.

—Ms. Amelia A. Slabaugh, Wisconsin

Peanut Butter Cookies [1]

2 c. white sugar
2 c. brown sugar
2 c. butter
4 eggs
2 tsp. vanilla
inch of salt
2 c. peanut butter
6 c. flour
4 tsp. baking soda

Mix in order given. Chill 1 hour. Form into balls and flatten to 1/4" thick. Bake at 350°. This was my mom's recipe.

—Mrs. Samuel (Katie) Herschberger, Michigan

Kindness is becoming
at any age.

Peanut Butter Cookies [2]

4 eggs
2 c. brown sugar
2 c. white sugar
2 c. butter
2 c. lard
4 tsp. baking soda
4 tsp. cream of tartar
8 c. flour
¾ c. peanut butter

Mix eggs, sugars, butter and lard. Combine baking soda, cream of tartar and flour. Mix together. Add peanut butter and mix well. Form into balls and flatten on cookie sheet with back of finger. Bake.

—Mrs. Albert (Laura) Borntreger, Wisconsin

Peanut Butter Blossoms

1 c. shortening
1 c. peanut butter
1 c. brown sugar
1 c. white sugar
2 eggs
¼ c. milk, optional
1-2 tsp. vanilla
3-3½ c. flour
½ tsp. salt
2 tsp. baking soda
1 tsp. baking powder
1 pkg. Hershey's kisses

Cream shortening and peanut butter. Add sugars and continue to beat. Add eggs, milk and vanilla. Beat until fluffy. Sift flour, salt, baking soda and baking powder together. Gradually add sifted dry ingredients to creamed mixture and mix thoroughly. Chill dough for several hours. Shape dough into balls. Place on cookie sheet and press flat with a fork or potato masher. Bake at 375° for 12-15 minutes. Place Hershey's Kiss in the middle of a hot cookie. Let cool before you remove from tray. Do not overbake. Makes 6 doz.

—Ms. Emma A. Rabaugh, Wisconsin
—Mrs. Atlee (Susan) Yoder, Ohio

Byler Cookies

26 c. flour
6 Tbsp. + 2 tsp. baking soda
2 tsp. cinnamon
2 tsp. nutmeg
2 tsp. cloves
dash of salt
2 tsp. allspice
8 c. brown sugar
4 c. lard
8 eggs beaten with
 4+ c. cold water
2 c. blackstrap molasses
2 lb. raisins

Sift dry ingredients together. Cut in lard. Add water and eggs 1 at a time. Add molasses and raisins. Form into balls and flatten with a fork.

—Mrs. Andy (Ada) Mast, New York

Snickerdoodles

1 c. shortening
1½ c. sugar
2 eggs
2 tsp. vanilla
2½-3 c. flour
2 tsp. cream of tartar
1 tsp. baking soda
½ tsp. salt
2 Tbsp. sugar
2 tsp. cinnamon

Cream shortening, sugar and eggs and vanilla together. Add flour, cream of tartar, baking soda and salt. Roll into balls. Mix 2 Tbsp. sugar and cinnamon. Roll balls in mixture. Place on an ungreased cookie sheet 2" apart. Bake at 400° for 8-10 minutes.

—Mrs. John (Gertie) Kurtz, Wisconsin
—Mrs. Henry (Clara) Miller, Kentucky
—Ms. Lydia A. Mast, New York

Pumpkin Cookies

1 c. sugar
1 c. shortening
1 c. pumpkin
1 egg
1 tsp. vanilla
1 tsp. baking powder
1 tsp. baking soda
2½ c. flour
½ c. nuts or raisins

Combine in order given. Bake.

—Mrs. John (Esther) Brock, Iowa

Buttermilk Cookies

1 c. shortening
2 c. sugar
3 eggs
1 tsp. baking soda
1 c. buttermilk or sour cream
2 tsp. baking powder
4 c. (or less) flour
1 tsp. salt
nutmeg
1 tsp. vanilla
lemon flavoring
maple flavoring, optional

Mix shortening, sugar and eggs well. Mix baking soda with buttermilk and add. Add dry ingredients and flavorings. Drop on cookie sheet. Bake at 350° for 15 minutes or until slightly browned. Sprinkle sugar on top or frost.

Frosting:
1 egg, beaten
2 Tbsp. butter, melted
2 tsp. cream
powdered sugar for right consistency

Combine and mix well.

—Mrs. David (Naomi) Herschberger, Michigan

Mattie Mast Buttermilk Cookies

½ c. lard
½ c. butter
1 c. white sugar
1½ c. brown sugar
2 eggs
2 tsp. baking soda
1 c. buttermilk
1 tsp. vanilla
2 tsp. baking powder
6 c. (or less) flour
nutmeg
lemon

Cream lard, butter, sugars and eggs. Combine baking soda and buttermilk and add. Add remaining ingredients. It may not take all the flour. Dough should not be too stiff. Chill overnight. Cut out and sprinkle sugar on top before baking at 400° for 10 minutes.

—Mrs. David (Naomi) Herschberger, Michigan

Butterscotch Cookies

4 eggs, beaten
4 c. brown sugar
1 c. butter
1 c. lard
2 tsp. vanilla
1½ Tbsp. baking soda dissolved in
  2 Tbsp. water
2 Tbsp. cream of tartar
7¼ c. flour
18 oz. butterscotch chips

Mix in order given. Dough will be stiff, so you may need to use your hands to finish mixing. Roll in balls and bake at 350° until light brown. Enjoy!

—Mrs. John (Susan) Miller, New York

Butterscotch Delight Cookies

- 2½ c. white sugar
- 2½ c. brown sugar
- 2 c. shortening
- 5 eggs
- 2½ tsp. baking soda
- 2½ tsp. baking powder
- 2 tsp. salt
- 5 c. flour
- 5 c. quick oats
- 2 Tbsp. vanilla
- ¼ c. milk

Mix sugars and shortening. Add eggs, then dry ingredients, vanilla and milk. Form into balls. Roll in **powdered sugar** and press flat onto baking sheets. Bake.

—Mrs. Levi (Barbara) Mast, Pennsylvania

Old Timer Sugar Drops

- 2 c. butter
- 2 c. white sugar
- 2 c. brown sugar
- 4 eggs
- 2 tsp. vanilla
- 1 tsp. maple flavoring
- ½ tsp. salt
- 2 tsp. baking soda
- 2 Tbsp. baking powder
- 2 c. milk
- 9 c. flour

Mix butter and sugars. Add eggs, vanilla and maple flavoring. Next add remaining ingredients. Drop and bake. Sprinkle **Jell-O** on top or frost.

—Mrs. Eli (Emma) Yoder, Michigan

Grandma's Church Cookies

1 c. shortening
1 c. butter
2 c. white sugar
2 c. brown sugar
4 eggs
salt
vanilla
coconut flavoring
9 c. flour
4 tsp. baking soda
5 tsp. baking powder
2 c. buttermilk

Cream shortening, butter, sugars, eggs, salt and flavorings. Sift flour, baking soda and baking powder together. Add alternately with milk. Roll out to ¼"-½" thick. Sprinkle with sugar. Cut and bake at 375°.

—Mrs. Amos (Ella) Beechy, Ohio

Brown Sugar Cookies

4 c. brown sugar
2 c. butter
6 eggs
4 tsp. baking soda
2 tsp. cream of tartar
3 Tbsp. + 1 tsp. cold water
2 tsp. vanilla
7 c. flour

Mix in order given. Good when frosted with brown sugar frosting.

—Mrs. Andy (Anna) Hershberger, Ohio

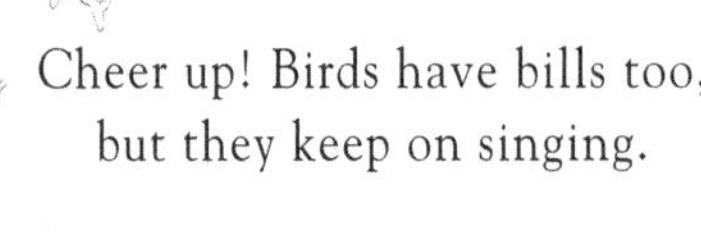

Cheer up! Birds have bills too,
but they keep on singing.

Ohio Fruit Bar Cookies

1½ c. raisins
1½ c. water
3 c. brown sugar
2 c. white sugar
5 eggs
½ c. blackstrap molasses
vanilla
1 Tbsp. cinnamon
2 tsp. baking soda
5-6 c. bread flour

Cook raisins in water. Mix in remaining ingredients. Bake at 500°.

—Mrs. Sam (Frany) Mast, Wisconsin

Sour Cream Cookies

1 c. lard
3 c. brown sugar
4 eggs
2 c. thick sour cream
2 tsp. vanilla
1 tsp. salt
2 tsp. baking soda
½ tsp. nutmeg
1 tsp. baking powder
6-7 c. flour

Cream lard and sugar well. Add eggs, stirring well after each addition. Add sour cream and vanilla. Add remaining ingredients. Bake at 375°.

—Mrs. Levi (Mattie) Yoder, Michigan

Strawberry Creme Cookies

1 c. butter, softened
1 c. sugar
3 oz. cream cheese
1 egg
1 Tbsp. vanilla
2½ c. flour
¼ tsp. salt
½ tsp. baking powder
strawberry jam at room temp.

Cream butter, sugar and cream cheese together. Add egg and vanilla; mix well. Add dry ingredients. Chill dough. Shape into 1" balls and place on an ungreased cookie sheet. Using a floured thimble, press a dent in the center of each cookie and fill with ½ tsp. jam. Bake at 350° for 10-12 minutes. Top with your favorite icing, leaving center with jam exposed.

—Ms. Rachel D. Mast, New York

Honey Cookies

2 c. honey
1 c. butter
4 tsp. baking soda
2 eggs, beaten
½ tsp. cinnamon
2 tsp. vanilla
½ tsp. allspice
8 c. flour

Cook honey and butter for 1 minute. Do not cook longer. Remove from heat and add baking soda. Pour in a large saucepan as it will rise. Let stand until cold. Add remaining ingredients. Can be rolled out and cut into desired shapes or dropped. Bake at 350°.

—Mrs. Paul (Edna) Brenneman, Michigan

Maple Creams

5 c. sugar
½ c. corn syrup
⅓ c. butter
2 c. cream
2 Tbsp. maple flavoring
1 Tbsp. vanilla

Stir together and bring to a boil. Do not stir while boiling! Boil until 240°. Remove from heat and let cool until lukewarm. Stir until light in color and put on a buttered stainless steel tray. Makes two 9" x 13" pans of candy or approx. 4 lb.

—Ms. Rachel J. Hochstetler, Wisconsin

Sandwich Cookies

Vanilla:
½ c. butter
1 c. sugar
1 egg
1 tsp. vanilla
1½ tsp. baking soda
½ tsp. salt
1 Tbsp. cream
2¾ c. sifted flour

Chocolate:
¾ c. butter
1 c. sugar
1 egg
2 c. sifted flour
1 tsp. baking powder
½ tsp. salt
⅔ c. cocoa
¼ c. milk
½ tsp. vanilla

Mix vanilla and chocolate parts separately in given order. Chill a few hours. Roll out and cut the size of sandwich cookies. Bake at 400°. When cool, take 1 vanilla and 1 chocolate and spread with frosting in between.

Frosting:
5 Tbsp. butter
3-4 Tbsp. cream
1 tsp. vanilla
¼ tsp. salt
about 3 c. powdered sugar

Combine and mix well.

—Mrs. Amos (Emma) Hershberger, Ohio

Cry Baby Cookies

1 c. + 2 Tbsp. shortening
1 c + 2 Tbsp. sugar
1 c. molasses
2 eggs, well beaten
4¾ c. cake flour or
4¼ c. all-purpose flour
1 Tbsp. baking powder
1 tsp. salt
1½ tsp. baking soda
2 c. coconut
2 c. walnuts
1½ c. raisins
1 c. candied cherries, optional
1 c. milk

Cream shortening, sugar, molasses and eggs together. Sift flour, baking powder, salt and baking soda. Combine with coconuts, walnuts, raisins and cherries if desired. Add dry ingredients alternately with milk to creamed mixture. Drop on an ungreased cookie sheet. Wait a minute before removing to wire rack to cool. Makes 100 cookies.

—Mrs. Mary L. Hershberger, Ohio

Coconut Cookies

2 c. brown sugar
1 c. butter
2 eggs
2 c. flour
1 tsp. baking soda
1 tsp. baking powder
¼ tsp. salt
3 c. finely shredded coconut
2 tsp. vanilla

Mix well. Form into balls and roll in finely shredded coconut to cover. Do not flatten. If cookies are too thin or flat, add more flour.

Filling:
3 egg whites, beaten
1 tsp. vanilla
3 c. powdered sugar
1 c. shortening

Combine and mix well.

—Mrs. Levi (Fannie) Mast, Ohio

Candy Cane Cookies

1 c. butter
1 c. sugar
1 egg
1 tsp. vanilla
¼ tsp. peppermint extract
2½ c. sifted flour
½ tsp. salt
½ c. crushed candy canes
2 Tbsp. sugar

Beat butter and sugar together. Add egg, vanilla and peppermint extract. Add flour and salt next. Wrap dough in waxed paper and chill for 1 hour. When ready to shape, mix crushed candy with sugar. Roll 1 Tbsp. dough on surface sprinkled with a little candy mixture to make a 6" rope. Place on greased baking sheet. Curve 1 end to make handle of cane. Repeat until dough and candy have all been used up. Bake in a moderate oven until lightly browned. Makes 3½ doz.

—Mrs. Noah (Lovina) Miller, Wisconsin

$250 Cookies

2 c. butter
2 c. brown sugar
2 c. white sugar
4 eggs
2 tsp. vanilla
4 c. flour
5 c. oatmeal
1 tsp. salt
2 tsp. baking powder
2 tsp. baking soda
24 oz. chocolate chips
8 oz. Hershey's bar, chopped
3 c. nuts

Cream butter and sugars. Add eggs and vanilla. Mix with flour, oatmeal, salt, baking powder and baking soda. Add chocolate chips, Hershey's bar and nuts. Roll into balls and place 2" apart on cookie sheet. Bake at 375° for 10 minutes. Makes 9-9½ doz.

—Mrs. John (Elizabeth) S. Mast, New York

Frosted Pineapple Cookies

⅔ c. butter, softened
1½ c. brown sugar
1 (20 oz.) can crushed pineapple, well drained, reserving juice
1 tsp. vanilla
2 eggs
2½ c. all-purpose flour
1 tsp. baking soda
1 tsp. baking powder
½ tsp. salt
½ c. chopped walntus

In a large bowl, beat butter and brown sugar until light and fluffy. Add pineapple, vanilla and eggs; mix well. Add flour, baking soda, baking powder and salt. Mix well. Stir in walnuts. Drop by teaspoon on greased cookie sheets. Bake at 350° for 8-12 minutes. Frost cooled cookies. Makes 5 doz.

Brown Butter Frosting:
2 c. powdered sugar
6 Tbsp. butter, no substitutes
3-4 Tbsp. pineapple juice

Place powdered sugar in a small bowl. Heat butter in heavy skillet until golden brown. Pour into powdered sugar. Stir, adding enough pineapple juice for desired spreading consistency.

—Mrs. Daniel (Gertie) Mast, New York

Worry pulls tomorrow's cloud
over today's bright sunshine.

Raisin Wheel Cookies

1 c. butter
1 c. white sugar
1 c. brown sugar
3 eggs
4 c. flour
1 tsp. baking soda
¼ tsp. salt

Roll in a rectangle and spread with filling. Cool overnight before baking.

Filling
1 c. raisins
½ c. sugar
½ c. water
a little flour to thicken

Cook and cool.

—Mrs. Eli (Anna) Mast

Raisin-Filled Cookies [1]

1 c. butter
2 c. brown sugar
3 eggs
2 tsp. vanilla
1 Tbsp. lemon juice
4 c. flour
1 tsp. salt
1 tsp. baking soda
1 tsp. baking powder

Cream butter and sugar. Add eggs, vanilla and juice. Beat well. Stir in remaining ingredients. Roll out cookie dough to about ⅛"-¼" thick. Cut out cookies with cutter. Place on cookie sheet. Put about 1 Tbsp. filling (depending on size of cookie) on each cookie. Do not spread filling to edges. Put another cookie on top and gently press around edge. A hole may be cut in center of cookie if you wish. Bake at 375° until slightly browned.

Filling:
1½ c. raisins
1½ c. sugar
1½ c. water
1½ tsp. salt
4½ tsp. flour

Grind raisins. In a saucepan, combine raisins, sugar, water and salt. Bring to a boil. Use a little water to make a paste with the flour and add to the boiling mixture. Cook until thickened. Cool.

—Mrs. Enos (Ada) Mast, New York

Raisin-Filled Cookies [2]

2 c. white sugar
1 c. lard
2 eggs
1 c. sweet milk
2 tsp. baking soda
2 tsp. baking powder
2 tsp. cream of tartar
¼ tsp. salt
5 c. flour

Mix and roll out thinly. Fill like sandwich cookies before baking.

Filling:

1 lb. raisins, ground
1 c. brown sugar
1 c. boiling water
2 Tbsp. flour as thickening

Boil together and cool.

—Mrs. Samuel (Edna) Mast, Pennsylvania

Raisin-Top Cookies

2 c. brown sugar
2 eggs
1 Tbsp. vanilla
¼ tsp. salt
1 c. shortening
¼ c. milk
1 tsp. baking soda
4 c. all-purpose flour

Mix all together. Chill. Make little balls and make a little well in middle of cookie and put 1 Tbsp. jelly in cookie. Bake at 375°.

Filling:

1 c. ground raisins
¾ c. brown sugar
1 c. water
¼ tsp. salt
2 Tbsp. clear jel
maple flavoring

Cook raisins, brown sugar, water and salt together. Thicken with clear jel. Add maple flavoring.

—Mrs. Mosie (Lizzie) Mast, New York

Banana Whoopie Pies

1½ c. brown sugar
1 c. shortening
2 eggs
2 c. mashed bananas
1 tsp. baking soda
1 tsp. vanilla
3½ c. flour
1 tsp. salt
1 tsp. baking powder
1 tsp. cinnamon

Mix all together then drop by teaspoonful onto cookie sheets. Bake at 350° for 10 minutes. When cool sandwich together with icing.

Icing:
1 egg white, beaten
2 Tbsp. flour
1 Tbsp. milk
1 c. powdered sugar
1 tsp. vanilla
½ c. shortening
1 c. powdered sugar

Cream together first 5 ingredients, then add shortening and the additional powdered sugar.

—Mrs. Amanda J. Mast, New York

Double Stuffed Oreos

1 chocolate cake mix
2 eggs
2 Tbsp. vegetable oil
2 Tbsp. water
Nestlé's Quik

Blend cake mix, eggs, oil and water. Chill thoroughly. Form ½" balls. Roll in Nestlé's Quik. Flatten with glass and bake at 350° for 8 minutes. Spread icing between 2 cookies, forming a sandwich.

Icing:
½ env. Knox gelatin
¼ c. cold water
1 c. shortening
2-3 c. powdered sugar
1 tsp. vanilla

Dissolve gelatin in cold water. Combine with other ingredients and beat.

—Mrs. Ida J. Yoder, Ohio

Chocolate Mint Wafers

2/3 c. butter, no substitutes
1/2 c. sugar
1/2 c. brown sugar
1/4 c. milk
1 egg
2 c. all-purpose flour
3/4 c. baking cocoa
1 tsp. baking powder
1/2 tsp. baking soda
1/4 tsp. salt

Filling:
2 3/4 c. powdered sugar
1/4 c. half and half cream
1/4 tsp. peppermint extract
1/4 tsp. salt
green food coloring

In a mixing bowl, cream softened butter and sugars. Add milk and egg; mix well. Combine dry ingredients. Gradually add to creamed mixture and mix well. Cover and chill for 2 hours or until firm. Roll chilled dough on a floured surface to 1/8" thick. Cut with a 1 1/2" cookie cutter and place 1" apart on greased baking sheets. Bake at 375° for 5-6 minutes or until edges are lightly browned. Combine filling ingredients. Spread between 2 cookies to form a sandwich.

—Mrs. Daniel (Gertie) Mast, New York

Cream Wafers

1/2 c. butter
1 c. brown sugar
3 Tbsp. cream
2 eggs, beaten
1 1/2 tsp. baking soda
1 tsp. vanilla
1/3 tsp. cinnamon
1/2 tsp. salt
2 3/4 c. (more or less) flour

Mix all together. Use in cookie press. Variation: For chocolate, use 2 Tbsp. cream instead of 3 and 2 sq. melted chocolate.

—Mrs. Dannie (Anna) Hershberger, Michigan

Brownies

¾ c. butter
½ c. white sugar
¼ c. brown sugar
3 egg yolks, reserve whites for topping
¼ tsp. salt
1 tsp. vanilla
2 c. flour
1 tsp. baking powder

Mix and spread in a cake pan.

Topping:
3 egg whites
1 c. brown sugar
nuts, chocolate chips or butterscotch chips

Beat egg whites until frothy. Add brown sugar. Make like a meringue. Spread on batter. Sprinkle with nuts, chocolate chips or butterscotch chips. Bake at 350° for 30-40 minutes. Delicious with ice cream!

—Mrs. Ora (Rachel) Beechy, Michigan

Chocolate Crunch Brownies

1 c. butter, softened
2 c. sugar
4 eggs
6 Tbsp. cocoa
1 c. all-purpose flour
2 tsp. vanilla
½ tsp. salt
1 (7 oz.) jar marsmallow creme
1 c. creamy peanut butter
2 c. semi-sweet chocolate chips
3 c. crisp rice cereal

In a mixing bowl, cream butter and sugar. Add eggs. Stir in cocoa, flour, vanilla and salt. Spread into a greased 9" x 13" x 2" baking pan. Bake at 350° for 25 minutes or until a toothpick inserted comes out clean. Cool. Spread marshmallow creme over cooled brownies. In a small saucepan, melt peanut butter and chocolate chips over low heat, stirring constantly. Remove from heat and stir in cereal. Spread over marshmallow layer. Chill before cutting. Makes 3 doz.

—Ms. Rachel A. Mast, Ohio

Chocolate Blonde Brownies

2/3 c. butter, softened
2 c. brown sugar
2 Tbsp. hot water
2 eggs
2 tsp. vanilla
2 c. flour
1 tsp. baking powder
1/4 tsp. baking soda
1 tsp. salt
1/2 c. chocolate chips

Cream butter and sugar. Add hot water, eggs and vanilla. Beat well. Add dry ingredients. Spread in a greased 9" x 13" pan. Sprinkle chocolate chips over top. Bake at 350° for 25-30 minutes. Cool slightly and cut in squares. Serves 12 people.

—Ms. Clara J. Herschberger, Wisconsin

Cinnamon Brownies

3/4 c. cocoa
1/2 tsp. baking soda
1/2 c. butter, melted, divided
1/2 c. boiling water
2 c. sugar
2 eggs, beaten
1 tsp. vanilla
1 1/3 c. all-purpose flour
1 1/2 tsp. cinnamon
1/4 tsp. salt
1 c. semi-sweet chocolate chips

In a mixing bowl, combine cocoa and soda. Blend in 1/3 c. melted butter. Add boiling water, stirring until thickened. Stir in sugar, egg, vanilla and remaining butter. Add flour, cinnamon and salt. Fold in chocolate chips. Pour into a greased 9" x 13" x 2" baking pan. Bake at 350° for 40 minutes until brownies test done. Cool. Makes 3 doz.

Frosting:
6 Tbsp. butter
1/2 c. cocoa
2 2/3 c. powdered sugar
1 tsp. cinnamon
1/3 c. evaporated milk
1 tsp. vanilla

Cream butter in a mixing bowl. Combine cocoa, sugar and cinnamon. Add alternately with milk. Beat to a spreading consistency. Add vanilla. Add more milk if necessary. Spread over brownies.

—Mrs. Alvin (Emma) Mast, Pennsylvania

Cookie Dough Brownies

2 c. sugar
1½ c. flour
½ c. cocoa
½ tsp. salt
1 c. vegetable oil
4 eggs
2 tsp. vanilla
½ c. chopped walnuts, optional

In a mixing bowl, combine sugar, flour, cocoa and salt. Add oil, eggs and vanilla; beat at medium speed for 3 minutes. Stir in walnuts if desired. Pour into a greased 9" x 13" x 2" baking pan. Bake at 350° for 30 minutes or until brownies test done. Spread filling over the brownies. Spread glaze over filling. Sprinkle **nuts** on immediately.

Filling:
½ c. butter, softened
½ c. brown sugar
¼ c. sugar
2 Tbsp. milk
1 tsp. vanilla
1 c. flour

Cream butter and sugars in a mixing bowl. Add milk and vanilla; mix well. Beat in flour.

Glaze:
1 c. semi-sweet chocolate chips
1 Tbsp. shortening

Melt until smooth.

—Mrs. Daniel (Gertie) Mast, New York

Cream Cheese Brownies

1 pkg. chocolate cake mix
8 oz. cream cheese
1 egg
½ c. white sugar
½ c. chocolate chips

Mix cake mix as directed. Pour batter in pan. Mix remaining ingredients. Drop by tablespoon onto batter. Cut through batter to marbleize. Sprinkle with additional chocolate chips if desired. Bake at 350° for 25-30 minutes. Delicious warm or cold.

—Ms. Cassie H. Mast, Ohio

Simply Fudgy Brownies

½ c. vegetable oil
¼ c. cocoa
1 c. sugar
2 eggs, lightly beaten
1 tsp. vanilla
¾ c. flour
⅛ tsp. salt
½ c. walnuts
½ c. vanilla chips

In a small bowl, combine oil and cocoa until smooth. Add sugar, eggs and vanilla. Stir in flour and salt only until moistened. Fold in walnuts. Pour into an 8" x 10" greased pan. Sprinkle with vanilla chips. Put in 325° oven for several minutes until chips are melted. Take out and swirl chips into dough. Return to oven for 30 minutes. Do not overbake. Very good! Serves 6 people.

—Mrs. Atlee (Susan) Yoder, Ohio

Susie Q's [1]

3 c. flour
2 c. sugar
½ c. cocoa
2 tsp. baking soda
1 tsp. salt
2 c. water
1 c. vegetable oil
2 tsp. vinegar
2 tsp. vanilla

Mix dry ingredients well. Add remaining ingredients. Grease a 13" x 17" cookie sheet and pour a thin layer in pan ½" thick. Bake at 350° for 20-30 minutes. Cool. Cut in half. Spread filling on half of layer. Top with second half. Cut in 2" squares. Serves 24 people. A family favorite!

Filling:
16 oz. whipped topping
8 oz. cream cheese
½ c. powdered sugar

Mix well.

—Mrs. Melvin (Emma) Herschberger, Ohio

Suzi Q's [2]

1 chocolate cake mix
½ c. instant vanilla pudding
4 eggs
½ c. vegetable oil
1 c. water

Combine cake mix, pudding, eggs, oil and water. Mix well. Spread on 2 cookie sheets lined with waxed paper. Bake at 300° for 15-20 minutes. Fill with filling and cut in squares. Serves 12 people.

Filling:
1¼ c. milk
5 Tbsp. flour
1 c. shortening
1 c. white sugar
2 c. powdered sugar
vanilla

Cook milk and flour until thick. Cream shortening and white sugar. Add to flour mixture and stir until fluffy. Add powdered sugar and vanilla.

—Mrs. Eli (Mattie) Yoder, Ohio

Marshmallow Bars

1 c. brown sugar
½ c. butter
1 egg
1 tsp. vanilla
¼ c. cocoa
2 c. flour
½ tsp. baking soda
½ tsp. salt
½ c. milk
miniature marshmallows

Combine sugar, butter, egg and vanilla. Add dry ingredients and milk. Spread on a greased cookie sheet. Bake at 375° for 8 minutes or more. Remove from oven and sprinkle with miniature marshmallows over the top. Return to oven for 1 minute.

Icing:
⅓ c. butter
1 c. brown sugar
2 Tbsp. cocoa
¼ c. milk

Combine and boil until it forms large bubbles. Cool and add powdered sugar to thicken. Spread thinly over bars.

—Mrs. Amos (Ella) Beechy, Ohio

Disappearing Marshmallow Bars

½ c. butter
1 c. butterscotch chips
⅔ c. brown sugar
1½ c. flour
2 tsp. baking powder
2 eggs
1 tsp. maple flavoring
1 c. chocolate chips
2 c. marshmallows
1 c. M&M's
1 c. pecans

Melt the butter and butterscotch chips in a saucepan. Cool and add brown sugar, flour, baking powder, eggs and maple flavoring. Mix well, then fold in chocolate chips, marshmallows, M&M's and pecans.

—Mrs. Noah (Malinda) Raber, New York

Chocolate Marshmallow Bars

½ c. butter
1 c. brown sugar
1 egg
1 tsp. vanilla
¼ c. cocoa
2 c. flour
½ tsp. baking soda
½ tsp. salt
½ c. milk
marshmallows

Combine first 4 ingredients, then add dry ingredients alternately with milk. Spread on a greased cookie sheet. Bake for 8 minutes at 375°. Remove from oven and sprinkle marshmallows on top. Bake again for 1 minute.

—Ms. Mattie J. Yoder, Ohio

Never pray for money. The Lord is your shepherd, not your banker.

Crispy Mallow Bars

½ c. margarine
¾ c. sugar
2 eggs
2 tsp. vanilla
1 c. flour
¼ tsp. baking powder
½ c. nuts
2 Tbsp. cocoa
¼ tsp. salt
2 c. miniature marshmallows

Cream margarine and sugar. Beat in eggs and vanilla. Add flour, baking powder, nuts, cocoa and salt. Bake for 15-20 minutes. Cover with marshmallows and return to oven for 2-3 minutes. Set aside to cool. Spread topping over marshmallows and cut into squares.

Topping:
½ c. chocolate chips
1 c. peanut butter
1 c. Rice Krispies

In a saucepan, combine chocolate chips and peanut butter. Stir until melted. Add Rice Krispies.

—Ms. Miriam D. Herschberger, Michigan

Twix Cookie Bars

1 c. butter
1 c. brown sugar
½ c. milk
⅔ c. white sugar
2 c. graham cracker crumbs
Club crackers

Mix butter, brown sugar, milk, white sugar and graham cracker crumbs together and bring to a boil. Place a layer of Club crackers on the bottom of a 9" x 13" pan. Pour half of boiled mixture over crackers. Add another layer of crackers. Pour remaining boiled mixture over crackers. Top with another layer of crackers. Cool. Pour frosting over bars.

Frosting:
1 c. butterscotch chips
¾ c. peanut butter
1 c. chocolate chips

Melt together.

—Ms. Barbara F. Yoder, New York

Cookie Bars

2 c. raisins
water
3½ lb. flour
2 lb. white sugar
1 lb. butter
5 eggs
2 c. baking molasses
egg, beaten
3 Tbsp. baking soda
1 Tbsp. salt

Boil raisins in water and allow to cool. Mix flour, sugar and butter in a big dishpan and mix like pie dough. Drain raisins and reserve liquid. Add raisins to crumbs. Beat eggs and add along with molasses and salt. Dissolve baking soda in raisin water and add. Mix but don't overbeat. Pour into a cookie sheet. Brush with beaten egg. Bake at 350°. Cut into bars once cooled. Very good and will keep for months. May need more flour especially if cane or Brer Rabbit molasses is used.

—Mrs. Henry (Sarah) Mast, Ohio

Coffee Bars

2⅔ c. brown sugar
1 c. vegetable oil
2 eggs
1 c. coffee or 1 tsp. instant
1 tsp. vanilla
3 c. flour
1 tsp. salt
1 tsp. baking soda
2 c. chopped pecans
2 c. chocolate chips

Stir sugar, vegetable oil and eggs together. Mix well. Add coffee and vanilla and mix well. Then add flour, salt and baking soda. Pour into 9" x 13" pan. Sprinkle with chopped pecans and chocolate chips. Bake at 350° for 20-30 minutes. Do not overbake.

—Ms. Miriam D. Herschberger, Michigan

Filled Coffee Bars

1 c. butter
1½ c. white sugar
4 eggs
1 tsp. vanilla
3 c. flour
1½ tsp. baking powder
½ tsp. salt
2 c. any flavor pie filling

Cream butter and sugar. Add eggs one at a time. Beat well after each one. Add vanilla. Sift flour, baking powder and salt. Add to first mixture. Spread ¾ of dough in a jelly-roll pan. Cover with pie filling and spoon remaining batter on top. Bake at 350° for 30-40 minutes. Drizzle with glaze while still warm.

Glaze:
1½ c. powdered sugar
2 Tbsp. butter
½ tsp. vanilla
enough milk to make a thin consistency

—Mrs. Henry (Sarah) Yoder, Michigan

Cherry Cake Bars

1 c. butter
1¾ c. sugar
4 eggs
3 c. flour
1½ tsp. baking powder
½ tsp. salt
1 tsp. vanilla
1 can cherry pie filling

Cream butter, sugar and eggs together. Add flour, baking powder, salt and vanilla. Spread half of batter on a greased 10½" x 15½" pan. Pour cherry pie filling over top. Pour rest of batter over filling. Bake at 350° for 50 minutes or until done. Glaze with a thin powdered sugar frosting. Scrumptious if not burned!

—Mrs. Daniel (Katie) Mast, Wisconsin

Treasure Bars

1 c. flour
½ c. brown sugar
½ c. butter
2 eggs, beaten
1 c. brown sugar
1 tsp. vanilla
½ tsp. baking powder
¼ tsp. salt
1 Tbsp. flour
1 c. chopped walnuts
1 c. coconut
½ c. chocolate chips

Combine flour, ½ c. sugar and butter. Press into a slightly greased pan and bake at 350° for 12 minutes. While this is baking, beat eggs. Add 1 c. sugar and beat until fluffy. Add vanilla and remaining ingredients. Spread over baked crust. Bake for 25-30 minutes. Do not overbake.

—Mrs. Mosie (Lizzie) Mast, New York
—Mrs. Allee (Edna) Yoder, Wisconsin

Lemon Bars

Crust:
2 c. flour
½ c. powdered sugar
1 c. butter

Mix flour, powdered sugar and butter well. Press into a 9" x 13" pan and bake at 350° for 15 minutes.

2 c. sugar
4 eggs
6 Tbsp. lemon juice
2 Tbsp. flour
1 tsp. baking powder

Combine and pour on top of baked crust and bake another 20-30 minutes. Cool and cut into bars.

—Mrs. Uria (Sara) Miller, Michigan

Lemon Squares

Crust:

½ c. shortening
¼ c. powdered sugar
4 c. flour
pinch of salt

Mix. Press into a pan and bake at 350° for 15 minutes. Set aside.

Filling:

2 eggs, beaten
1 c. sugar
2 Tbsp. flour
3-4 Tbsp. lemon juice

Mix and pour over baked crust. Bake another 50 minutes at 350°. Sprinkle with **powdered sugar**.

—Ms. Miriam Herschberger

Peanut Butter Squares

½ c. white sugar
½ c. brown sugar
½ c. butter, softened
⅓ c. crunchy peanut butter
1 egg, beaten
1 c. flour
1 c. quick oats
½ tsp. baking soda
¼ tsp. salt

Cream sugars, butter, peanut butter and eggs. Stir dry ingredients together and blend into creamed mixture. Spread in a greased 9" x 13" pan. Bake at 350° for 17-22 minutes or until golden brown. Frost when cool. Makes 4 doz.

Frosting:

1½ c. powdered sugar
¼ c. crunchy peanut butter
3 Tbsp. milk, divided
3 Tbsp. cocoa

Cream powdered sugar and peanut butter. Stir in 2 Tbsp. milk ½ Tbsp. at a time until spreading consistency. Reserve ⅓ c. of mixture. Add cocoa and 1 Tbsp. milk to remaining frosting. Frost squares with cocoa frosting. Drop peanut butter frosting by teaspoon on top and swirl for a marbled effect.

—Mrs. Henry (Edna) Hershberger, Ohio

Coconut Love Bars

1 c. flour
3 Tbsp. brown sugar
½ c. butter
1½ c. coconut
1½ c. brown sugar
¼ c. flour
2 eggs, beaten
1 tsp. vanilla

Mix first 4 ingredients and pat evenly in a greased 7" x 15" pan. Bake at 325° for 10 minutes. Mix remaining ingredients and pour over baked crumbs. Bake for another 30 minutes or more. Cool and cut into squares.

—Ms. Clara M. Herschberger, Wisconsin

Halfway Bars

1¼ c. brown sugar, divided
½ c. white sugar
1 c. butter
2 eggs, separated
2 c. flour
1½ tsp. baking soda
1 pkg. chocolate chips

Mix ½ c. brown sugar, white sugar, butter, egg yolks, flour and baking soda and put in 9" x 13" pan. Sprinkle chocolate chips on top and press in. Bake at 350° for 15 minutes. Beat egg whites stiffly with remaining ¾ c. brown sugar. Spread over top and brown.

—Ms. Mary S. Herschberger, Michigan

The best way to knock a chip off someone's shoulder is with a pat on the back.

Pecan Bars

6 c. flour
1½ c. sugar
1 tsp. salt
2 c. butter, no substitutes

In a large bowl, combine the flour, sugar and salt. Cut in butter until crumbly. Press onto the bottom and up the sides of 2 greased 15" x 10" x 1" baking pans. Bake at 350° for 18-22 minutes or until the edges of the crust are beginning to brown and bottom is set. Pour filling over crust. Bake for 25-30 minutes longer or until edges are firm and center is almost set. Cool on wire racks. Cut into bars. Makes 6-8 doz.

Filling:
8 eggs
3 c. sugar
3 c. corn syrup
½ c. butter, melted
1 Tbsp. vanilla
5 c. chopped pecans

Combine eggs, sugar, corn syrup, butter and vanilla in a large bowl; mix well. Stir in pecans.

—Mrs. Chris (Ella) Borntreger, Wisconsin

Butter Pecan Turtle Bars

2 c. flour
1 c. brown sugar
½ c. butter
1 c. chopped pecans
1 c. chocolate chips

Preheat oven to 350°. Combine first 3 ingredients and pour in an ungreased 9" x 13" x 2" pan. Sprinkle pecans evenly over crust. Pour caramel layer over top. Bake until the entire layer is bubbly and the crust is a light golden brown. Remove from oven and sprinkle with chocolate chips. Allow chocolate to melt then swirl with a knife.

Caramel Layer:
10 Tbsp. butter
½ c. brown sugar

Boil together for ½-1 minute, stirring constantly.

—Ms. Laura R. Borntreger, Wisconsin

Cowboy Bars

1 c. brown sugar
1 c. white sugar
1 c. butter
2 eggs
1½ tsp. vanilla
¼ c. milk
2 c. flour
½ tsp. salt
1½ tsp. baking powder
2 c. oatmeal
1 c. coconut
¾ c. nuts
1½ c. chocolate chips

Cream sugars and butter. Add remaining ingredients. Mix well and spread evenly in a large jelly-roll pan. Press lightly. Bake at 350° for 20-30 minutes or until done.

—Ms. Anna F. Mast, New York

Zucchini Bars

3 eggs
1 c. white sugar
1 c. brown sugar
1 c. vegetable oil
2 c. grated zucchini
2 c. flour
1 Tbsp. cinnamon
1 tsp. salt
2 tsp. baking soda
1 tsp. baking powder
nuts, optional

Slightly beat eggs. Add sugars and oil. Mix well. Add zucchini alternately with sifted dry ingredients. Mix well. Bake on a greased cookie sheet or loaf pan at 350° for 30 minutes. Spread frosting on cooled bars. Sprinkle with nuts if desired.

Frosting:
4 oz. cream cheese
½ c. butter, softened
2 c. powdered sugar
1 tsp. vanilla

Mix well.

—Mrs. Joseph (Martha) Miller, Ohio

Chocolate Chip Cheesecake Bars

¾ c. butter
¾ c. white sugar
⅓ c. brown sugar
1 egg
vanilla
flour
½ tsp. salt
¾ tsp. baking soda
1½ c. chocolate chips
¾ c. chopped pecans

Heat oven to 350°. Cream butter and sugars. Beat in egg and vanilla. Combine flour, salt and baking soda. Add to creamed mixture and mix. Add chocolate chips and nuts. Set aside ⅓ of dough and press remaining dough into a greased 9" x 13" x 2" baking pan and bake for 10 minutes. Spoon filling over crust. Drop reserved dough by teaspoon over filling. Bake for 35-40 minutes or until golden brown. Serves 36 people.

Filling:
16 oz. cream cheese
¾ c. sugar
2 eggs
1 tsp. vanilla

Beat cream cheese and sugar until smooth. Add eggs and vanilla.

—Mrs. Reuben (Irene) Brock, Wisconsin

Chocolate Chip Bar Cookies

1 c. shortening
1¾ c. sugar
2 eggs
1 tsp. baking soda
1 tsp. baking powder
1 c. coffee
3½ c. flour
1 c. chocolate chips
½ c. nuts

Pour in cookie sheet and bake at 350°. Frost and cut into squares. Delicious!

—Mrs. Rebecca O. Mast, Ohio

Scrumptious Chocolate Caramel Bars

Crust:
1 c. all-purpose flour
½ c. butter, softened
⅓ c. sugar

Heat oven to 350°. In a small bowl, combine all crust ingredients. Beat at low speed until mixture is crumbly. Press in the bottom of a greased 9" square pan. Bake for 12-17 minutes or until edges are slightly browned.

Filling:
½ c. sugar
¼ c. crunchy peanut butter
½ c. light corn syrup
2 eggs
¼ tsp. salt
½ tsp. vanilla
½ c. coconut
½ c. chocolate chips

Combine filling ingredients until well mixed. Pour over top. Return to oven and continue baking for 20-30 minutes or until filling is set and golden brown.

—Mrs. Aaron (Elizabeth) Yoder, Wisconsin

Double Chocolate Bars

½ c. butter
¾ c. white sugar
2 eggs
1 tsp. vanilla
¼ tsp. baking powder
¾ c. flour
2 Tbsp. cocoa
¼ tsp. salt
2 c. marshmallows

Combine all ingredients except marshmallows. Bake at 350° for 15-20 minutes. Sprinkle marshmallows on top and bake 2 minutes longer. Cool. Spread topping on top of cooled bars. Chill and cut into bars.

Topping:
6 oz. chocolate chips
1 c. peanut butter
1½ c. Rice Krispies

Combine chocolate chips and peanut butter in a saucepan. Melt, then add Rice Krispies.

—Ms. Ida A. Yoder, Ohio

Yum Yum Bars

Crust:
2 c. flour
½ c. brown sugar
½ c. butter

Mix thoroughly and press firmly in a large cookie sheet.

Filling:
3 eggs
2 c. brown sugar
½ tsp. salt
1 c. coconut
½ c. chopped nuts
2 Tbsp. flour
¼ tsp. baking powder
1 tsp. vanilla

Mix together and spread over crust. Bake at 350° for 20 minutes or until brown. Cut into bars when cooled. Delicious!

—Mrs. Henry (Fannie) Miller, Ohio

Bewitched Oatmeal Bars

¾ c. butter
1½ c. brown sugar
1 egg
¾ tsp. vanilla
2 c. flour
½ tsp. baking soda
¼ tsp. salt
1 c. oatmeal
1½ c. marshmallows
1 c. chocolate chips

Beat butter, sugar, egg and vanilla together. Add flour, baking soda and salt. Stir in oatmeal and marshmallows. Press in a 9" x 12" pan and sprinkle chocolate chips on top. Bake at 350° for 18-20 minutes or until done. Do not overbake!

—Ms. Emma M. Hershberger, Ohio

Yummy Granola Bars

¼ c. butter
¼ c. vegetable oil
1½ lb. marshmallows
½ c. honey
¼ c. crunchy peanut butter
9½ c. Rice Krispies
1 c. graham cracker crumbs
5 c. oatmeal
1½ c. raisins
1 c. coconut
1 c. chocolate chips or M&M's

Melt butter and oil on very low heat. Add marshmallows and stir until melted. Remove from heat. Add honey and peanut butter. In a large bowl, mix dry ingredients and make a well in the middle. Pour marshmallow mixture over it and mix well. Press into 2 greased cookie sheets. Cool and cut into bars. Makes 4 doz.

—Mrs. Levi (Susan) Mast, New York

Granola Bars [1]

¼ c. butter
1 pkg. marshmallows
½ c. peanut butter
1 c. oatmeal
5 c. Rice Krispies
½ c. chocolate chips
½ c. butterscotch chips

Melt butter, marshmallows and peanut butter together. Add remaining ingredients. Press into pan. Cool and cut into bars.

—Mrs. Amos (Mattie) Garber, Ohio

You can live without music,
You can live without books,
But show me the one
Who can live without cooks!

Granola Bars [2]

5 c. oatmeal
4½ c. Rice Krispies
2 pkg. graham crackers, crushed
1 c. coconut
2 pkg. marshmallows
1 c. butter
¼ c. peanut butter
½ c. chocolate chips
½ c. M&M's

Mix oatmeal, Rice Krispies, graham crackers and coconut in a large bowl. Melt marshmallows, butter and peanut butter together. Add to dry ingredients. Stir in chocolate chips and M&M's. When it's cooled a bit, press in cookie sheets. When cold, cut in squares and store in an air-tight container.

—Mrs. Simon (Malinda) Yoder, Ohio

Granola Bars [3]

1 c. butter, softened
1 egg
1 c. brown sugar
½ tsp. baking soda
1 tsp. vanilla
½ tsp. salt
1½ c. flour
1 c. oatmeal
½ c. coconut
½ c. chocolate chips
¼ c. nuts

Mix butter, egg, sugar, baking soda, vanilla, salt and flour together. Add remaining ingredients. Press into a pan and bake for 20 minutes or until done. Cut in squares.

—Mrs. Mahlon (Mary) Miller, Michigan

Pumpkin Bars

4 eggs
2 c. sugar
1 c. vegetable oil
2 c. pumpkin
2 c. flour
1 tsp. salt
2 tsp. baking soda
2 tsp. cinnamon

Combine eggs, sugar and oil in a large bowl. Beat well. Blend in pumpkin. Sift flour, salt, baking soda and cinnamon. Add to the pumpkin mixture. Pour into a large cookie sheet. Bake at 350° for 20-25 minutes. Spread frosting on bars while still a little warm.
Variation: Mattie tops the bars with ¼ c. chocolate chips when almost done instead of frosting.

Emma's Frosting:
3 oz. cream cheese
¼ c. shortening
1 tsp. vanilla
1½ c. powdered sugar

Combine.

Edna's Frosting
3 oz. cream cheese, softened
1 tsp. vanilla
6 Tbsp. butter, softened
1 tsp. milk
about ¾ lb. powdered sugar

Combine.

—Mrs. Albert (Emma) Autzman, Ohio
—Mrs. Levi (Mattie) Yoder, Michigan
—Mrs. Atlee (Edna) Yoder, Wisconsin

If you were born lucky, even your rooster would lay eggs.

Peanut Butter Fingers

1 c. shortening
2 c. brown sugar
⅔ c. peanut butter
2 eggs
1 tsp. vanilla
½ tsp. salt
1 tsp. baking soda
2 c. oatmeal
2 c. flour

Mix in order given. Bake at 350° for 15-20 minutes or until brown. Cool slightly. Spread glaze on bars. Cut and remove from pan. Serves 12 people.

Glaze:
3 Tbsp. water
2 Tbsp. butter
⅓ c. cococa
1 c. powdered sugar
½ tsp. vanilla

Combine water and butter in a saucepan and bring to a full boil. Remove from heat and add cocoa. Mix well. Add powdered sugar and vanilla. Stir until smooth.

—Mrs. Clara F. Herschberger, Wisconsin

Sour Cream Raisin Bars

7 c. quick oats
7 c. flour
4 c. brown sugar
4 tsp. soda
3 c. butter

Preheat oven to 300°. Combine ingredients and mix well. Pat ⅔ of crumb mixture in 2 cookie sheets. Bake for 15 minutes. Pour filling over baked crust. Sprinkle remaining crumbs on top. Bake for another 15-20 minutes.

Filling:
8 egg yolks
¼ c. cornstarch
6 c. sour cream
3 c. raisins
1½ c. brown sugar

Mix all ingredients in a saucepan. Boil for 5-10 minutes, stirring constantly.

—Mrs. Edna F. Yoder, Ohio

'Tis Saturday morn
And time to bake.
Let's start with cookies
And end with a cake.

Sometimes to decide
On what cookies to make
Takes almost as long
As it does to bake.

Mom wants butterscotch,
Oatmeal for Sarah and chips for me,
Finally Mom decides
Chocolate crinkle it'll be.

Now to make the cake
It really isn't hard.
You will be done
Almost as soon as you start.

A Happy Home

4 c. love
2 c. loyalty
2 spoons of faith
2 spoons of tenderness
5 spoons of hope
1 barrel of laughter
1 c. friendship

Take love and loyalty. Mix with faith. Blend with tenderness, kindness, understanding and hope. Sprinkle abundantly with laughter and friendship. Bake in sunshine. Serve daily with generous helpings.

—Mrs. Sarah Mast

Pies
Sweet Heart

- Set foil pan in Pyrex pan to bake pie crust. This will make the crust brown better.
- Add a tablespoon of vinegar to the pie dough and a bit of sugar to keep it from drying out when storing for later use. Store in a plastic bag or dish in a cool, dry place.
- When pie crust shrinks, rinse the pan in cold water before putting in the crust.
- For streusel pie, mix ⅓ c. peanut butter and ¾ c. powdered sugar. Spread this on the bottom of a baked pie shell. Top it with your favorite cream pie filling and meringue or whipped cream.
- For best results, pie dough should be worked very lightly after the water has been added.
- Pie crust will have a browner crust when milk is used in the dough. Milk can also be brushed over the top before baking.
- To glaze pies or cookies, brush the top with a beaten egg white.
- If a custard recipe calls for several eggs, 1 or more may be left out if ½ Tbsp. cornstarch is added for each egg omitted.
- Brush the inside of an unbaked pie crust with an egg white and bake a few minutes before adding the filling. This will keep it from becoming soggy.
- Meringue on pies will stand up high if a generous pinch of baking soda is added to beaten egg whites.
- Brush pie crust with cream, then sprinkle with sugar. The pie will brown beautifully.
- To prevent bottom of pie crusts from becoming soggy, grease pie pans with butter. The crust will be soft and flaky.

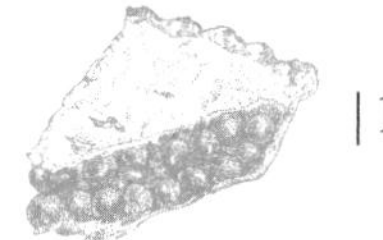

Pie Crust [1]

4 c. flour
1 Tbsp. salt
½ tsp. baking powder
1½ c. lard
1 egg
½ c. water
1 Tbsp. vinegar

Combine flour, salt, baking powder and lard. Beat egg. Add water and vinegar. Pour over flour mixture. Mix until right consistency. Makes 8 pie crusts.

—Ms. Sarah M. Hershberger, Wisconsin
—Ms. Laura R. Borntreger, Wisconsin

Pie Crust [2]

1⅓ c. flour
½ tsp. salt
½ c. butter-flavored shortening
3 Tbsp. ice water

Combine flour and salt. Cut in shortening. Add water, a little at a time with a fork. Roll out. Makes a nice, flaky crust. Very simple and easy!

—Mrs. Moses (Amelia) Gingerich, Ohio

Never-Fail Pie Crust

3 c. flour
1 tsp. salt
1¼ c. shortening
1 egg, beaten
5 Tbsp. water

Mix flour and salt with shortening. Moisten with beaten egg and water.

—Mrs. John (Anna) Yoder, Michigan

Pie Dough Mix

9 lb. pastry flour
4 lb. lard
1 c. cornstarch
2 c. powdered sugar
1 Tbsp. baking powder
1 Tbsp. salt

Mix well.

—Mrs. Levi (Barbara) A. Mast, Pennsylvania

Chocolate Pie Crust

1¼ c. flour
½ tsp. salt
⅓ c. sugar
¼ c. cocoa
½ c. shortening
½ tsp. vanilla
2-3 Tbsp. cold water

Sift flour, salt, sugar and cocoa together. Cut in shortening. Add vanilla. Sprinkle with water. Form into a ball. Roll out and put in pie pan. Also bake trimmings and crumble for crumb topping. Fill baked shell with vanilla pudding.

—Mrs. Dan (Anna) Raber, Ohio

Chocolate Pie

2 c. milk
1 c. sugar
1 Tbsp. (heaping) cocoa
3 egg yolks
2 Tbsp. cornstarch
¼ tsp. salt
1 tsp. vanilla
3 Tbsp. butter, melted

Cook and pour into a baked pie shell. Top with whipped cream or meringue. Serves 6 people.

—Mrs. Eli (Rachel) Mast, New York

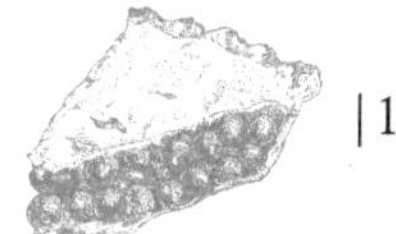

Chocolate Marshmallow Pie

16 lg. or 5 oz. miniature marshmallows
½ c. milk
4 sm. Hershey's bars
1 c. cream, whipped

Melt marshmallows and milk in double boiler. Add Hershey's bars. Stir until melted. Cool and add whipped cream. Pour into a baked pie crust or graham cracker crust. Serves 6 people.

—Ms. Clara J. Herschberger, Wisconsin

Chocolate Chiffon Pie

1 Tbsp. gelatin
¼ c. cold water
½ c. white sugar
2 Tbsp. cocoa
½ c. hot milk
½ c. light coffee
½ tsp. salt
1 tsp. vanilla
1 c. whipping cream

Soak gelatin in water for 5 minutes. Boil sugar, cocoa, milk, coffee and salt. Add gelatin to this mixture, stirring thoroughly. Cool until slightly thick, then add vanilla and whipped cream. Pour in a baked pie shell and chill for 1 hour. Serves 6 people.

—Mrs. Eli (Mattie) Yoder, Ohio

Chocolate Mocha Pie

1 Tbsp. unflavored gelatin
¼ c. cold water
1 tsp. instant coffee
¾ c. white sugar
1¼ c. cold milk
⅛ tsp. salt
1 c. heavy cream
1 tsp. vanilla
nuts, optional

Soften gelatin in cold water while you bring coffee, sugar, milk and salt to a boil, stirring constantly. Remove from heat and add gelatin. Cool until slightly thickened. Beat cooked mixture until smooth. Whip cream and vanilla. Fold whipped cream into cooked mixture. Pour into a baked pie shell. Top with nuts if desired.

—Mrs. Floyd (Katie) Beechy, Michigan

Chocolate Cream Cheese Pie

8 oz. cream cheese
½ c. brown sugar
2 eggs, separated
¾ c. chocolate chips, melted
1 c. whipped cream

Mix cream cheese and brown sugar. Add egg yolks 1 at a time. Add melted chocolate chips. Beat egg whites and add to mixture. Fold in whipped cream. This is enough to fill a little over 1 pie or 1 large pie.

—Mrs. Levi (Esther) Kisley, Ohio

Chocolate Cheese Pie

6 oz. chocolate chips or sweet chocolate
8 oz. cream cheese
¾ c. browns sugar, divided
⅛ tsp. salt
1 tsp. vanilla
2 eggs, separated
1 c. heavy whipping cream

Use a 9" chilled graham cracker or pie crust. Melt chocolate over hot, not boiling water. Cool for 10 minutes. Blend cream cheese, ½ c. brown sugar, salt and vanilla. Beat in egg yolks 1 at a time. Add cooled chocolate and blend well. Beat egg whites until stiff but not dry. Slowly beat in remaining ¼ c. brown sugar. Beat until very stiff. Whip cream and fold in chocolate mixture. Pour into crust and chill overnight.

—Ms. Elmina C. Kauffman, Wisconsin

Be careful what you think; your thoughts are heard in Heaven.

Vanilla Pie

3 Tbsp. flour
1 egg
1 c. sugar
1 c. light corn syrup
1 pt. water
1 tsp. vanilla

Boil flour, egg, sugar, corn syrup and water together until thick. When cool add vanilla. Top with crumbs. Serves 12 people.

Crumbs:
2 c. flour
½ c. sugar
½ c. lard
1 tsp. baking soda
½ tsp. salt

Combine.

—Ms. Mary L. Hershberger, Ohio

Vanilla Crumb Pie

2 c. brown sugar
1½ c. white sugar
½ c. corn syrup
4 c. water
¼ c. flour
2 eggs
2 tsp. vanilla
1 tsp. cream of tartar
2 tsp. baking soda

Boil first 5 ingredients together for 1 minute. Set aside. In a large bowl, mix remaining ingredients. Mix together. Divide into 4 unbaked pie shells. Top with crumbs. Bake at 350° for 45 minutes.

Crumbs:
4 c. pastry flour
2 c. brown sugar
1 c. lard
1 tsp. baking soda
2 tsp. cream of tartar

Combine and mix well.

—Mrs. Eli (Sarah) Mast, New York

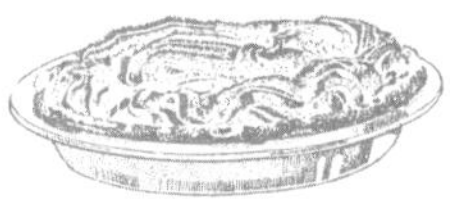

Vanilla Crumb Pie

1 c. brown sugar
1 c. light corn syrup
3 Tbsp. (heaping) flour
2 eggs, beaten
2 c. water
1 tsp. vanilla

Cook first 5 ingredients together. Cool and add vanilla. Bake crust until almost done before adding filling. Bake until golden brown. Makes 2 pies.

Crumbs:
1 c. flour
½ c. brown sugar
¼ c. butter
1 tsp. baking soda

Combine.

—Mrs. Albert (Lizzie) Miller, New York

Vanilla Tarts

Filling:
1 pt. cold water
1 c. sugar
1 c. syrup
1 egg
vanilla

Pour filling into an unbaked pie shell. Drop topping by spoonsful onto filling. Bake. Makes 2 lg. or 3 sm. pies. We used to make this at home.

Topping:
2 c. sugar
½ c. butter or lard
1 egg
1 c. sour milk
1 tsp. baking soda
3 c. flour
vanilla

Cream together like you would for a cake.

—Mrs. John (Edna) Herschberger, Wisconsin

Caramel Pie

2 egg whites, beaten
1 c. brown sugar
1 Tbsp. flour
¼ tsp. salt
1 c. milk
1 c. cream
vanilla
maple flavoring

Beat egg whites until stiff. Mix remaining ingredients separately and add. Bake at 500° or a little over. Makes 1 pie or 6 servings.

—Mrs. Sam (Frany) Mast, Wisconsin
—Ms. Amelia A. Stabaugh, Wisconsin

Caramel Custard Pie [1]

1 Tbsp. (heaping) flour
1 c. brown sugar
1 c. cream
1 c. milk
2 eggs, separated
½ tsp. maple flavoring
a little salt

Mix flour, sugar and some cream. Add egg yolks, flavoring, salt and enough cream to make a thin batter. Bring the milk to a boil and add to remaining ingredients. Beat the egg whites and add last of all. A few nuts are good on top if you wish. Makes 1 pie.

—Mrs. Henry (Sarah) Mast, Ohio

Caramel Custard Pie [2]

1 c. brown sugar
1 Tbsp. flour
pinch of salt
1 c. rich milk or cream
2 Tbsp. butter, browned
2 eggs, separated
1 tsp. vanilla

Mix ingredients in order given, beating egg whites until stiff and adding last. Bake at 350°-400°. Makes 1 pie or 6-8 servings.

—Mrs. Reuben (Irene) Mast, Wisconsin

Custard Pie [1]

3 eggs
1 c. sugar
2 c. (scant) milk
1 tsp. vanilla
cinnamon

Beat eggs. Add sugar, milk and vanilla. Pour in an unbaked pie shell and top with cinnamon. Bake at 450° for 10 minutes. Reduce heat to 350° and bake until set. Best if filling does not cook before it sets. Serves 6 people.

—Mrs. Monroe (Mary) Hershberger, Wisconsin

Custard Pie [2]

4 eggs
7 Tbsp. sugar
1 tsp. vanilla
pinch of salt
2 c. milk

Beat eggs. Add sugar, vanilla and salt. Add milk last. Pour in a 9" pie shell and bake in a moderate oven.
Variation: Beat egg whites and add last.

—Mrs. Aden (Mary) Mast, New York

Great-Grandma's Custard Pie

1½ c. white sugar
¾ c. brown sugar
6 Tbsp. flour
6 eggs, beaten
6 c. milk
1 tsp. vanilla

Mix sugars and flour together. Stir in eggs. Add milk and vanilla. Makes 3 pies.

—Mrs. Dannie (Anna) Hershberger, Michigan

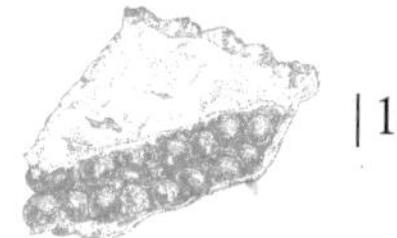

Butterscotch Pie [1]

1 Tbsp. butter
1 c. brown sugar
1¾ c. milk, divided
3 Tbsp. flour
2 eggs, separated
1 tsp. vanilla
pinch of salt

Brown butter in a kettle. Add brown sugar and ¼ c. milk. Cook for 5 minutes. In a bowl, mix flour, egg yolks, vanilla, salt and remaining 1½ c. milk. Mix well and add to sugar mixture. Cool a little before putting in a baked pie crust. Beat egg whites and put on top. Yum, yum!

—Mrs. David (Lisbet) Mast, Wisconsin

Butterscotch Pie [2]

⅓ c. butter
1½ c. brown sugar
1 c. water
3 Tbsp. flour
2 eggs, separated
pinch of salt
1 c. rich milk
1 tsp. vanilla
¼ tsp. cream of tartar
sugar

Put butter in skillet and add brown sugar. Stir until melted and brown. The browner it is, the better it tastes. Add water and bring to a boil. Mix flour, egg yolks, salt and milk to a smooth paste. Pour into boiling mixture and stir until thick. Remove from heat and add vanilla. Pour into a baked pie shell. Beat egg whites with cream of tartar. Add sugar a little at a time. Spread on top of pie and brown in oven. Makes 1 pie.

—Mrs. John (Edna) Herschberger, Wisconsin

May you live all the
days of your life.

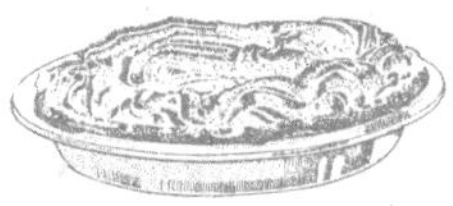

Butterscotch Pie [3]

3 Tbsp. butter
2 c. brown sugar
½ tsp. baking soda
6-8 c. water
3 Tbsp. flour
1 Tbsp. white sugar
2 Tbsp. cornstarch
pinch of salt
milk that you can stir
1 tsp. vanilla

Brown butter. Add brown sugar and stir until melted. Dissolve baking soda in water and add. Thicken with dry ingredients. Add milk and vanilla. Makes 2 pies.

—Mrs. Alvin (Elizabeth) Mast, New York

Butterscotch Wedding Pie

1½ c. butter, no substitutes
4 c. brown sugar
2 c. water
6 c. milk
4 egg yolks
6 Tbsp. (heaping) cornstarch
1 can evaporated milk
vanilla

Brown butter into a heavy saucepan and brown. Add sugar and stir until melted. Add water and milk, reserving some of the liquid. Moisten egg yolks and cornstarch. Stir into boiling syrup. Cook until thickened. Add evaporated milk and vanilla last. Makes 5 pies.

—Mrs. Aden (Mary) Mast, New York

I not only use all the brains I have, but all I can borrow.

Pumpkin Chiffon Pie

1 env. gelatin
¼ c. water
¾ c. brown sugar
½ tsp. salt
½ tsp. nutmeg
1 tsp. cinnamon
½ c. milk
1 c. cooked pumpkin
3 eggs, separated
¼ c. sugar

Dissolve gelatin in water. Mix everything except egg whites and ¼ c. sugar together. Pour into a saucepan and heat over medium heat for 10 minutes, stirring constantly. Remove from heat and cool until partially set. Beat egg whites until stiff. Add sugar and fold into pumpkin mixture. Top with whipped cream. Makes one 9" pie or 6 servings.

—Mrs. Jacob (Sadie) Hershberger, Wisconsin

Mother's Pumpkin Pie

⅔ c. sugar
1 Tbsp. butter, melted
1 Tbsp. flour
¼ tsp. cinnamon
½ tsp. salt
½ c. stewed pumpkin or squash
1 egg, separated
2 or 3 drops vanilla
¾ c. cream
¾ c. milk

Beat sugar, butter, flour, cinnamon, salt, pumpkin and egg yolk together. Add vanilla, cream and milk. Beat egg white and fold into mixture. Pour into unbaked crust and bake slowly as for custard. Serves 6 people.

—Mrs. Atlee (Fannie) Miller, New York

Pumpkin Pie [1]

1½ Tbsp. flour
1 c. brown sugar
1 c. white sugar
¾ tsp. nutmeg
¾ tsp. cinnamon
¾ tsp. salt
1 pt. pumpkin
6 eggs, separated
3½ c. cream
3 c. milk

Mix flour, sugars and spices. Add salt, pumpkin and egg yolks and stir. Add cream and milk. Last beat egg whites and stir in. Pour into 3 unbaked pie shells and bake at 350° for 20 minutes, then at 300° until done.

—Ms. Elizabeth J. Herschberger, Michigan

Pumpkin Pie [2]

3 Tbsp. flour
3 c. brown sugar
1 Tbsp. pumpkin pie spice
4 eggs, separated
3 c. pumpkin
5 c. milk

Mix flour, sugar and spice together. Add egg yolks. Gradually add pumpkin. Then add milk. Beat egg whites and add last. Bake at 400°. Makes four 8" pies. Our favorite—good anytime!

—Ms. Mary S. Herschberger, Michigan

Pumpkin Pie [3]

4 eggs, separated
2 c. (scant) white sugar
2 c. brown sugar
3 Tbsp. flour
1 Tbsp. pumpkin pie spice
5 c. milk
3 c. pumpkin

Separate eggs. Beat egg yolks and add sugars, flour, pumpkin pie spice, milk and pumpkin. Beat egg whites and add last. Makes 3 large pies.

—Mrs. David (Barbara) Hershberger, Michigan

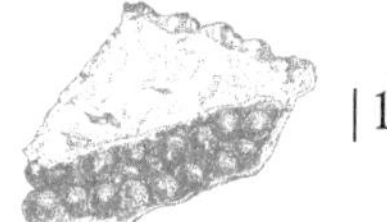

Buttermilk Pie

4 eggs
1½-2 c. sugar
6 Tbsp. butter, melted
2 Tbsp. flour
1 tsp. vanilla
½ tsp. salt
¾ c. buttermilk
⅓ c. chopped walnuts

Beat eggs. Add sugar, butter, flour, vanilla and salt. Slowly add buttermilk and blend well. Pour into 9" unbaked pie shell. Sprinkle walnuts on top. Bake at 350° for 40-45 minutes or until a knife comes out clean and top is golden. Keep refrigerated.

—Mrs. David (Naomi) Herschberger, Michigan

Peanut Butter Pie [1]

4 oz. cream cheese, softened
¼ c. creamy peanut butter
¼ c. white sugar
1 tsp. vanilla
1 c. Rich's topping, whipped

Cream together cream cheese, peanut butter, sugar and vanilla. Fold in whipped topping last. Pour in a baked pie crust or graham cracker crust. I also like to put chocolate chips or Oreo cookies in bottom of pie crust before filling. Makes 1 pie.

—Mrs. Alvin (Elizabeth) Mast, New York

After dinner rest a while.
After supper walk a mile.

Peanut Butter Pie [2]

Filling:
1 c. sugar
1 Tbsp. (heaping) clear jel
2 c. milk
3 egg yolks, slightly beaten; reserve whites
1 Tbsp. butter
1 tsp. vanilla

Mix sugar and clear jel with some milk. Add slightly beaten egg yolks, butter and vanilla. Bring remainder of milk to a boil. Stir in your first mixture. Remove from heat. Put ¾ of crumbs into a 10" baked pie shell. Pour pudding on top of crumbs. Top with meringue. Sprinkle remainder of crumbs over it. Brown slightly at 350°.

Crumbs:
1 c. powdered sugar
⅓ c. peanut butter

Combine.

Meringue:
¼ tsp. vanilla
3 egg whites
¼ tsp. cream of tartar

Beat well.

—Ms. Edna A. Slabaugh, Wisconsin

Coconut Pie [1]

5 eggs, beaten
1 c. white sugar
2 Tbsp. flour
¼ c. butter, melted
2 c. light corn syrup
2 tsp. vanilla
¼ tsp. salt
2 c. milk
2 c. coconut

Mix in order given. Pour in an unbaked pie shell. You can omit ¼ c. sugar if the coconut is sweetened. Bake at 350° for 30 minutes or until done.

—Mrs. Dannie (Lizzie) Yoder, Michigan

Coconut Pie [2]

1½ c. sugar
5⅓ Tbsp. butter
2 Tbsp. flour
3 eggs
1½ c. milk
1 c. coconut

Mix first 5 ingredients and stir in coconut. Put in an unbaked pie shell.

—Mrs. Rudy (Ella) Borntreger, Wisconsin

Coconut Oatmeal Pie

9 eggs, beaten
1¾ c. water
2 c. sugar
pinch of salt
6 Tbsp. butter
1 Tbsp. vanilla
1½ c. coconut
1½ c. oatmeal

Mix all ingredients together and put in an unbaked pie shell. Bake at 375° until done. Makes 2 pies.

—Mrs. Mahlon (Sarah) Gingerich, Ohio

Rice Krispie Ice Cream Pie

¼ c. light corn syrup
2 Tbsp. brown sugar
3 Tbsp. margarine
3½ c. Rice Krispies
¼ c. peanut butter
¼ c. chocolate syrup
1 Tbsp. corn syrup
vanilla ice cream

Mix ¼ c. corn syrup, sugar and margarine and bring to a boil. Add Rice Krispies. Mix and pat into serving dish. Combine peanut butter, chocolate and 1 Tbsp. corn syrup. Mix and pour onto Rice Krispies. Top with ice cream and freeze until served.

—Ms. Lovina A. Mast, New York

Rice Krispie Pie [1]

4 eggs
1½ c. corn syrup
1 tsp. vanilla
¼ tsp. salt
2 Tbsp. butter
2 Tbsp. water
2 Tbsp. brown sugar
1 Tbsp. flour
1 c. Rice Krispies

Beat eggs. Add remaining ingredients. Bake at 350° for 1 hour. Pour into an unbaked pie crust. Serves 6 people.

—Mrs. Dan (Anna) Raber, Ohio

Rice Krispie Pie [2]

2 eggs
1½-2 c. milk
⅔ c. sugar
½ c. corn syrup
2 Tbsp. flour
¼ tsp. salt
1 tsp. vanilla
3 Tbsp. butter, melted
1 c. Rice Krispies

Beat eggs and milk. Add sugar, corn syrup, flour, salt, vanilla and melted butter. Fold in Rice Krispies. Pour in an unbaked pie crust. Bake at 375° for 35-40 minutes. Do not overbake! Makes 1 pie or 6 servings.

—Mrs. Eli (Emma) Yoder, Michigan
—Ms. Fannie L. Raber, Ohio
—Mrs. Alvin (Susie) Yoder, Ohio
—Mrs. Andy (Anna) Hershberger, Ohio
—Mrs. Levi (Esther) Troyer, Ohio

Maple Nut Pie

½ c. milk
1 c. maple syrup
2 eggs, separated
1 Tbsp. gelatin
a little cold water
1-2 tsp. maple flavoring
1 c. whipped cream
½-¾ c. chopped nuts
¼ tsp. salt, optional

Heat milk and maple syrup. Add slightly beaten egg yolks. Cook a little. Soften gelatin in a little cold water and add. Add maple flavoring and chill until the mixture begins to thicken. Fold in stiffly beaten egg whites. Add whipped cream, chopped nuts and salt. Pour into a baked pie shell. Freeze. If you double this recipe, it makes three 8" pies. This tastes like maple nut ice cream.

—Mrs. Henry (Fannie) Miller, Michigan
—Ms. Rachel M. Coblentz, Minnesota

Nut Pie

3 eggs, beaten
1 c. light corn syrup
¾ c. brown sugar
¼ c. (scant) butter
½ c. pecans
pinch of salt
1 tsp. vanilla

Beat eggs. Add corn syrup, brown sugar, butter, pecans, salt and vanilla. Bake at 350°-400° until set. Makes 1 small pie.

—Mrs. Albert (Laura) Borntreger, Wisconsin

A quiet answer quiets anger,
but a harsh one stirs it up.
(Proverbs 15:11)

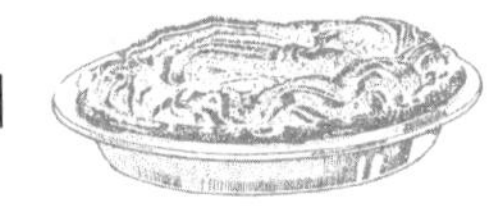

Pecan Pie [1]

2 eggs, beaten
½ c. brown sugar
1 c. molasses
1 Tbsp. flour
½ c. milk
2 Tbsp. butter, melted
1 c. chopped pecans or coconut
1 tsp. vanilla
pinch of salt

Pour in an unbaked pie shell. Bake.

—Ms. Lizzieann E. Mast, Michigan

Pecan Pie [2]

3 eggs, slightly beaten
½ c. brown sugar
1 c. light corn syrup with a little water added
1 Tbsp. flour
1 Tbsp. butter, melted
½ tsp. salt
1 tsp. vanilla
1 c. pecans

Mix all together, adding pecans last. Pour in an unbaked pie crust and bake as you would for a custard pie. Bake for about 45 minutes. Makes 1 pie.

—Ms. Amanda J. Mast, New York

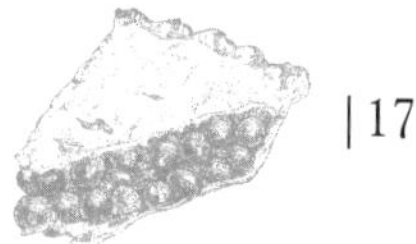

My Mother-in-Law's Favorite Pecan Pie

¼ c. butter
½ c. brown sugar
1 c. dark corn syrup
3 eggs, beaten
1 tsp. vanilla
¼ tsp. salt
1½ c. pecan halves

Cream butter and sugar together until fluffy. Add corn syrup, eggs, vanilla and salt. Sprinkle pecans on bottom of pie shell. Pour filling over pecans. Bake at 450° for 10 minutes. Reduce heat and continue baking until done. Fills one 9" pie pan.

—Mrs. Merle (Emma) Coblentz, Ohio

Kentucky Pecan Pie

1 c. corn syrup
½ c. brown sugar
⅓ c. butter, melted
1 tsp. vanilla
⅓ tsp. salt
3 eggs, beaten
1 c. pecans

Mix together in order given. Bake in 1 unbaked pie shell. Bake at 350° for 35-40 minutes or until done.

—Mrs. Mattie J. Yoder, Ohio

Happiness is not having
what you want but wanting
what you have.

Pecan Cream Cheese Pie

8 oz. cream cheese
¼ c. sugar
1 egg, beaten
1 tsp. vanilla
¼ tsp. salt
½ c. nuts

Syrup:
½ c. sugar
2 eggs, beaten
2 Tbsp. flour
2 Tbsp. butter
1 c. light corn syrup
¼ c. water

Pour syrup mixture on top of cream cheese mixture and bake at 350°.

—Mrs. Henry (Clara) Miller, Kentucky

Raisin Cream Pie [1]

2 c. milk
2 egg yolks, beaten
½ c. white sugar
½ c. brown sugar
¼ c. flour
1 c. raisins, cooked
1 tsp. vanilla
1 Tbsp. butter
pinch of salt
½ c. whipped topping

Bring milk to almost boiling. Make a paste of egg yolks, sugars, flour and a little of the milk and stir into milk. Boil again a little. Last add raisins, vanilla, butter and salt. Cool and pour in a baked pie shell. Top with whipped topping once cold.

—Mrs. Henry (Sarah) Yoder, Michigan

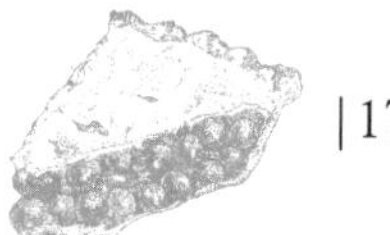

Raisin Cream Pie [2]

2 c. raisins
water
4 c. milk, divided
1 c. white sugar
1 c. brown sugar
4 egg yolks, beaten
¾ c. flour
2 Tbsp. butter

Cook raisins in water for 5 minutes. Boil 3 c. milk in a saucepan. Beat 1 c. milk, sugars, egg yolks and flour. Add to boiled milk and cook until thick. Last add butter and raisins. Pour in a baked crust. Makes 2 pies.

—Ms. Ida J. Yoder, Ohio

Holmes County Pie

4 eggs, separated
1½ c. sugar
4 c. sweet milk
1 c. sweet cream
1 Tbsp. (heaping) flour
1 tsp. cinnamon
1 tsp. nutmeg
1 tsp. cloves
1 c. raisins

Mix egg yolks and remaining ingredients. Spread in pan. Beat egg whites until soft peaks form and add some **sugar**. When removed from oven, top with beaten egg whites and return to oven to brown. Makes 3 pies.

—Mrs. Levi (Barbara) Mast, Pennsylvania

A great many open minds
should be closed for repairs.

Fresh Lemon Meringue Pie

1½ c. sugar
¼ c. + 2 Tbsp. cornstarch
¼ tsp. salt
½ c. cold water
½ c. freshly squeezed lemon juice
3 eggs, separated
2 Tbsp. butter
1½ c. boiling water
1 tsp. grated lemon peel
¼ tsp. cream of tartar
6 Tbsp. sugar

In a saucepan, thoroughly combine sugar, cornstarch and salt. Gradually stir in cold water and lemon juice. Blend in egg yolks. Add butter and boiling water. Bring to boil over medium heat, stirring constantly. Reduce heat and boil for 1 minute. Remove from heat. Stir in lemon peel. Pour into a baked pie shell while hot. Beat egg whites until foamy. Add cream of tartar and continue beating until soft peaks form. Gradually add sugar 1 Tbsp. at a time. Spread meringue over hot filling. Be sure to cover filling to the edges. Brown in oven. Makes 1 pie.

—Mrs. John (Edna) Herschberger, Wisconsin

Lemon Meringue Pie Supreme

7 Tbsp. cornstarch
1½ c. sugar
¼ tsp. salt
1½ c. hot water
3 egg yolks, beaten
3 Tbsp. butter
1 tsp. grated lemon peel
½ c. fresh lemon juice

Combine cornstarch, sugar and salt. In a saucepan, gradually stir in hot water. Cook until thick and clear. Remove. Stir ½ c. hot mixture into yolks. Mix into remaining hot mixture. Stir in butter, lemon peel and juice. Cool. Pour into a baked pie shell.

Meringue:
3 egg whites
¼ tsp. cream of tartar
6 tbsp. white sugar

Beat egg whites until foamy. Add cream of tartar and continue beating until soft peaks form. Gradually add sugar. Spread over hot filling. Brown in oven.

—Mrs. Allee (Edna) Yoder, Wisconsin

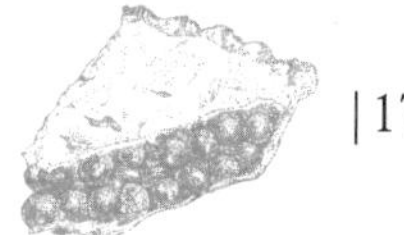

Lemon Sponge Pie

1 c. sugar
1 Tbsp. flour
2 eggs, separated
1 c. milk
grated rind and juice of 1 lemon
pinch of salt

Mix sugar, flour and beaten egg yolks. Add milk, lemon rind and juice and salt. Beat egg whites stiffly and fold in last. Bake.

—Mrs. John (Anna) Yoder, Michigan

French Rhubarb Pie

1 egg
1 c. sugar
1 tsp. vanilla
2 c. chopped rhubarb
2 Tbsp. flour

Mix and pour into an unbaked pie shell. Cover with crumbs. Bake.

Crumb Topping:
¾ c. flour
½ c. brown sugar
⅓ c. margarine

Combine.

—Mrs. Samuel (Edna) Mast, Pennsylvania

Rhubarb Custard Pie

1 c. (heaping) rhubarb, finely chopped
¾ c. white sugar
1½ Tbsp. flour
¼ tsp. salt
2 eggs, separated
1 c. milk
1 Tbsp. butter, melted
1 tsp. vanilla
2 Tbsp. sugar

Place finely chopped rhubarb in an unbaked pie shell. Mix ¾ c. sugar, flour, salt, beaten egg yolks, milk, melted butter and vanilla. Pour over rhubarb. Bake until firm. Cover with egg whites beaten with 2 Tbsp. sugar. Brown.

—Mrs. Mosie (Lizzie) Mast, New York

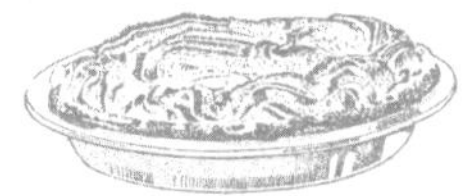

Rhubarb Strawberry Pie

1½ c. chopped rhubarb
¾ c. sugar
¼ c. water
⅓ c. strawberry Jell-O
1 c. whipping cream

Cook rhubarb, sugar and water together. Add Jell-O. Cool until thick. Whip cream and mix together. Pour in 1 baked pie shell. Very good!

—*Mrs. John (Susan) Miller, New York*

Fresh Fruit Pie

approx. 3 c. fresh fruit
1 c. brown sugar
1 c. white sugar, optional
½ c. flour
3 c. sweet cream
pinch of salt
1 tsp. vanilla

Line 2 crusts with fruit. Mix remaining ingredients and pour over fruit. Bake at 350° until done. If apples are used, add a pinch of nutmeg and sprinkle cinnamon over top. Delicious! Do not overbake.

—*Mrs. David (Naomi) Herschberger, Michigan*
—*Mrs. David (Barbara) Hershberger, Michigan*

Swallow your pride occasionally.
It's non-fattening.

Special Apple Pie

Crust:
1¾ c. flour
¼ c. white sugar
1 tsp. cinnamon
½ tsp. salt
½ c. + 2 Tbsp. butter
¼ c. water

Mix and roll out. This is enough for one 10" pie or 2 smaller ones.

Filling:
8 med. McIntosh apples
1⅔ c. sour cream
1 c. sugar
⅓ c. flour
1 egg, beaten
2 tsp. vanilla
¼ tsp. salt

Mix and pour into shells. Bake at 450° for 10 minutes, then at 350° for 30 minutes. Remove from oven.

Crumbs:
½ c. chopped walnuts
½ c. flour
⅓ c. white sugar
⅓ c. brown sugar
1 tsp. cinnamon
pinch of salt
½ c. butter

Immediately after removing from oven, top with crumbs. Bake another 15 minutes until lightly browned.

—Mrs. Levi (Susan) Mast, New York

Apple Pie

3-4 c. sliced apples
1 c. sugar
2 Tbsp. instant clear jel
1 tsp. cinnamon
2 Tbsp. butter
½ c. water

Combine all ingredients. Put in pie shell and top with crust.

—Mrs. Samuel (Naomi) Miller, Wisconsin

Dutch Apple Pie

3 c. sliced apples
1 c. brown sugar
3 Tbsp. flour
½ tsp. cinnamon
1 egg, beaten
1 c. light cream
1 tsp. vanilla
½ c. chopped nuts
1 Tbsp. butter

Place apples in pie shell. Mix sugar, flour and cinnamon. Combine egg, cream and vanilla. Add sugar mixture and mix well. Pour over apples. Sprinkle with nuts and dot with butter. Bake at 350° for 45-50 minutes or until apples are tender.

—Mrs. Ephraim (Amanda) Mast, Michigan

Farm Apple Pan Pie

Egg Yolk Pastry:
5 c. all-purpose flour
4 tsp. sugar
2 tsp. salt
½ tsp. baking powder
1½ c. shortening
2 egg yolks, lightly beaten
¾ c. cold water

Mix flour, sugar, salt and baking powder. Cut in shortening. Mix egg yolks and water and add, mixing just until moistened. Divide dough in half. On a lightly floured surface, roll half of dough to fit a 15" x 10" x 1" baking pan.

Filling:
5 lb. tart apples, peeled and thinly sliced
4 tsp. lemon juice
¾ c. white sugar
¾ c. brown sugar
1 tsp. cinnamon
½ tsp. nutmeg
¼ tsp. salt
milk
sugar

Sprinkle apples with lemon juice; arrange half of them over dough. Combine sugars, cinnamon, nutmeg and salt. Sprinkle half over apples. Top with remaining apples. Sprinkle with remaining sugar mixture. Roll remaining pastry to fit pan. Place on top of filling and seal edges. Brush with milk and sprinkle with sugar. Cut vents in top of pastry. Bake at 400°.

—Ms. Barbara F. Yoder, New York

Sour Cream Apple Pie

1 egg
¾ c. white sugar
¼ tsp. salt
½-1 tsp. vanilla
2 Tbsp. flour
¼ tsp. nutmeg, optional
2 c. chopped apples
1 c. sour cream

Beat egg and add remaining ingredients. Bake at 350° for 30 minutes. Top with crumbs and bake 15 minutes longer.

Crumbs:
⅓ c. brown sugar
1 tsp. cinnamon
⅓-½ c. flour
¼ c. butter

Mix together until crumbly.

—Mrs. Noah (Edna) Brenneman, Michigan
—Mrs. Levi (Mattie) Yoder, Michigan

Sour Cream Cherry Pie

1 c. sugar
3 Tbsp. flour
3 oz. cream cheese
1 c. sour cream
2½ c. cherry pie filling

Combine sugar, flour, cream cheese and sour cream. Blend well. Pour fruit in an unbaked pie shell. Pour cream cheese mixture over fruit. Top with crumbs. Bake at 425° for 15 minutes. Reduce heat to 350° and bake until done.

Crumbs:
1 c. flour
¼ c. butter
½ c. sugar

Mix together until crumbly.

—Ms. Elizabeth J. Yoder, Ohio

Strawberry Angel Pie

1 (3 oz.) pkg. strawberry Jell-O
1¼ c. boiling water
1 c. whipping cream
1 c. sliced fresh strawberries

Dissolve Jell-O in boiling water. Chill until gelatin mixture is partially set. Whip cream until soft peaks form. Fold cream and strawberries into gelatin mixture. Chill until mixture mounds slightly when spooned. Pile into pie shell. Chill 4-6 hours or overnight. Top with additional whipped cream and berries if desired. Serves 8 people.

—Ms. Saloma E. Mast, New York

Old-Fashioned Rhubarb Pie

2 eggs, beaten
1 c. (heaping) rhubarb
1 c. white sugar
6 white crackers, crushed
¼ tsp. salt
2 tsp. butter
¾ c. cream

Beat eggs well. Add remaining ingredients. Pour in a shell and top with a lattice pie crust.

—Mrs. Eli (Emma) Yoder, Michigan

Cleaning house while children are growing is like shoveling snow while it's snowing.

Lancaster Shoofly Pie

Filling:
½ c. molasses
1 c. hot water
¼ c. + 2 Tbsp. brown sugar
½ tsp. baking soda
1 egg, beaten
⅛ tsp. salt

Combine ingredients and mix well. Pour filling in unbaked pie crust. Top with crumbs. Bake slowly until done.

Crumbs:
1 c. flour
⅓ c. butter
⅓ c. brown sugar
¼ tsp. baking soda
⅓ tsp. cream of tartar

Mix together until crumbly.

—Mrs. Eli (Rachel) Mast, New York

Potato Cheese Pie

Crust:
2-2½ c. cooked, mashed potatoes
2 Tbsp. flour
1 tsp. baking powder
1 egg
2 Tbsp. butter, melted
salt
pepper

Mix ingredients thoroughly and pat into a large greased pie plate as if dough.

Filling:
2 eggs
1 c. cream
salt
pepper
¾ c. grated Velveeta cheese

Beat the eggs. Stir in cream and seasonings. Pour into potato crust and top with cheese. Bake at 350° for 20 minutes or until a knife inserted in the center comes out clean.

—Ms. Saloma E. Mast, New York

Fry Pies [1]

9 c. Velvet cake flour
3 c. SuperFry shortening
1 Tbsp. salt
2 Tbsp. sugar, optional, dissolved in 2 c. water

Glaze:
8 lb. powdered sugar
2½ c. warm water
½ c. cornstarch
1 tsp. vanilla

Mix like pie dough. Roll out dough and cut into circles or use a fry pie press. Fill with 1 Tbsp. pie filling. Wet edges all around and press together. Deep fry at 375° in SuperFry shortening. Glaze while still warm.

—Mrs. Andrew (Emma) Yoder, Ohio
—Mrs. Ora (Rachel) Beechy, Michigan
—Ms. Saloma E. Mast, New York

Pineapple Custard Pie

2 eggs, separated
⅔ c. sugar
¾ c. pineapple
1 T. flour (scant)
2 T. melted butter
½ c. cream and/or water

Mix like custard. Fold in beaten egg whites last. Pour into unbaked pie shell and bake in a 300° oven for 15-30 minutes, until nicely baked. Makes one pie.

—Mrs Moses (Martha (Troyer, Wisconsin

A man with ambition can do more with a rusty screwdriver than a loafer with a shop full of tools.

Desserts

- Marshmallows can be nicely cut by using scissors dipped in water.
- To soften brown sugar, put in a warm oven or put a piece of soft bread in the sugar container. Keeping a raw apple in your container will also keep the sugar soft.
- Store cottage cheese upside down in the refrigerator. It will keep twice as long.
- To keep strawberries fresh longer, place them in a Tupperware, cover them with a paper towel and cover. The paper towel absorbs the moisture.
- A few drops of lemon juice added to whipped cream helps it to whip faster and better.
- When you use fresh farm milk for instant pudding, bring it to a boil and let it cool before adding to the instant pudding mix. If you don't heat it first, the pudding will taste soapy.
- Try sprinkling a few grains of salt on your banana when you eat it. Not only does it make it easier to digest, but it also gives it more flavor.
- Cream whipped ahead of time will not separate if you add a touch of unflavored gelatin. Add 1 tsp. per cup of cream.
- A pinch of salt added to cream before whipping helps the cream stiffen more quickly.
- A pinch of salt added to Jell-O improves the flavor.
- Never cook tapioca fast. Just simmer it. It will become stringy if cooked too fast. Do not stir while cooling.
- To beat eggs quickly, add a pinch of salt.
- When cream will not whip, add an egg white. Thoroughly chill cream and egg. Try again, and it will whip easily.

Angel Food Cake Pudding [1]

- 4 egg yolks
- ½ c. butter, melted
- 2 c. powdered sugar
- 2 c. whipped cream
- 3 Butterfinger candy bars, crushed
- 1 angel food cake, cubed

Beat egg yolks, butter and powdered sugar well. Add whipped cream. Crush candy bars and fold half into pudding. Layer angel food cake and pudding. Top with remainder of candy bar crumbs. Refrigerate. Serves 12 people.

—Mrs. Samuel (Katie) Herschberger, Michigan
—Mrs. Albert (Laura) Brontreger, Wisconsin

Angel Food Cake Pudding [2]

- 1 angel food cake
- 4 egg yolks
- 2 c. powdered sugar
- 2 c. whipped cream
- ½ c. butter, softened
- 3 Butterfinger candy bars, crushed

Cut angel food cake in small pieces in a bowl. Beat egg yolks and powdered sugar well. Add whipped cream and butter. Fold half of the crumbs in pudding and sprinkle other half on top of pudding.

—Mrs. Moses (Martha) Troyer, Wisconsin

Happiness is like jam. You can't even spread a little without getting some on yourself.

Dirt Pudding

1 (12 oz.) pkg. Oreo cookies
3 (3 oz.) pkg. instant vanilla pudding
4½ c. milk
8 oz. cream cheese
8 oz. whipped topping

Crush cookies. Mix pudding and milk. Refrigerate for 10 minutes. Mix cream cheese and whipped topping. Add pudding. Pour pudding over crumbs, reserving some crumbs for the top.

—Mrs. Levi (Esther) Troyer, Ohio

Pretzel Pudding

2½ c. crushed pretzels
½ c. butter, melted
1 c. brown sugar
2 pkg. Jell-O, flavor of your choice
½ c. boiling water
2 c. whipped cream
8 oz. cream cheese
1 c. powdered sugar
2 tsp. vanilla

Mix pretzels, butter and brown sugar. Line a 9" x 13" pan, reserving some for top. Mix Jell-O with boiling water. Whip cream until stiff. Beat cream cheese, powdered sugar and vanilla. Fold in whipped cream. Beat in Jell-O and cream filling. Pour into pan. Sprinkle remainder of pretzels on top.

—Ms. Sarah F. Brock, Iowa

Blessed is the one who is too busy to worry in the daytime and too sleepy to worry at night.

Date Pudding

1 c. boiling water
1 c. finely chopped dates
1-2 tsp. baking soda
1 c. sugar
1 Tbsp. butter, softened
1 egg
1-1½ c. flour
¼ tsp. baking powder
½ tsp. salt
1 c. chopped nuts

Pour hot water over dates and baking soda. Let stand until cool. Mix together sugar, butter and egg. Add flour, baking powder, salt and chopped nuts. Bake in a greased 9" x 13" pan at 325° for 30-40 minutes. Cut in squares. Layer cake, sauce and whipped cream. Serves 10 people.

Laura's Sauce:
1 c. butter
4 c. brown sugar
4 c. water
1 tsp. salt
¾ c. clear jel
2 c. cold water
vanilla

Melt butter. Add brown sugar, 4 c. water and salt and bring to a boil. Combine clear jel, 2 c. water and vanilla. Add when first mixture boils. Boil 5 more minutes, then cool.

Edna's Sauce:
1 Tbsp. butter
1½ c. brown sugar
1½ c. boiling water

Bring to a boil.

—Mrs. Eli (Sarah) Mast, New York
—Mrs. Albert (Laura) Borntreger, Wisconsin
—Mrs. Samuel (Edna) Mast, Pennsylvania

Pineapple Pudding

2 c. graham cracker crumbs
2 c. powdered sugar
1 tsp. vanilla
2 egg yolks
1 Tbsp. butter
1 c. whipped cream
1 c. crushed pineapples, drained
½ c. nuts

Put graham cracker crumbs on a large platter. Mix powdered sugar, vanilla, egg yolks and butter. Add some pineapple juice or milk if too thick to spread. Spread on top of crumbs. Mix whipped cream, pineapples and nuts and put on top.

—Mrs. Andy (Martha) Kauffman, Wisconsin

Mandarin Orange Pudding

5 c. water
5 Tbsp. minute tapioca
½ c. instant vanilla pudding
⅔ c. orange Jell-O
1 (6 oz.) can mandarin oranges
8 oz. whipped topping

Bring water, tapioca, pudding and Jell-O to a boil, stirring constantly. Chill 3-4 hours. Add oranges and whipped topping. Bananas, pineapple, etc. may also be added if desired. Serves 8 people.

—Mrs. Eli (Mattie) Yoder, Ohio

Mystery Pudding

2 c. sugar
2 c. flour
2 tsp. baking soda
2 eggs
2 tsp. vanilla
1 qt. fruit cocktail
1 c. nuts
1 c. brown sugar

Mix first 6 ingredients and pour in a cake pan. Mix nuts and brown sugar. Sprinkle on top of cake. Bake at 325° for 40 minutes.

—Ms. Lovina D. Herschberger, Michigan

Butterscotch Tapioca [1]

6 c. boiling water
1 tsp. salt
1½ c. pearl tapioca
2 c. brown sugar
2 eggs, beaten
½ c. white sugar
1 c. milk
1 Tbsp. vanilla
1 Milky Way candy bar, crushed
whiped topping

Cook boiling water, salt and tapioca for 15 minutes. Add brown sugar. Cook until tapioca is clear, stirring often. Mix beaten eggs, white sugar and milk together. Add this to the tapioca mixture. Cook until it bubbles. Add vanilla and candy bar and mix well. Cool and add whipped topping. Serves 15 people.

—Mrs. Eli (Sarah) Mast, New York

Butterscotch Tapioca [2]

4 c. boiling water
1 tsp. salt
1½ c. pearl tapioca
2 c. brown sugar
1 egg, beaten
½ c. white sugar
4 c. milk
1 Tbsp. vanilla
1 c. whipped cream

Cook water, salt and tapioca for 30 minutes. Add brown sugar and cook until tapioca is clear, stirring often. Mix egg, white sugar and milk. Add to tapioca, then cook until bubbly. Add vanilla and cool. Add whipped cream. Miniature candy bars—Milky Way, Snickers or whatever you choose—make this pudding extra delicious if you cut them up in small pieces and add with whipped cream.

—Mrs. Emma A. Stabaugh, Wisconsin

Butterscotch Tapioca [3]

¼ c. butter
2 c. brown sugar
6 c. boiling water
1 tsp. salt
1 c. pearl tapioca
2 eggs, beaten
½ c. sugar
1 c. milk
1 tsp. vanilla
1 c. whipped topping
4 Milky Way candy bars, chopped, optional

Brown butter. Add brown sugar, boiling water, salt and tapioca. Cook until tapioca is clear. Mix eggs, sugar and milk together. Add to tapioca and cook until it bubbles. Add vanilla. Cool. Add whipped cream and candy bars.

—Mrs. Samuel (Dora) Mast, New York

Caramel Tapioca

2 c. tapioca
¼ tsp. salt
10 c. boiling water
2 c. brown sugar
3 eggs, beaten
1 c. cream
1 c. sugar
2 Tbsp. butter, browned
1 tsp. vanilla
whipped cream

Add tapioca and salt to boiling water. Cook until half clear. Add brown sugar. Cook until clear. Add beaten eggs, cream and sugar. Bring to a boil. Remove from heat and add butter and vanilla. Cool and add whipped cream.

—Mrs. Elizabeth J. Yoder, Ohio

Caramel Dumplings

Sauce:
2 Tbsp. butter
1½ c. brown sugar
1½ c. water

In a skillet, heat butter, brown sugar and water to boiling. Reduce to a simmer.

Dumplings:
1¼ c. flour
½ c. sugar
2 tsp. baking powder
½ tsp. salt
2 Tbsp. butter
½ c. milk
½ c. chopped, peeled apples

Meanwhile mix dumpling ingredients together. Drop by teaspoon into simmering sauce. Cover tightly and simmer for 20 minutes. Do not lift lid. Serve warm with ice cream. Serves 10 people.

—Mrs. Dan (Anna) Raber, Ohio

Hot Caramel Dumplings

1 Tbsp. butter
1½ c. boiling water
⅛ tsp. salt
1 c. brown sugar
1¼ c. flour
1½ tsp. baking powder
¼ c. sugar
⅛ tsp. salt
1 Tbsp. butter
½ c. milk
½ tsp. vanilla

Make a sauce of butter, boiling water, salt and brown sugar. Put all in a 8 qt. shallow saucepan and let come to a boil while preparing dough. Sift dry ingredients together. Cut in butter. Add milk and vanilla and mix. Drop by rounded teaspoonsful into boiling sauce. Boil lightly over low heat for 10 minutes. Do not lift lid while boiling. Good with whipped cream or ice cream.

—Ms. Sarah M. Hershberger, Wisconsin

Different Apple Dumplings

2 c. flour
2 tsp. baking powder
1 tsp. salt
⅔ c. shortening or
½ c. butter
½ c. milk
chopped apples

Mix flour, baking powder and salt. Cut in shortening or butter. Mix in milk just until moistened. Roll out into rectangular shape. Cover with as many chopped apples as you like. Roll up as for cinnamon rolls. Slice and lay in a greased pan. Cover with boiling syrup and bake until apples are tender and crust is done. We like these with milk or ice cream. Serves 8 people.

Syrup:
2 c. hot water
2 c. sugar
1 tsp. cinnamon
1 tsp. nutmeg

Bring to a boil.

—Mrs. Andy (Barbara) Schwartz, Ohio

Pineapple Delight

Layer 1:
2½ c. graham cracker crumbs
½ c. butter, melted

Press into an 8" x 10" pan. Bake at 320° for 15 minutes.

Layer 2:
½ c. butter
1½ c. powdered sugar
2 egg yolks

Beat until light and fluffy. Spread on cooled crust.

Layer 3:
1 can crushed pineapple, drained
1 c. whipped cream

Fold well-drained pineapples into cream. Spread on top of second layer. Chill and cut into squares.

—Ms. Lizzieann E. Mast, Michigan

Old-Fashioned Apple Dumplings

2 c. flour
½ tsp. salt
2½ tsp. baking powder
⅔ c. shortening
½ c. milk
6 apples, peeled and halved

Combine first 3 ingredients. Cut in shortening. Add milk. Roll out dough and cut into squares. Place 1 apple half on each square. Wet edge of dough and press into a ball around the apple. Or, put 2 halves together and fill cavity with **brown sugar**. Place dumplings 1" apart in baking pan and pour sauce over them. Bake at 375° for 35-40 minutes. Baste occasionally during baking. Serves 6 people.

Sauce:
2 c. brown sugar or maple syrup
2 c. water
¼ c. butter
½ tsp. cinnamon

Cook for 5 minutes.

—Mrs. Andy (Ada) Mast, New York
—Mrs. Noah (Susie) Gingerich, Ohio

Ideas are funny little things—they don't work unless you do.

Brown Betty

1 c. quick oats
1 c. whole wheat flour
¼ c. brown sugar
½ tsp. salt
½ tsp. baking soda
¼ c. shortening
1 qt. canned apple pie filling or any other fruit

Mix quick oats, whole wheat flour, brown sugar, salt and baking soda in a bowl. Cut in shortening. Pour apple pie filling or fruit of your choice into an 8" x 8" baking pan. Top with first mixture. Bake at 350° for 45 minutes or until browned. Serve warm with milk.

—Mrs. Levi (Mary) Beller, Michigan

Rhubarb Crumble

¾ c. brown sugar
¾ c. oatmeal
1 c. flour
½ c. butter
cinnamon
2½ c. diced rhubarb
1 c. sugar
2 Tbsp. cornstarch
1 c. water
1 tsp. vanilla

Mix brown sugar, oatmeal, flour, butter and cinnamon until crumbly. Press half in pan. Cover with rhubarb. Mix sugar and cornstarch. Add water and vanilla. Cook until clear and pour over rhubarb. Sprinkle remaining crumbs on top. Bake at 350° for 1 hour.

—Mrs. Andrew (Emma) Yoder, Ohio

Rhubarb Cake Dessert

2 c. flour
2 Tbsp. sugar
1 c. butter

Combine flour and sugar. Cut in butter until crumbly. Press into a greased 13" x 9" x 2" baking dish. Bake at 350° for 20 minutes. Cool.

Custard:
2 c. sugar
¼-⅓ c. all-purpose flour
1 tsp. salt
6 egg yolks, beaten
1 c. whipping cream
5 c. sliced rhubarb

In a bowl, combine sugar, flour and salt. Stir in egg yolks and cream. Add rhubarb. Pour over crust. Bake at 350° for 50-60 minutes or until set.

Mrs. Andy's Meringue:
6 egg whites
½ tsp. cream of tartar
¾ c. sugar
1 tsp. vanilla

In a mixing bowl, beat egg whites and cream of tartar on medium speed until soft peaks form. Gradually beat in sugar 1 Tbsp. at a time until stiff peaks form. Beat in vanilla. Spread over hot filling. Bake for 12-15 minutes or until golden brown. Refrigerate before serving. Serves 12 people.

Mrs. Eli's Meringue:
6 egg whites
¼ c. cornstarch
¾ c. sugar
2 Tbsp. vanilla
pinch of salt

In a mixing bowl, beat egg whites and cornstarch on medium speed until soft peaks form. Gradually beat in sugar 1 Tbsp. at a time until stiff peaks form. Beat in vanilla and salt. Spread meringue on top of baked filling before it is completely done and finish baking.

—Mrs. Andy (Anna) Hershberger, Ohio
—Mrs. Eli (Anna) Mast, Wisconsin
—Mrs. Samuel (Malinda) Mast, Pennsylvania
—Mrs. John (Susan) Miller, New York

Striped Delight

35 Oreo cookies, finely crushed (3 c.)
6 Tbsp. butter, melted
8 oz. cream cheese, softened
¼ c. sugar
2 Tbsp. milk
1½ c. whipped cream, divided
3¼ c. cold milk
2 pkg. instant chocolate pudding

Mix cookies and butter in a medium bowl. Press firmly into the bottom of a 9" x 13" pan. Refrigerate for 15 minutes. Beat cream cheese, sugar and 2 Tbsp. milk in a bowl with wire whisk until smooth. Gently stir in 1¼ c. whipped cream. Spread over crust. Pour 3¼ c. milk into a large bowl. Add pudding mixture. Beat with a wire whisk for 1-2 minutes. Pour over cream cheese layer. Let stand 5 minutes. Spread remaining ¼ c. cream over pudding.

—Ms. Rachel M. Coblentz, Minnesota

Fruit Pizza

Crust:
½ c. butter
½-1 c. brown sugar
1 egg
1⅓ c. flour
1 tsp. baking powder
¼ tsp. salt

Combine and mix well. Press dough into a pan. Bake at 350° for 10 minutes.

Filling:
8 oz. cream cheese
½ c. powdered sugar
½ tsp. vanilla
1 c. cream

When cooled, combine cream cheese filling and spread on baked dough. Top with any fruit you wish. We like to thicken pineapple juice with clear jel and mix with crushed pineapple and plenty of apples or any kind of raw fruit.

Glaze:
2 c. pineapple juice
½ c. sugar
1 Tbsp. (heaping) clear jel
pineapple Jell-O

Bring to a boil. Cool and spread over fruit.

—Ms. Ada F. Herschberger, Wisconsin
—Mrs. Dannie (Anna) Herschberger, Michigan

Peach Cobbler

6-8 lg. ripe peaches
2½ Tbsp. cornstarch
1 c. sugar

Peel and slice peaches. Combine peaches, cornstarch and sugar. Pour into a greased 9" x 13" baking pan.

Crust:
1 c. all-purpose flour
2 eggs, separated
¼ c. butter, melted
1 tsp. baking powder
1 c. sugar

Combine all ingredients except egg whites in a bowl. Gently fold egg whites into batter. Spread over peaches. Bake at 375° for about 45 minutes or until the fruit is bubbling around the edges and top is golden. Serves 12 people.

—Ms. Lovina D. Herschberger, Michigan

Blueberry Buffet

½ c. butter
½ c. sugar
1 egg
½ c. milk
2 c. flour
2½ tsp. baking powder
1 tsp. salt
2 c. blueberries

Mix butter, sugar and egg. Add milk, then dry ingredients. Fold in blueberries. Top with crumbs and bake at 350°. Serve warm with milk.

Crumbs:
½ c. flour
½ c. sugar
¼ c. butter

Mix together until crumbly.

—Mrs. Lewis (Elizabeth) Yoder, New York

Blueberry Cobbler

1½ c. sugar
¾ c. shortening
3 eggs
4½ tsp. baking powder
1 tsp. salt
1 tsp. vanilla
1½ c. milk
½ c. wheat flour
2 c. pastry flour
1 can blueberry or cherry pie filling

Cream sugar, shortening and eggs together. Add baking powder, salt, vanilla, milk and flour. Put ⅔ of dough in cake pan. Top with pie filling. Spread remaining dough on top. Bake. Serve warm or cold with milk.

—Mrs. David (Barbara) Hershberger, Michigan

Elder-n-Blueberry Cobbler

1¼ c. sugar
2 c. berries
1 Tbsp. lemon juice
1¾ c. all-purpose flour
4 tsp. baking powder
¾ tsp. salt
½ c. brown sugar
butter
1 egg, beaten
1c. milk

Mix ¾ c. sugar, berries and lemon juice. Pour into a greased 8" x 8" baking pan. Mix flour, baking powder, salt and brown sugar. Add butter. Mix until crumbly, then add beaten egg and milk. Pour on top of berries and bake at 350° until a toothpick inserted comes out clean. Serve with milk or whipped cream. A delicious supper!

—Mrs. John (Anna) Yoder, Michigan

Apple Goodie

½ c. sugar
2 Tbsp. flour
¼ tsp. salt
1 tsp. cinnamon
1½ qt. sliced apples

Mix sugar, flour, salt and cinnamon. Add to apples and mix. Put in bottom of a greased pan.

Crumbs:
1 c. oatmeal
½ c. brown sugar
1 c. flour
¼ tsp. baking soda
⅓ tsp. baking powder
⅔ c. butter

Mix until crumbly. Put on top of apples and pat firmly. Bake at 350° until brown and a crust is formed. Serve with milk.

—Mrs. Alvin (Emma) Mast, Pennsylvania

The reason a dog has so many friends is he wags his tail instead of his tongue.

Fresh Strawberry Dessert

Crust:

1¼ c. flour
½ c. butter, melted
¾ c. chopped pecans

In a mixing bowl, combine crust ingredients. Pat evenly over the bottom of a greased 9" x 13" x 2" baking pan. Bake at 300° for 25 minutes. Cool.

Filling:

1 c. butter, softened
8 oz. cream cheese, softened
2 c. powdered sugar
1 tsp. vanilla
2 qt. halved fresh strawberries

Cream butter, cream cheese, powdered sugar and vanilla in a mixing bowl until light and fluffy. Spread over crust. Arrange strawberries over filling.

Glaze:

1 c. sugar
3 Tbsp. cornstarch
1 c. water
3 Tbsp. strawberry Jell-O
2 tsp. lemon juice
whipped cream

Combine sugar and cornstarch in a saucepan. Stir in water; cook and stir over medium heat until thickened and bubbly. Remove from heat and stir in Jell-O until dissolved. Stir in lemon juice. Pour glaze over berries. Top with whipped cream. Serves 12 people.

—Mrs. Chris (Ella) Borntreger, Wisconsin

The only time people really care which side of their bread is buttered on is when they drop it on the floor.

Banana Split Dessert

Crust:

2 c. crushed graham crackers
½ c. margarine, melted
4 tsp. sugar

Mix together and press into a 12" x 8" x 3" pan.

Filling:

½ c. margarine
8 oz. cream cheese, softened
2 c. powdered sugar
5 bananas
1 or 2 cans crushed pineapple
whipped topping
maraschino cherries
nuts

Mix margarine, cream cheese and powdered sugar with beater and pour over crust. Slice bananas over filling. Drain pineapple and pour over bananas. Cover with whipped topping. Sprinkle with maraschino cherries and nuts. Chill 4-5 hours. Serves 12-15 people.

—Mrs. Enos (Ada) Mast, New York

Friendly Flora Yogurt

1 gal. milk
¼ c. gelatin
1 c. cold milk
1 c. plain yogurt
1-2 c. sugar
½ c. any flavor Jell-O
1 qt. pie filling, optional

Pour milk into a 6 qt. kettle and heat to 180°, stirring often. Remove from heat. Dissolve gelatin in cold milk, then add to hot milk. Cool down to 98° and put through a strainer to take off the skin. Beat in yogurt, sugar and Jell-O and pie filling if desired. Let set on stove shelf for 8 hours, then cool before serving. Makes 4 qt.

—Mrs. Noah (Edna) Brenneman, Michigan

Yogurt

1 gal. milk
¾-1½ c. sugar
3-4 Tbsp. Jell-O dissolved in hot water
2 Tbsp. gelatin dissolved in water
¼ c. yogurt

Heat milk to 190°, then cool to 130°. Add sugar, Jell-O, gelatin and yogurt. Beat well. Pour in jars and let set where it's 85° for 8 hours. Chill overnight. Temperature is very important. If plain yogurt is desired, add vanilla instead of Jell-O. When chilled, mix with fruit or pie filling. Delicious!

—Mrs. Noah (Lovina) Miller, Wisconsin
—Mrs. Andy (Barbara) Schwartz, Ohio

Homemade Yogurt

1 gal. milk
3 Tbsp. Jell-O
¼ c. yogurt
2 c. sugar
1 Tbsp. gelatin
1 c. water

Heat milk to 190°, then cool to 130°. Add flavoring and yogurt. Add sugar and gelatin which has been dissolved in water. Dissolve Jell-O in a little boiling water. Add. Beat well and pour into five 1 qt. jars. Put flat lids on but don't screw on rings. Put where it's 85° for 8 hours. The shelf of a cookstove works. Refrigerate.

—Mrs. Daniel (Gertie) Mast, New York

Orange Slush

2 c. white sugar
3 c. hot water
6 oz. frozen orange juice or orange drink or Jell-O
1 c. crushed pineapple
6 bananas

Dissolve sugar in hot water. Add orange juice. Combine pineapples and bananas. Mix together and freeze. A refreshing dessert. We like to freeze it an ice cream freezer but can also be set outside to freeze in the winter.

—Mrs. John (Esther) Miller, Ohio

Ice Cream Sandwiches [1]

½ c. sugar
3 eggs, separated
1 c. whipping cream
1 tsp. vanilla
maple flavoring, optional
graham crackers

Whip some sugar into egg whites and some into cream. Mix whipped egg whites, whipped cream, egg yolks and flavoring together. Put a layer of graham crackers in bottom of cake pan. Pour in ice cream mixture and put another layer of graham crackers on top. Try to match the bottom ones. Put it out to freeze overnight or a couple hours. Cut in squares to eat. They're best if temperature is 0° or below.

—Mrs. Dannie (Anna) Hershberger, Michigan
—Mrs. Andy (Ada) Mast, New York
—Ms. Elmina C. Kauffman, Wisconsin

Ice Cream Sandwiches [2]

½ c. butter, melted
2 c. graham cracker crumbs
½ c. sugar
3 eggs, separated
1⅓ c. powdered sugar
vanilla
1 pt. whipping cream

Mix butter, graham cracker crumbs and sugar. Put half of crumb mixture in bottom of pan. Separate eggs. Beat egg yolks until light. Add powdered sugar and beat well. Beat egg whites until stiff and add vanilla. Fold into egg yolk mixture. Last, whip cream and add to other mixture. Pour on top of graham cracker crumbs and top with remaining crumbs. Set out to freeze. These work best if temperature is below 0°.

—Mrs. Danny (Edna) Borntrager, Wisconsin
—Ms. Lovina A. Mast, New York

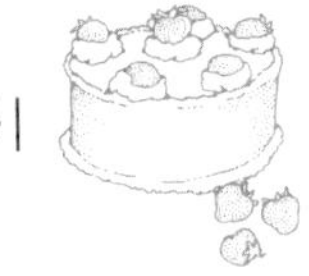

Dairy Queen Ice Cream [1]

2 Tbsp. gelatin
½ c. cold water
4 c. whole milk
2 c. sugar
1 tsp. salt
2 tsp. vanilla
3 c. cream, whipped

Soak gelatin in cold water. Heat milk until hot but not boiling. Remove from heat. Add gelatin mixture and sugar, salt and vanilla. Cool, then add whipped cream. Let set a couple hours before freezing. Chocolate may also be added. Makes 1 gal.

—Mrs. Simon (Clara) Miller, Michigan
—Mrs. Perry (Rebecca) Herschberger, Wisconsin

Dairy Queen Ice Cream [2]

3 qt. milk
¼ c. gelatin
¾ c. cold water
¼ c. vanilla
3 c. sugar
1 qt. cream

Heat milk just to boiling point but do not boil. Dissolve gelatin in cold water and stir into hot milk. Cool. Add remaining ingredients and freeze. Very good! Makes enough for 2 gal.

—Mrs. Mary S. Herschberger, Michigan

Homemade Ice Cream

1 qt. milk
2 c. white sugar
3 Tbsp. flour
4 eggs, separated
a little milk
½ c. milk
1-2 c. cream, whipped
flavoring

Bring 1 qt. milk to a boil. Meanwhile, blend sugar, flour, beaten egg yolks and enough milk to make a paste. When milk comes to a boil, stir in mixture until it boils again. It will be a soft custard. Add ½ c. milk and beaten egg whites. When cool, add whipped cream. Put in can and freeze. The more cream, the creamier.

—Mrs. Henry (Sarah) Yoder, Michigan

Ice Cream

6 c. milk
2½ c. sugar
½ c. cornstarch
½ c. flour
½ c. sugar
milk
4 eggs
pinch of salt
vanilla

Heat 6 c. milk and sugar until boiling. Make a batter of the cornstarch, flour, ½ c. sugar, milk and eggs. Add this to boiling milk, stirring constantly, until it boils again. Add salt, vanilla and enough milk to fill 6-qt. freezer can ¾ full.

—Ms. Verna S. Mast, New York

Quick Ice Cream

2 c. sugar
¾ c. instant clear jel
1 tsp. salt
2 qt. whole milk
2 tsp. vanilla or flavoring of your choice
3 eggs, well beaten
1 box instant pudding, prepared as directed

Mix sugar, clear jel and salt thoroughly. Slowly pour cold milk into sugar mixture, stirring with a wire whip to blend well. Mix all ingredients together and pour into a 6 qt. freezer can. Add more milk if necessary to fill can 4" from the top. Variation: Substitute brown sugar and add maple flavoring and 1 can sweetened condensed milk.

—Ms. Lovina A. Mast, New York

Instant Ice Cream

1 doz. eggs
2-3 c. white sugar, divided
½ c. instant pudding
2 qt. cream

Separate eggs. Beat egg whites with 1 c. sugar and beat until stiff. Beat egg yolks separately. Add some sugar and instant pudding. Beat cream separately and mix all ingredients together. Put in pans and cover. Set out to freeze. Freezes faster on the porch, than in snow on the ground.

—Ms. Ada J. Herschberger, Wisconsin

Delicious Homemade Ice Cream

4 whole eggs
1½ c. white sugar
1½ c. brown sugar
pinch of salt
1½ c. instant pudding
milk
flavoring, optional

Beat together with an egg beater. Freeze.

—Ms. Lovina Herschberger, Michigan

Orange Ice Cream

5 eggs
2 c. sugar
2 c. heavy cream
2 pkg. orange Jell-O
1 c. boiling water
whole milk

Beat eggs, sugar and cream together. Dissolve Jell-O in boiling water. Add to first mixture and stir well. Add whole milk to fill a gallon freezer to within 2" of the top. Any other flavor of Jell-O may be used or unflavored gelatin with vanilla.

—Ms. Elizabeth R. Borntreger, Wisconsin

Sherbet Ice Cream

1 c. white sugar
2 c. water
1 c. (heaping) Jell-O
5 c. milk
1 c. cream
½ tsp. salt

Boil sugar and water together for 2 minutes. Add Jell-O. Cool and add milk, cream and salt. Delicious!

—Mrs. Andy (Martha) Kauffman, Wisconsin

Butterscotch Sauce

1½ c. brown sugar
½ c. light corn syrup
¼ c. butter
½ c. cream
1 tsp. vanilla

Heat brown sugar, syrup and butter over low heat to boiling, stirring constantly. Remove from heat. Stir in cream and vanilla. Stir just before serving. Makes about 1 cup.

—Mrs. Emanuel (Esther) Herschberger, Michigan

Gooey Cake

1 lb. brown sugar
3 Tbsp. butter
1½ c. water
1¼ c. sugar
2 Tbsp. butter
1 tsp. vanilla
2 tsp. cinnamon
1 c. milk
2 tsp. baking powder
1¾ c. sifted flour
nuts

Bring brown sugar, butter and water to a boil. Set aside to cool while mixing the remainder of the cake. Cream sugar, butter, vanilla, cinnamon and milk together. Add baking powder and flour. Pour dough into a greased and floured 9" x 13" loaf pan. Sprinkle nuts over dough and pour syrup over it. Bake at 275°. Serve warm with cake.

—Ms. Miriam D. Herschberger, Michigan

Caramel Pudding

1½ c. brown sugar
1 Tbsp. butter
1 tsp. vanilla
½ c. white sugar
½ c. sweet milk
1 Tbsp. butter
2 tsp. baking powder
flour

Mix brown sugar, 1 Tbsp. butter and vanilla. Pour into a small cake pan. Mix sugar, milk, 1 Tbsp. butter and baking powder. Add flour to make a stiff dough. Drop dough in by spoonful. Good with milk.

—Mrs. Eli (Emma) Yoder, Michigan

Baked Chocolate Fudge Pudding

3 Tbsp. butter
¾ c. white sugar
1 c. flour
1½ tsp. baking powder
½ tsp. salt
½ c. milk
½ c. nuts
1 c. brown sugar
1½ Tbsp. cocoa
¼ tsp. salt
1¼ c. water

Cream butter and sugar together. Add flour, baking powder, salt, milk and nuts. Put in an ungreased pan. Mix brown sugar, cocoa and salt. Sprinkle over top of batter. Do not stir. Pour hot water over top of batter. Bake at 350°. Serve warm with ice cream or cold with cream. Delicious!

—Mrs. David (Lisbet) Mast, Wisconsin

Cocoa Fudge Pudding

2 c. flour
1¼ c. white sugar
1 tsp. salt
¼ c. shortening
4 tsp. baking powder
1 c. milk
2 c. brown sugar
½ c. cocoa
3 c. hot water

Combine flour, white sugar, salt, shortening and baking powder in a bowl. Mix in the milk to make dough like a cake batter. Pour in a 9" x 13" cake pan. Mix brown sugar and cocoa. Sprinkle over cake batter. Pour hot water over it and bake at 350° for 45 minutes.

—Ms. Elmina C. Kauffman, Wisconsin

There aren't enough crutches in the world for all the lame excuses.

Brownie Pudding

1 c. flour
2 tsp. baking powder
½ tsp. salt
2 Tbsp. cocoa
½ c. sugar
½ c. milk
2 Tbsp. lard, softened
1 tsp. vanilla
½ c. brown sugar
2 Tbsp. cocoa
1 c. boiling water

Combine flour, baking powder, salt, cocoa and sugar. Add milk and lard. Beat well. Add vanilla. Mix together brown sugar and cocoa. Sprinkle over batter. Pour boiling water over all. Bake in a square cake pan at 350° for 20-30 minutes. Serves 4 people.

—Mrs. Moses (Amelia) Gingerich, Ohio

Saucy Fudge Pudding

1 c. sifted flour
½ tsp. baking soda
2 Tbsp. shortening
1 tsp. vanilla
¾ c. nuts, optional
½ tsp. salt
½ c. sugar
½ c. milk
1 Tbsp. cocoa
¾ c. brown sugar
1⅓ c. hot water
1 Tbsp. (scant) cocoa

Mix first 9 ingredients into a batter. Pour into an 8"-12" pan. Boil remaining ingredients together for 5 minutes. Pour over batter. Bake at 350° for 45 minutes or until done. Serve warm with milk or whipped cream.

—Mrs. Harvey (Katieann) Raber, New York

Chocolate Fudge Pudding

1 c. brown sugar
¼ c. cocoa
¼ tsp. salt
1 Tbsp. butter
1¾ c. boiling water
1 Tbsp. shortening
½ c. sugar
1 egg
milk
1 c. flour
1½ tsp. baking powder
½ tsp. salt

Combine brown sugar, cocoa, salt, butter and boiling water in a 9" x 12" cake pan. Cream shortening, sugar, egg and milk. Add flour, baking powder and salt. Mix well and drop by teaspoonful into sauce. Bake at 350° for 30 minutes. Serve warm with ice cream.

—Ms. Elizabeth J. Herschberger, Michigan

Yogurt

2 qts. milk
1 T. unflavored gelatin
⅓ c. water
½ c. starter yogurt
½ c. sugar

Heat milk to 180°. Dissolve gelatin in water. Add to milk and beat well. Set in sink of cold water until 110°. Add yogurt and beat again. Cover with wrap and set in gas oven or on top of refrigerator overnight. Add sugar and beat well again. Keep yogurt starter before adding sugar. Use within 10 days. Makes 2 quarts of yogurt or a little more.

—Mrs. Moses (Martha) Troyer, Wisconsin

Meats and
Main Dishes
Sweet Heart

- To keep vegetables colorful, add a pinch of baking soda to cooking water.
- Baked potatoes should be pricked with a fork to release the steam as soon as they are finished baking. This keeps them from becoming soggy.
- Leftover bologna pieces or dried beef can be used up if cut in pieces and soaked overnight, then cooked and made with gravy.
- Add raw rice to salt shaker to keep salt free-flowing.
- In damp weather when salt is difficult to use in a shaker, add 1 tsp. cornstarch to each cup of salt and mix thoroughly. The salt will run freely.
- Before you pour your cooked corn for cornmeal mush in a pan, rinse it with cold water. It won't stick to your pan when cutting the next morning.
- Hillbilly Hint—After fixing a turkey, put in 6 c. unpopped corn. Sew up tightly, put in oven and turn heat on high. Get out of kitchen and let her go. When the corn bursts the stitches, you'll know she's done a-poppin'. Git the broom and shovel.
- When cutting onions, do not cut off the roots. This helps to prevent watery eyes.
- Use spices and herbs sparingly. They are best if you have to guess which ones are really used.
- For perfect noodles, bring required water to a boil, add noodles, turn off heat and allow to stand for 20 minutes. This prevents them from boiling over and the chore of stirring. Noodles won't stick to the pan.
- A lump of butter added to water when boiling rice, noodles, spaghetti, potatoes and similar starches will keep it from boiling over.
- To prevent potatoes from boiling over, add 1 Tbsp. butter. A butter wrapper laid on top of potatoes will do the same.
- A little baking powder added to meatloaf will make it more fluffy. If you add about ½ c. milk to a pound of hamburger and let it set for 1½ hours before using it, it will be more juicy.
- Onion odor may be removed from hands by rubbing them with salt.
- To roast a juicy chicken, just put an apple inside before roasting it.
- For extra juicy, extra nutritious hamburgers, add ¼ c. evaporated milk per pound of meat before shaping.
- In a hurry to fry hamburgers? When forming the patties make a small hole in the center with your finger; this will speed up frying and will partially close when done.

Pizza Casserole [1]

1 lb. ground beef
1 sm. onion, chopped
1 Tbsp. butter
salt and pepper
10 oz. small shell macaroni or noodles
2 cans pizza sauce
1 sm. pkg. sliced pepperoni
1 can mushroom pieces
4 oz. shredded cheese or Velveeta cheese

Brown beef and onion in butter. Add salt and pepper to taste. Cook macaroni until soft. Combine all in a baking dish, topping with cheese. Bake at 350° for 1 hour.

—Mrs. Henry (Sarah) Mast, Ohio

Pizza Casserole [2]

2 (9") pie crusts
1 lb. pork sausage
½ c. minced onion
2 Tbsp. butter
2 Tbsp. flour
1 c. milk
1-2 c. cheese
salt and pepper
¼ tsp. oregano
1 can tomato soup or pizza sauce

Line pie plates with unbaked pastry. Fry sausage and onions until nicely browned. Make a white sauce with butter, flour and milk. Add cheese. Add salt, pepper and oregano if desired. Put sausage in bottom. Add tomato sauce and top with cheese sauce. Bake at 425° for 20-30 minutes. This makes a juicy pie!

—Mrs. Ora (Rachel) Beechy, Michigan

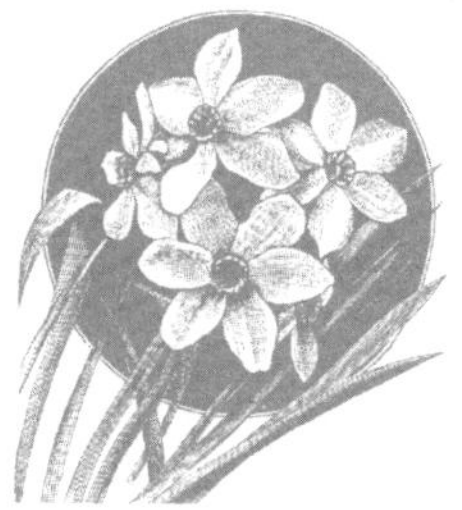

The optimist sees the doughnut.
The pessimist sees the hole.

Pizza Casserole [3]

1-2 lb. hamburger
salt and pepper
onion
8 oz. wide noodles
½ green pepper
1 c. mushroom soup
1 pt. pizza sauce
1 can mushrooms, undrained
¼ tsp. garlic powder
¼ tsp. oregano
¼ c. Parmesan cheese
mozarella cheese
pepperoni

Brown hamburger. Add salt, pepper and onion to taste. Cook noodles for 3-5 minutes. Drain. Place in bottom of baking dish. Add hamburger mixture and next 7 ingredients. Top with mozzarella cheese and pepperoni. Bake at 350° for 30 minutes.

—Ms. Anna J. Mast, New York

Pizza Casserole [4]

2 lb. hamburger
1 pt. pizza sauce
8 oz. sour cream or cream cheese
1 env. onion soup mix
3 cans biscuits
pizza cheese

Brown hamburger. Add pizza sauce, sour cream and onion soup mix. Bake biscuits. Layer biscuits, meat mixture and cheese. Repeat until all used.

A day of worry is more exhausting than a week of work.

Pizza Casserole [5]

3 lb. hamburger
1 sm. onion, chopped
½ c. spaghetti
1⅓ c. flour
2 tsp. baking powder
⅔ tsp. salt
½ c. milk
¼ c. vegetable oil
3 c. pizza sauce
1 c. sour cream
3½ Tbsp. salad dressing
2 c. grated cheese

Fry hamburger with onion. Cook spaghetti according to package directions. Mix flour, baking powder and salt together. Add milk and oil all at once and mix well. Press in bottom of a 9" x 13" pan. Place hamburger on top of crust, then layer spaghetti and pizza sauce. Mix sour cream, salad dressing and cheese together and spread on top. Bake in a moderate oven until crust is golden brown.

—Ms. Elizabeth R. Borntreger, Wisconsin

Breakfast Pizza [1]

1 lb. ground sausage
1 c. shredded potatoes
1 c. shredded cheese
5 eggs
½ c. milk
½ tsp. salt
⅛ tsp. pepper

Cook meat until browned. Drain off fat. Take your favorite biscuit recipe and roll out in a cake pan. Spoon meat over crust. Sprinkle with potatoes. Top with cheese. In a bowl, beat eggs, milk, salt and pepper. Pour into crust and bake at 370° for 25-30 minutes.

—Mrs. Alvin (Emma) Mast, Pennsylvania
—Mrs. Atlee (Fannie) Miller, New York

A man can do nothing if he waits
until he can do it so well that
no one can find fault with it.

Breakfast Pizza [2]

1 c. pastry flour
1 Tbsp. baking powder
¼ tsp. cream of tartar
¼ tsp. salt
1 Tbsp. sugar
shortening
1 egg, unbeaten
⅓ c. milk
sausage gravy
scrambled eggs
fried and crumbled bacon
shredded cheese

Mix flour, baking powder, cream of tartar, salt, sugar and shortening until crumbly. Add egg and milk. Stir just until dough clings together. Drop by Tbsp. onto cookie sheet. Bake at 350° until light brown. Cool to touch and crumble in a 7" x 11" pan. Top with sausage gravy, eggs, bacon and cheese. Return to oven for 15 minutes longer or until cheese is melted. Serves 6 people.

—Mrs. Eli (Mattie) Yoder, Ohio

Breakfast Pizza [3]

1 tube crescent biscuits
1 c. bacon or ham
1 c. shredded cheese
4 eggs scrambled in
½ c. milk
salt and pepper to taste
chopped onions, optional
mushrooms, optional
diced peppers, optional

Spread biscuits in bottom of baking pan. Layer with bacon or ham, shredded cheese, eggs and onions. May also add mushrooms or peppers if desired. Bake until done.

—Mrs. Perry (Rebecca) Herschberger, Wisconsin

Mom's Breakfast Pizza

biscuits
sausage gravy
scrambled eggs
fried smoked sausage wieners
fried bacon
cheese

Layer in order given. Place in oven until heated.

—Ms. Ida J. Yoder, Ohio

Pizza Sandwiches

1 qt. hamburger
1 c. pizza sauce
½ c. brown sugar
6 slices bread
cheese

Mix and heat hamburger, pizza sauce and brown sugar to make sloppy joe mixture. Butter bread and put on cookie sheet, buttered side down. Spread meat on top. Bake at 375° until bread is toasted. Remove from oven and top with a layer of cheese. Bake again until cheese is melted. Quick and easy to fix. Serves 6 people.

—Mrs. David (Barbara) Hershberger, Michigan

Every family needs at least three books in their home—a cookbook, a checkbook and the Good Book.

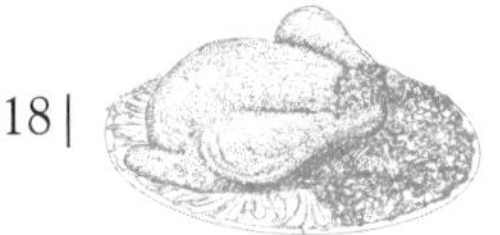

Vegetable Pizza

Crust:
¼ c. butter
2 Tbsp. sugar
¼ c. boiling water
1 Tbsp. active dry yeast
¼ c. warm water
1 egg, beaten
1½ c. all-purpose flour
1 tsp. salt

Combine butter, sugar and boiling water in a mixing bowl. Stir until butter is melted. Dissolve yeast in water, then add yeast and beaten egg to butter mixture. Add flour and salt and mix well. Spread evenly on a well-greased 10" x 15" pan. Bake at 325° just till golden brown. Cool.

Dressing:
8 oz. cream cheese
1 pkg. dry Hidden Valley Ranch dressing mix
8 oz. sour cream
1 Tbsp. sugar
shredded carrots
diced green peppers
minced broccoli
minced cauliflower
minced onions
shredded cheese

Soften cream cheese to room temperature. Add next 3 ingredients and spread on cooled crust. Top with carrots, green peppers, broccoli, cauliflower and onions. Top with shredded cheese. Cut into squares and serve. I prefer cutting it into squares before adding vegetables.

—Ms. Amanda F. Miest, New York

How come some lemonade is flavored with artificial lemon while furniture polish and dish soap are made with real lemon?

Cheesy Pizza

Crust:

1 Tbsp. yeast
1 c. warm water
2 Tbsp. sugar
2 Tbsp. vegetable oil
2½ c. flour
1 tsp. salt

1 pt. pizza sauce
3 c. crumbled meat
1 lb. shredded cheese

Dissolve yeast in warm water. Add remaining ingredients and let set for 5 minutes. Press into a greased cookie sheet. Spread pizza sauce on dough. Sprinkle with meat. Bake at 375° for 25-30 minutes. Remove from oven and sprinkle with cheese. Bake for 5 more minutes.

—Mrs. Henry (Sarah) Yoder, Michigan

Mo Tos

1 c. flour
2 tsp. seasoned salt
¼ tsp. garlic powder
1 tsp. paprika
1 tsp. baking powder
¼ tsp. pepper
¼ c. Parmesan cheese
6 med. potatoes, cut French-fry style
milk
½ c. butter, melted

Put first 7 ingredients in a plastic bag and mix. Dip potatoes into milk then shake in flour mixture. Place in a single layer on a cookie sheet. Drizzle with melted butter. Bake at 400° for 1 hour or until golden brown. Very good!

—Mrs. Floyd (Katie) Beechy, Michigan

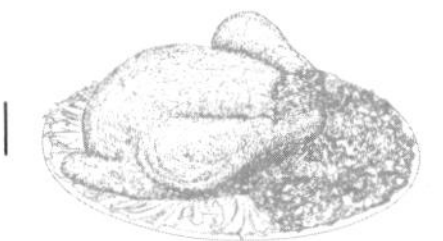

Stromboli

1 Tbsp. yeast
1 c. warm water
1/4 c. vegetable oil
1 tsp. salt
3 c. flour
diced ham
white American cheese
pizza sauce
thinly sliced onion, optional
diced green peppers, optional
butter
seasoned salt

Dissolve yeast in water. Mix in oil, salt and flour. Roll out. Put half on cookie sheet and fill with ham and white American cheese and onion and peppers if desired. Put in layers. Pour a little pizza sauce on and fold over with remaining dough. Spread a thin layer of pizza sauce on top. Bake at 350° for 20-25 minutes. Brush with butter and sprinkle lightly with seasoned salt.

—Mrs. Ora (Rachel) Beechy, Michigan

Breakfast Casserole [1]

3 c. cubed bread
3 c. diced ham, sausage or bacon
3 c. shredded cheese
chopped onion
6 eggs
1 Tbsp. flour
2 Tbsp. butter, melted
3 c. milk

Grease a 7" x 10" pan. Layer bread, meat, cheese and onion. Beat eggs. Add flour, butter and milk. Pour over mixture in pan. Refrigerate overnight. Bake uncovered at 325° for 1 hour.

—Mrs. Henry (Fannie) Miller, Michigan

Food for Thought—
Only people who do things make mistakes.

Breakfast Casserole [2]

bread slices
cheese slices
ham, bacon or sausage
6 eggs
3 c. milk
1 tsp. salt
1 tsp. black pepper
1½ c. crushed cornflakes
¼ c. butter, melted

Generously butter a 9" x 13" pan. Arrange bread slices on bottom of pan. Layer cheese and meat on top. Beat eggs and milk. Add salt and pepper. Pour over everything. Let set overnight or several hours. When ready to bake, mix cornflakes with butter and spread over top. Bake at 350°.

—Mrs. Amos (Mattie) Garber, Ohio

Breakfast Casserole [3]

12 slices bread
6 slices bologna
6 slices cheese
6 eggs
3 c. milk
1 tsp. onion flakes
1 tsp. powdered mustard
1 tsp. salt
½ c. butter
1 c. crushed cornflakes

Butter bread. Arrange 6 slices bread in a regular cake pan buttered side down. Top with bologna, cheese and remaining 6 slices bread buttered side down. Beat eggs and add milk, onion flakes, powdered mustard and salt. Pour over bread. Set in a cool place overnight. The next morning, melt butter and mix in crushed cornflakes. Spread over everything and bake for 30-45 minutes or until browned.

—Ms. Elmina C. Kauffman, Wisconsin

Cheeseburger Macaroni

1½ lb. ground beef
1 sm. onion, chopped
½ c. barbecue sauce
2¾ c. water
2 c. macaroni, uncooked
8 oz. Velveeta cheese
1 lg. tomato, chopped
½ c. bacon bits, optional

Brown meat and onion in a large skillet with butter. Drain. Add barbecue sauce and water and mix well. Bring to a boil and add macaroni. Cook for 8-10 minutes or until tender. Stir in cheese until melted. Top with tomatoes and bacon. Serves 6 people.

—Mrs. Noah (Lovina) Miller, Wisconsin

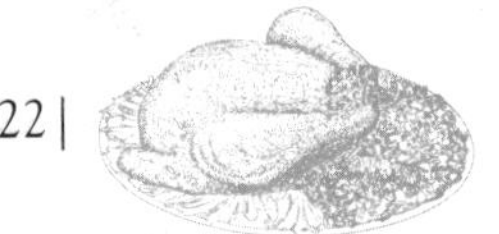

Baked Macaroni and Cheese

8 oz. macaroni
3 Tbsp. butter
3 Tbsp. flour
2 c. milk
½ tsp. salt
⅛ tsp. pepper
1 c. dry bread crumbs
½ lb. Velveeta cheese

Cook macaroni in salt water. Make a sauce with the next 5 ingredients. Add ⅔ of the cheese to the sauce and stir until melted. Combine cooked macaroni with the sauce and pour into greased baking dish. Chopped **pepper**, **onion**, **celery** or **parsley** may be added for variation. Sprinkle crumbs and remaining cheese over top. Bake at 325°-350° for 15-20 minutes.

—Mrs. Levi (Esther) Troyer, Ohio

Chicken Casserole

9 slices bread, crumbled
4 c. cooked, chopped chicken
1 c. butter, melted
½ c. salad dressing
1 tsp. salt
4 eggs, beaten
1 c. milk
1 c. chicken broth
9 slices cheese
2 cans cream of celery soup
buttered bread crumbs

Put crumbled bread slices in bottom of a 9" x 13" cake pan or small roaster. Top with chicken. Mix melted butter, salad dressing, salt, eggs, milk and chicken broth and pour over chicken. Top with cheese and celery soup. Top with buttered bread crumbs. Cover and refrigerate overnight. Bake 350° for 1½ hours.

—Ms. Rachel D. Mast, New York

Though life's trials pull
us apart, Jesus' love
holds us together!

Chicken Rice Casserole

1½ c. rice
2 c. water
1 pt. chicken pieces and broth
salt
6 slices Velveeeta
1 can cream of mushroom soup

Cook rice, water and chicken together until rice is done. Add salt, cheese and cream of mushroom soup. Put in casserole dish with cheese and cracker or cornflake crumbs on top. Serves 4 people.

—Mrs. Andy (Barbara) Schwartz, Ohio

Chicken Potpie

2 qt. chicken with broth
4 med. potatoes, diced
1 onion, chopped
parsley
salt and pepper

Pastry Dough:
2 c. flour
⅓ c. shortening
½ tsp. salt
1 tsp. baking powder
½ c. milk

Put chicken in kettle and add broth and water to cover. Make pastry dough and take ¾ of it and roll out to size of bowl. Line bottom and sides. Put chicken pieces in bottom, then diced potatoes and chopped onion. Sprinkle with parsley, salt and pepper. Repeat layers. Make pastry lid and cut slits in top. Fasten sides securely. Bake at 350° for 1 hour.

—Mrs. Rebecca O. Mast, Ohio

Impossible Cheeseburger Pie

1 lb. ground beef or sausage
½ c. chopped onions
½ tsp. salt
¼ tsp. pepper
1½ c. milk
3 eggs
¾ c. Bisquick
1 c. pizza sauce
1 c. shredded cheese

Brown meat and onions together. Add salt and pepper and spread in cake pan. Beat milk, eggs and Bisquick until smooth. Pour over meat and bake at 400° for 25-30 minutes. Top with pizza sauce and cheese. Bake until a knife comes out clean.

—Ms. Mattie J. Yoder, Ohio

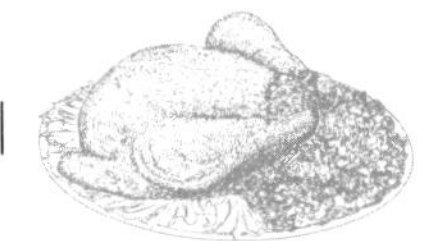

Yummasetti [1]

1 lb. noodles
2 cans cream of chicken soup
1 lb. smoked bacon
1½ lb. hamburger
1 onion, diced
1 can mushroom soup
1 lb. Velveeta cheese

Cook noodles in plain salt water. Add chicken soup. Heat bacon, hamburger and onion in skillet. Add mushroom soup. Layer in roast pan. Top with cheese. Bake at 300° for 1½ hour.

—Ms. Lovina D. Herschberger, Michigan

Yummasetti [2]

1 lg. pkg. noodles, cooked
3 lb. hamburger, fried
1 pt. peas
2 cans cream of mushroom soup
1 can cream of chicken soup
1 c. sour cream
½ loaf bread, toasted

Reserve some crumbs for top. Mix all together and pour in a greased baking dish. Top with reserved crumbs. Bake at 350° for 1 hour.

—Mrs. Henry (Clara) Miller, Kentucky

Mexican Dish

2 lb. hamburger
1 med. onion, chopped
1 sm. can pizza sauce
1 can cream of mushroom soup
½ c. chopped hot peppers
2 c. uncooked rice
1 bag corn chips, crushed
Velveeta cheese

Brown hamburger with onion. Add pizza sauce, mushroom soup and hot peppers. Cook rice until soft, then add to first mixture. Place in a greased casserole dish. Top with crushed corn chips and place cheese slices over the top. Bake at 325° for 30 minutes. Serves 8-10 people.

—Ms. Rachel M. Coblentz, Minnesota

Penny Supper

6 wieners, thinly sliced
4 med. potatoes, diced and cooked
2 Tbsp. minced onion
¼ c. butter, softened
1 c. cooked peas
1 Tbsp. prepared mustard
salt and pepper to taste
1 can cream of mushroom soup

Mix some wieners with potatoes, onions and butter in a casserole. Mix remaining ingredients and toss with wiener mixture. Dot with reserved wiener pennies. Cover and bake at 350° for 30 minutes. Serves 6 people.

—Mrs. Chris (Ella) Borntreger, Wisconsin

El Paso Casserole

½ lb. white sugar
1 c. flour
½ gal. milk
1¾ lb. Velveeta cheese
2 lb. chipped ham
1½ lb. noodles
toasted bread crumbs

Make a white sauce of sugar, flour and milk. Add cheese to melt. Put everything in baking dish, putting toasted bread crumbs on top.

—Mrs. Noah (Edna) Brenneman, Wisconsin

Have you heard of the new garlic diet? You don't lose weight, but you look thinner from a distance.

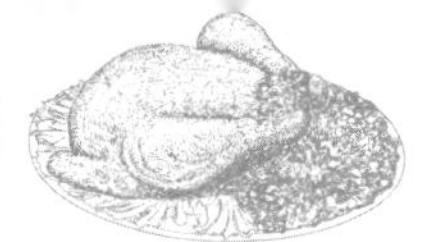

Underground Ham Casserole

4 c. cooked, chunked ham
¼ c. butter
½ c. chopped onion
1 Tbsp. Worcestershire sauce
2 cans cream of mushroom soup
1 c. milk
2 c. Velveeta cheese
4 qt. mashed potates
1 pt. sour cream
crumbled bacon

Combine ham, butter, onion and Worcestershire sauce. Cook until onions are tender. Place in the bottom of a medium-sized roaster. In a saucepan, heat soup, milk and cheese together until cheese melts. Place on top of onion mixture. Mash potatoes, using no salt or milk. Mix with sour cream. Spread over top of cheese mixture and sprinkle with bacon. Bake at 350° for 20 minutes. Mushroom soup and cheese mixture comes on top when done.

Variation: Put a layer of noodles between ham and cheese layer.

—Mrs. John (Elizabeth) Mast, New York
—Mrs. Aaron (Elizabeth) Yoder, Readstown, Wisconsin

Velveeta Broccoli Casserole

1 Tbsp. butter
1 lb. ham
½ tsp. salt
½ tsp. pepper
½ c. water
3 c. broccoli florets
3 med. potatoes, chunked
8 oz. Velveeta cheese, chunked
1 (10¾ oz.) can cream of mushroom soup
¼ tsp. ground nutmeg

Heat a large skillet. Add butter and brown ham which has been cut into bite-sized pieces. Season with salt and pepper. Add water, broccoli and potatoes and stir. Cover and cook for 5-7 minutes, stirring frequently. Stir in remaining ingredients. Cook until cheese is melted, stirring frequently. Serves 6 people.

—Mrs. Noah (Lovina) Miller, Wisconsin

Cheesy Zucchini Casserole

3 c. grated raw zucchini
1½ c. white cracker crumbs
½ c. butter
1 sm. onion, chopped
1 c. shredded cheese
3 eggs, beaten
½ tsp. salt
1 c. milk

Mix all together. Bake uncovered at 300° for 1 hour.

—Mrs. Levi (Fannie) Mast, Ohio

Eggplant Casserole

2½ c. peeled, cubed eggplant
18 Saltine crackers
½ c. shredded sharp cheddar cheese
¼ c. chopped celery
2 Tbsp. chopped pepper
1 Tbsp. butter
½ tsp. salt
⅛ tsp. black pepper
1 c. light cream or evaporated milk

Cook eggplant in boiling water for 10 minutes and drain. Combine remaining ingredients. Turn into 1 qt. casserole dish. Bake in moderate oven. Serves 6 people.

—Mrs. David (Naomi) Herschberger, Michigan

Love in your heart wasn't put there to stay.
Love isn't love until you give it away.

Scalloped Potatoes with Ham

2 qt. milk
¾ c. flour
2 Tbsp. salt
½ tsp. pepper
¾ c. butter
½ lb. cheese
10 lb. potatoes, cooked and diced or shredded
5 lb. ham, diced

Bring milk to a boil. Thicken with flour. Add salt, pepper and butter. Boil well. Add cheese. Mix sauce with potatoes and ham. Bake at 450° for 30 minutes, then at 350° for another 30 minutes or until done. Serves 30 people.

—*Ms. Rachel J. Hochstetler, Wisconsin*

Potluck Potatoes

2 lb. potatoes
¼-½ c. butter
1 (6 oz.) can cream of mushroom or chicken soup
1 pt. sour cream or sweet cream
1 tsp. seasoned salt
1 tsp. onion salt
¼ tsp. black pepper
½ c. chopped onion, optional
2 c. Velveeta or cheddar cheese
2 c. crushed cornflakes
½ c. butter, melted

Boil potatoes in jackets, peel and cube or shred. Combine butter, mushroom soup, sour cream, seasoned salt, onion salt, pepper, onion and cheese. Heat until cheese is melted. Put potatoes and heated mixture in layers in a casserole dish and cover with cornflakes and melted butter. Bake at 350° for 45 minutes. Serves 6 people.

—*Mrs. Allen (Fannie) Miller, New York*
—*Mrs. Jacob (Sadie) Hershberger, Wisconsin*
—*Mrs. Amos (Emma) Hershberger, Ohio*
—*Mrs. Andrew (Ella) Mast, Ohio*

Tater Tot Casserole [1]

1 lb. hamburger
1 sm. onion, chopped
1 pkg. frozen peas
2 cans cream of mushroom soup
1 soup can milk
cheese, optional
10 oz. tater tots

Brown hamburger. Add onion, peas, soup, milk and cheese. Put in casserole dish. Cover with tater tots. Bake uncovered at 400° until tater tots are done.

—Ms. Barbara J. Yoder, New York

Tater Tot Casserole [2]

2 lb. hamburger
½ c. diced onions
2 tsp. diced green peppers
2 cans mushroom soup
Velveeta cheese
1 lg. pkg. tater tots

Brown hamburger, onions and peppers. Add 1 can mushroom soup. Put in a roaster and cover with the remaining can mushroom soup. Put cheese on top and arrange tater tots tightly over cheese. Bake at 350° for 1 hour. Tater tots should be brown. You can add any kind of vegetable you wish.

—Mrs. John (Elizabeth) Mast, New York

Tater Tot Casserole [3]

3 lb. hamburger
1 sm. onion, diced
1 can cream of mushroom soup
½ c. water
32 oz. frozen mixed vegetables
32 oz. tater tots
Velveeta cheese

Fry hamburger and onions until brown; season. Add mushroom soup diluted with water. Put in bottom of casserole dish. Next add vegetables. Last add tater tots. Bake at 350° for 1½ hours or until done. When ready to serve, top with Velveeta cheese and return to oven until melted.

—Ms. Cassie H. Mast, Ohio

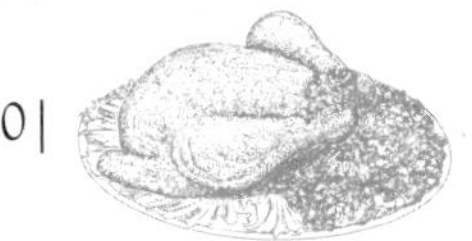

Sausage and Egg Casserole

1 lb. bulk sausage
6 eggs
2 c. milk
1 tsp. salt
1 tsp. ground mustard
6 bread slices, cubed
1 c. shredded cheese

In a skillet, brown and crumble sausage; drain. In a large bowl, beat eggs. Add milk, salt and mustard. Stir in bread cubes, cheese and sausage. Pour into a greased 11" x 7" x 2" baking dish. Cover and refrigerate for 8 hours or overnight. Remove from refrigerator 30 minutes before baking. Bake uncovered at 350° for 40 minutes or until done. Serves 8-10 people.

—Mrs. Andrew (Ella) Mast, Ohio

Wet Burrito

1½ c. sour cream
1 c. mushroom soup
1-2 lb. hamburger
1 onion, chopped
1 diced green pepper, optional
1 sm. can mushrooms, diced
1 pkg. taco seasoning
1 (16 oz.) can refried beans
1 lg. pkg. soft taco shells
4 c. shredded cheese

Mix sour cream and mushroom soup. Put half of mixture in bottom of 9" x 13" pan. Fry hamburger, onion and green pepper. Add mushrooms, taco seasoning and beans. Heat until warm. Fill shells, roll up and place in pan. Put the remaining mixture on top and top with cheese. Bake at 350° for 10 minutes. Makes 10 burritos.

—Mrs. Rebecca O. Mast, Ohio

It is better to fill a little place,
than a big place wrong.

Chicken Lasagna

1 can cream of mushroom soup
1 can cream of chicken soup
½ c. sour cream
¼ c. salad dressing
¼ tsp. garlic powder
1 c. shredded cheddar cheese
1 c. shredded mozarella cheese
1 med. onion, chopped
6 lasagna noodles, cooked
4 c. cooked, diced chicken

Mix soups, sour cream, salad dressing and garlic powder all together. Add cheese and onion. Cook lasagna noodles according to package directions. Cool in cold water. Layer sour cream mixture, noodles and chicken and bake at 350° for 30 minutes.

—Mrs. David (Naomi) Herschberger, Michigan

Lasagna

1½-2 qt. spaghetti sauce
1 pkg. lasagna noodles
1½ lb. hamburger, browned
cottage cheese
16 oz. shredded mozzarella cheese

Grease a large baking pan. Pour in spaghetti sauce to cover bottom, then layer noodles, hamburger, cheese and spaghetti sauce in 3 or 4 layers. Be generous with sauce as noodles absorb it. Bake at 350° for approximately 1½ hours.

—Mrs. Eli (Anna) Mast, Wisconsin

Delicious Beans

3 c. navy beans, cooked
1 c. cream
3 Tbsp. butter
5 slices Velveeta cheese
½ c. ketchup
½ c. brown sugar
2 tsp. mustard
diced onion
1 tsp. Worcestershire sauce
1 tsp. salt

If desired, add ham, hot dogs or bacon. If soupy, more beans may be added.

—Mrs. Dannie (Lizzie) Yoder, Michigan

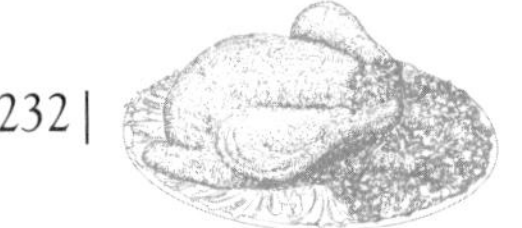

Speedy Baked Beans

6 slices bacon, diced
2 med. onions, minced
3 (1 lb. 3 oz.) cans baked beans
⅓ c. chili sauce
1½ tsp. prepared mustard

In a large skillet, cook and stir bacon and onion until bacon is crisp. Stir in remaining ingredients. Heat until it bubbles. Simmer uncovered, stirring occasionally, for 15-20 minutes or until liquid is absorbed. Or, pour into ungreased 2-qt. casserole dish and bake uncovered at 350° for 45 minutes.

—Mrs. Emanuel (Esther) Herschberger, Michigan

Baked Beans

4 qt. dried beans
2 Tbsp. salt
4 lb. wieners
3 lg. onions, chopped
3½ qt. tomato juice
2 c. ketchup
2½ lb. brown sugar
1 c. molasses

Soak beans overnight. In the morning, add salt and water to cook until tender. Slice wieners and fry with the onions in plenty of butter. Add tomato juice, ketchup, brown sugar and molasses. Boil for 5 minutes or until beans are tender. Add onions and bring to a boil. Put in jars and cold pack for 1 hour.

—Mrs. Jake (Anna) Herschberger, Michigan

Hamburger-Bean Hot Dish

1 lb. hamburger
½ lb. bacon
1 lg. onion, chopped
½ c. brown sugar
½ c. ketchup
2 tsp. vinegar
1 tsp. salt
1 tsp. prepared mustard
1 can pork and beans
1 can kidney beans
1 can butter beans, drained

Brown hamburger, bacon and onion. Mix brown sugar, ketchup, vinegar, salt and mustard. Pour the mixture over the hamburger mixture. Stir thoroughly. Add beans. Put in casserole dish and bake at 350° for 1 hour. Serves 6-8 people.

—Ms. Rachel M. Coblentz, Minnesota

Hamburger Skillet Supper

1½ lb. ground beef
¼ c. chopped onion
¼ c. chopped green pepper
1 c. chopped celery
1 Tbsp. Worcestershire suace
¾ tsp. salt
⅛ tsp. pepper
2 cans tomato sauce

Fry ground beef in skillet with onions, peppers and celery until brown and soft. Add remaining ingredients and simmer for 10 minutes.

Parsley Drop Biscuits:
1¾ c. flour
1 Tbsp. parsley flakes
1 Tbsp. baking powder
1 tsp. salt
⅓ c. shortening
1 c. milk

Mix all dry ingredients together. Cut in shortening and make like pie crumbs. Add milk and stir until crumbs are moistened. Drop by teaspoonful on top of hamburger mixture. Serves 6-8 people.

—Mrs. John (Elizabeth) Mast, New York

Chicken Gumbo

9 slices bread
4 c. cooked, chopped chicken
¼ c. butter, melted
½ c. salad dressing
4 eggs, beaten
1 c. milk
1 c. chicken broth
salt to taste
9 slices Velveeta cheese
cream of celery soup
buttered bread crumbs

Butter bottom of medium roaster. Put bread in bottom. Add chicken. Mix butter, salad dressing, beaten eggs, milk, broth and salt. Pour over bread and chicken. Top with Velveeta cheese and celery soup. Cover with bread crumbs. Bake at 350° for 1½ hours. Stir several times.

Variation: Use hamburger and cheddar cheese soup instead of chicken and broth.

—Mrs. Emma J. Yoder, Michigan

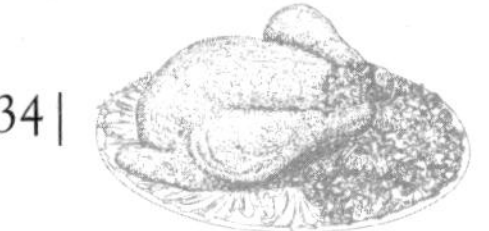

Zucchini Vegetable Mix

1 gal. cubed zucchini
4 med. onions, cubed
2 c. diced carrots
2 c. diced celery
2 red peppers, diced
2 heads cauliflower, cut into florets
½ c. salt

Syrup:
4 c. sugar
1½ tsp. tumeric
1½ tsp. celery seed
1 tsp. garlic salt
2 c. vinegar
1 c. water

Mix vegetables together and cover with salt. Cover and let stand for 3 hours, then drain. Mix syrup and pour over vegetables. Put in jars and seal. Variation: Use any amount of various vegetables to your liking.

—Mrs. Aaron (Elizabeth) Yoder, Wisconsin

Pigs in a Blanket

¼ oz. yeast
⅓ c. + 1 tsp. sugar, divided
⅔ c. warm milk
⅓ c. warm water
1 egg, beaten
3 Tbsp. shortening, melted
salt
2⅔ c. flour
10 wieners
1 pkg. American or Velveeta cheese

In a mixing bowl, dissolve yeast and 1 tsp. sugar in milk and water. Let stand for 5 minutes. Add egg, shortening, salt, remaining sugar and flour for a nice soft dough. Let rise in a warm place for 1 hour. Roll out thinly and cut in ¾" strips. Place wiener in a slice of cheese and roll into dough. You may also make your dough strips as big as you wish depending on the hot dog size. Let rise a little and bake until golden brown. Serves 10 people.

—Mrs. John (Elizabeth) Mast, New York

Dressing [1]

1½ doz. eggs
2 qt. vegetable mix of potatoes, carrots and celery
½ c. onions, chopped
3 Tbsp. (heaping) chicken bouillon
2 Tbsp. salt
1 Tbsp. pepper
2 Tbsp. Italian seasoning
2 qt. chicken and broth
milk
toasted bread

Beat eggs and add next 7 ingredients. Add enough milk and bread to fill 13-qt. mixing bowl. This is the recipe I use for a big group like at weddings, barn raisings, etc.

—Mrs. David (Naomi) Herschberger, Michigan

Dressing [2]

15 eggs, beaten
3-4 qt. milk
1 qt. chicken broth
2 Tbsp. chicken bouillon
2 Tbsp. salt
2 tsp. seasoned salt
1½ qt. cooked, diced potatoes
1 qt. raw diced celery
1 qt. cooked, diced carrots
1½ qt. chopped, deboned chicken
parsley to taste
1 tsp. lemon pepper
approx. 4 loaves bread, toasted and cubed

Beat eggs. Add milk and broth and mix well. Add remaining ingredients. Mix and allow to set for awhile. Add milk or bread as needed. Brown lightly in skillet with butter, then put in roaster and bake at 350° for 45 minutes or until done. Makes 13 qt.

—Mrs. Merle (Emma) Coblentz, Ohio

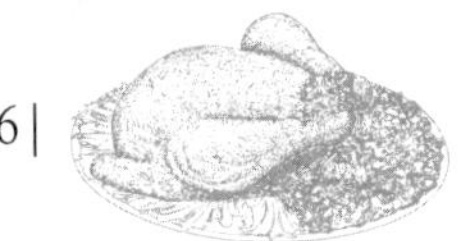

Dressing [3]

6 eggs, beaten
1½ c. deboned chicken
1½ c. cubed potatoes and carrots
1 qt. milk
1 tsp. chicken base
1 tsp. salt
½ tsp. black pepper
toasted bread crumbs

Mix everything except bread crumbs. Add toasted bread crumbs until right consistency. Make casserole dish only ¾ full. Bake for 45 minutes or until done. Mom often used this recipe at home with a family of 12 children.

—Mrs. Dannie (Anna) Hershberger, Michigan

Chicken Dressing

15 eggs
1 gal. milk
1 Tbsp. seasoned salt
2 Tbsp. chicken bouillon
2 Tbsp. salt
1 tsp. pepper
2 c. cooked, diced potatoes
2 c. cooked, diced carrots
2 c. finely chopped celery
bread cubes

Mix everything except bread cubes. Add bread as needed.

—Mrs. John (Anna) Yoder, Michigan

Good Turkey Stuffing

7 c. dry bread cubes
1 c. chopped onion
2 c. finely chopped celery or canned dressing mix
2 tsp. salt
½ tsp. black pepper
1½ tsp. sage or chicken bouillon
½ tsp. poultry seasoning
⅔ c. butter, melted
2 eggs, slightly beaten
1¼ c. turkey broth or milk

Mix all ingredients together. Stuff turkey and bake. It takes about 4 hours for a young turkey.

—Mrs. Perry (Rebecca) Herschberger, Wisconsin

You are never fully dressed
until you wear a smile.

Haystacks

6 baking powder biscuits
1 med. onion, diced
2 lb. ground beef
butter
flour
salt to taste
pepper to taste
taco seasoning to taste
shredded Velveeta cheese
noodles cooked in chicken broth
fresh potatoes cooked in skins
chopped lettuce
chopped tomatoes
diced onion
parsley

Crumble biscuits and put on bottom of plate. Brown onion and meat in butter and flour in skillet. Add salt, pepper and seasoning. Spoon on biscuits and top with shredded cheese. Add a thin layer of noodles and sliced potatoes. Spread with sauce, then lettuce, tomatoes, onion, parsley and more sauce. Delicious! Serves 6 people.
Variation: You can add any diced or chopped fresh vegetables that you want to.

Sauce:
1 Tbsp. butter
2 c. cream or half and half
1 tsp. cheese powder
2 Tbsp. flour
milk
salt to taste
black pepper to taste

Brown butter. Add cream and cheese powder. Dissolve flour in milk and use to thicken sauce. Add salt and pepper to suit taste. Variation: Cheese may be melted into sauce to make a cheese sauce.

—Mrs. Harvey (Lisbet) Mast, Pennsylvania

The grass is greener on the other side, but it's just as hard to mow!

Potato Haystack Casserole

1 c. sour cream
1 c. milk
2 pkg. Ranch dressing mix
4 lb. hamburger
¼ c. diced onion
2 pkg. taco seasoning
salt to taste
pepper to taste
10 potatoes, cooked and diced
cheese sauce
crushed nacho chips

Add sour cream and milk to dressing mix. Fry hamburger with onion and add taco seasoning, salt and pepper. Layer all ingredients except chips in casserole dish in order give, topping with cheese sauce. Bake until hot. Before serving top with crushed nacho chips. Serves 10 people.

—Mrs. Atlee (Susan) Yoder, Ohio

No-Cook Mush

1 c. cornmeal
2 Tbsp. (slightly rounded) flour
1 tsp. salt
2 c. boiling water (must be boiling)

Mix cornmeal, flour and salt in a small bowl. Add boiling water all at once. Stir well and drop by tablespoonsful into hot skillet with grease. When turning patties, flatten to desired thickness. Fries faster and isn't such a greasy mess like the old-fashioned cooked mush. A favorite, served with tomato gravy!

—Mrs. Andy (Fannie) Slabaugh, Wisconsin

Potato Puffs

1 c. leftover mashed potatoes
1 or 2 eggs, beaten
¼ tsp. salt
¼-½ c. flour
1 tsp. baking powder

Mix well and drop by teaspoon in deep lard or vegetable oil. Fry until brown on both sides.

—Mrs. Henry (Edna) Hershberger, Ohio

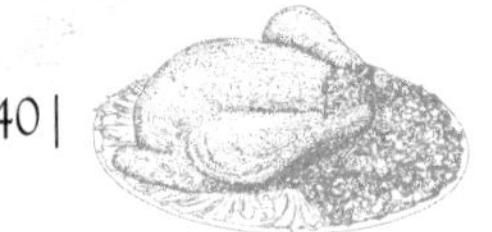

Juicy Meatloaf [1]

3 lb. ground beef
1½ c. quick oats
or crushed saltines
4 eggs, beaten
½ c. chopped onion
4 tsp. salt
½ tsp. pepper
2 c. tomato juice

Press in two 9" x 13" pans and bake at 350° for 1 hour.

Rachel's Sauce:
2 c. ketchup
⅓ c. brown sugar
½ c. chopped onion
2 Tbsp. liquid smoke
1 tsp. garlic powder

Mix together and put on top of baked meatloaf. Return to oven for 10 minutes.

Fannie's Sauce:
½ c. brown sugar
½ c. ketchup
¼ c. mustard

—Ms. Rachel J. Hochstetler, Wisconsin
—Mrs. Perry (Rebecca) Herschberger, Wisconsin
—Mrs. Levi (Fannie) Mast, Ohio

Faults are like crooked buggy wheels. We never notice our own; only those of the buggy ahead of us.

Juicy Meatloaf [2]

2 lb. ground hamburger
2 eggs, well beaten
3/4 c. tomato juice
3/4 c. quick oats
1/4 c. chopped onions
2 tsp. salt
1/4-1/2 tsp. pepper

Combine all ingredients thoroughly. Pack firmly into a loaf pan. Bake at 350° for 1 hour. If a sauce is desired, use the following recipe. This was used for a wedding.

Sauce:
2 Tbsp. ketchup
2 Tbsp. prepared mustard
2 Tbsp. brown sugar

Mix and spread over meatloaf before baking.

—Mrs. Floyd (Katie) Beechy, Michigan
—Mrs. Levi (Sadie) Yoder, Ohio

Meatloaf [1]

2 c. cracker crumbs
1/2 c. tomato juice
2 1/2 c. milk
diced onions
4 eggs
1 tsp. pepper
2 tsp. salt or more
2 tsp. seasoned salt
5 lb. hamburger

Mix crackers, juice and milk. Chop onion and add. Add eggs and seasonings and mix with hamburger. Mix well. Press into pans. Bake until almost done. Cut and top with sauce and return to oven until done.

Sauce:
1/3 c. ketchup
2 Tbsp. brown sugar
1 Tbsp. prepared mustard

—Mrs. David (Naomi) Herschberger, Michigan

Meatloaf [2]

10 lb. ground beef
1 Tbsp. pepper
¼ c. chopped celery, optional
5 eggs, beaten
½ c. diced onions
1 c. ketchup
3 c. milk
crushed crackers or oatmeal

Glaze:
2 c. ketchup
¾ c. brown sugar
2 Tbsp. prepared mustard

Mix first 7 ingredients well. Add soda crackers or quick oats. May also use half and half. Sometimes it takes more and sometimes it takes less, so it's better to not mix it all in at once. Top with glaze. Bake at 350° for 1 hour. Slice meatloaf and return to oven for a little.

—Mrs. Joseph (Martha) Miller, Ohio

Prize-Winning Meatloaf

1 lb. ground beef
¾ c. quick oats
¼ c. chopped onions
1½ tsp. salt
¼ tsp. black pepper
1 c. tomato juice or milk
2 eggs, beaten

Sauce:
⅔ c. ketchup
¼ c. brown sugar
2 Tbsp. prepared mustard

Combine all ingredients thoroughly. Pack firmly into an ungreased 8½" x 4½" x 2½" loaf pan. Bake at 350° for 1 hour. Spread with sauce and bake for 15 more minutes. Serves 8 people.

—Mrs. Jonas (Anna) Miller, Michigan

Taco Meatloaf

1 c. crushed saltines
1 pkg. taco seasoning
½ c. ketchup
1 sm. onion, chopped
1 can mushrooms, drained
2 eggs, beaten
2 Tbsp. Worcestershire sauce
2 lb. hamburger
salsa
sour cream
shredded cheddar cheese

Combine first 7 ingredients. Add hamburger and mix well. Press into a greased loaf pan. Bake at 350° for 1-1½ hours. Serve with salsa, sour cream and shredded cheddar cheese.

—Mrs. Perry (Elizabeth) Weaver, Ohio

Delicious Barbecued Meatballs

6 c. ground hamburger
1 c. milk
2 c. oatmeal
2 eggs
1 c. chopped onions
2 tsp. salt
½ tsp. pepper
¾ tsp. chili powder
½ tsp. garlic powder

Combine. Form into balls and place in a 9" x 13" x 2" cake pan or roaster. Pour sauce over meatballs and bake at 350° for 1 hour.

Sauce:
2 c. ketchup
1 c. brown sugar
2 tsp. liquid smoke
½ c. chopped onion
¼ tsp. chili powder

Mix together.

—Mrs. Samuel (Naomi) Miller, Wisconsin

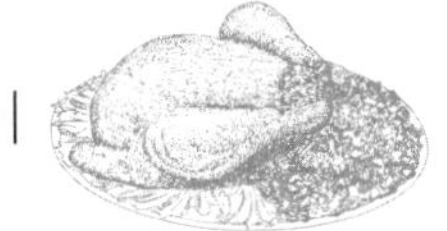

Sloppy Joes

1 lb. ground beef
1 med. onion, chopped
3 Tbsp. ketchup
3 Tbsp. prepared mustard
1 can chicken soup
6 slices bread, toasted

In a medium skillet, cook and stir ground beef and onion until meat is brown and onion is tender. Stir in ketchup, mustard and soup. Simmer for 15 minutes or until mixture thickens slightly, stirring occasionally. Spoon over bottom halves of bread. Top with remaining halves. Serves 6 people.

—Mrs. Emanuel (Esther) Herschberger, Michigan

Poor Man's Steak

2 lb. hamburger
2 c. cracker crumbs
2 c. milk
diced onion to taste
salt to taste
pepper to taste
1 can cream of mushroom soup
1 can water

Mix hamburger, cracker crumbs and milk. Add onions, salt and pepper to taste. Mix and press in a large flat pan. Let stand overnight, then cut in squares. Roll in flour and fry until brown. Put in casserole dish and cover with mushroom soup diluted with water. Bake slowly for 2 hours. It is necessary to set this overnight to make it firm.

—Ms. Lovina D. Herschberger, Michigan

If you have an unpleasant neighbor,
chances are he does too.

Mock Steak

3 lb. hamburger
1 c. oatmeal
1 c. tomato juice
1 Tbsp. salt
pepper to taste

Sauce:
1 can cream of mushroom soup
½ c. water
cheese

Mix together and fry. Put in roaster and cover with sauce. Bake at 350° for 1 hour.

—Mrs. Andy (Martha) Kauffman, Wisconsin

Fish Patties

2 eggs
1½ c. bread crumbs
½ c. cracker crumbs
¼ tsp. dry mustard
1 sm. onion, diced
½ tsp. salt
1 pt. salmon

Beat eggs and add remaining ingredients. Fry in hot skillet, turning when brown. Our favorite!

—Mrs. David (Barbara) Hershberger, Michigan

Chicken Patties

10 lb. chicken
5 c. crushed crackers
12 eggs
4½ c. water
1½ tsp. pepper
3 Tbsp. salt
a little diced onions
2-3 tsp. Worcestershire sauce

Mix together. Make patties and fry. You can also use this recipe for meatloaf, using hamburger instead of chicken.

—Mrs. Noah (Susie) Gingerich, Ohio

Barbecued Country Ribs

2½ lb. boneless pork ribs
2 tsp. liquid smoke, optional
½ tsp. salt
1 c. water

Barbecue Sauce:
⅔ c. chopped onion
1 Tbsp. vegetable oil
¾ c. water
¾ c. ketchup
⅓ c. lemon juice
3 Tbsp. sugar
3 Tbsp. Worcestershire sauce
2 Tbsp. mustard
½ tsp. salt
½ tsp. pepper
¼ tsp. liquid smoke

Place ribs in an 11" x 7" x 2" baking dish coated with nonstick cooking spray. Sprinkle with liquid smoke if desired and salt. Pour water over ribs. Cover and bake at 350° for 1 hour. Drain ribs.

Meanwhile in a saucepan, fry onions in oil until tender. Add remaining sauce ingredients. Bring to a boil. Reduce heat and simmer, uncovered, for 15 minutes. Top ribs with half of barbecue sauce. Cover and bake for another hour, basting every 20 minutes. Serve with remaining sauce. Serves 8 people.

—Ms. Anna J. Mast, New York

Country Pork Ribs

pork ribs
1 c. ketchup
¼ c. vinegar
2 Tbsp. brown sugar
3 Tbsp. Worcestershire sauce
½ c. water
2 Tbsp. prepared mustard
1 tsp. dry onion or chopped onion

Cook pork ribs until almost tender. Drain and trim off excess fat. Put into a large casserole dish. Combine remaining ingredients. Heat and pour over ribs. Bake covered at 350° for an hour.

—Ms. Rachel A. Mast, Ohio

Company Chicken

2 (3 lb.) fryers
1 c. flour
3 Tbsp. salt
¼ tsp. pepper
2 tsp. paprika
¼ c. lard
¼ c. butter
3 c. finely chopped celery
1 can cream of chicken soup
½ c. light cream
2 tsp. diced pimento
1 c. finely chopped American cheese
2 c. soft bread crumbs
½ c. slivered almonds, optional
2 Tbsp. butter, melted

Coat chicken with next 4 ingredients. Lightly brown in lard and butter. Put celery in greased 9" x 13" x 2" casserole dish with chicken on top. Combine soup, cream, pimento and cheese. Pour over chicken. Cover with bread crumbs and almonds. Pour melted butter over top. Bake at 350° for 1 hour. Serves 8 people.

—Mrs. Moses (Amelia) Gingerich, Ohio

Huntington Chicken

1 c. cooked chicken pieces
1 c. uncooked macaroni
3 c. toasted bread crumbs
½-1 lb. cheese
gravy from chicken broth

Put chicken in a casserole dish. Cook and drain macaroni and put on top of chicken. Top with bread crumbs. Melt cheese into gravy and pour over top. Bake at 300°-350° until done.

—Mrs. Neil (Esther) Kauffman, Wisconsin

Chicken Breading Mix

1 gal. flour
2 c. seasoned salt
1 Tbsp. pepper
3 Tbsp. salt

Mix all together. Takes about 3 ice cream pails for 225 lb. chicken.

—Mrs. John (Anna) Yoder, Michigan

Chicken Breading

2 boxes cornflakes
1 box white crackers
1½ c. whole wheat flour
½ c. sugar
½ c. seasoned salt
¼ c. salt
1 Tbsp. red pepper
1 tsp. black pepper
1 Tbsp. paprika
4 tsp. garlic powder
2 Tbsp. Ac'cent
1 c. butter, melted

Mix all together. This is good to roll any kind of meat in and fry. For a delicious flavor, dip your chicken in salad dressing or barbecue sauce first, then roll in breading and bake.

—Mrs. Henry (Sarah) Yoder, Michigan

Oven Baked Chicken

4 c. flour
4 c. white cracker crumbs
2 Tbsp. sugar
¼ c. vegetable oil
¼ c. salt
3 Tbsp. paprika
1 tsp. onion powder
1 tsp. garlic powder

Put in a bowl and mix well. Take out the needed amount and store the rest in a tight container in a cool place. It will keep for a long time. Dip chicken in milk then roll in crumbs. Put on a tray and brown on both sides, then put in a roaster until tender. Bake at 375°. Grease your tray to keep from sticking.

—Mrs. Henry (Fannie) Miller, Michigan

Chicken Crumbs

milk
1 egg
7 lb. finely crushed cornflakes
4½ lb. white crackers
3 oz. paprika
2¼ oz. onion salt
1½ oz. poultry seasoning
12 oz. seasoned salt
1½ jar celery salt
3 boxes Shake-N-Bake
2 c. flour
1 c. vegetable oil

Cover cookie sheet with tinfoil and spray with Pam. Beat milk and egg together. Dip chicken in mixture. Mix remaining ingredients. Drain chicken and coat with crumbs. Bake at 300°-400°. Turn once. Bake approximately 45 minutes or until done. Put in roaster, lined with tinfoil. Put ¼ c. water under foil. Put foil on top.

—Mrs. Alvin (Elizabeth) Mast, New York

Barbecue Sauce for Grilled Chicken

1 pt. vinegar
1 pt. water
½ c. butter
¼ c. salt
2 Tbsp. Worcestershire sauce
2 frying chickens

Heat first 5 ingredients in saucepan until butter is melted. Marinate chicken pieces in brine for several hours before grilling.

—Ms. Lovina A. Mast, New York

Happiness is a perfume you cannot pour on others without getting a few drops on yourself.

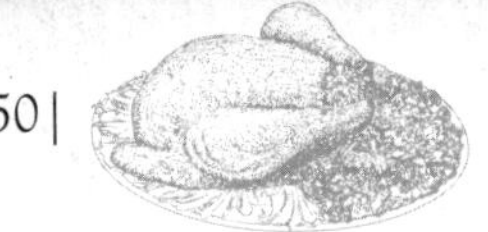

Deep Fried Fish

2 lb. fish fillets, steaks or pan-dressed fish
1 c. all-purpose flour
1 tsp. salt
1/8 tsp. pepper
2 eggs, beaten
1 c. dry bread crumbs or crushed cracker crumbs

Heat 3"-4" lard or oil to 375° in deep fat fryer or kettle. Stir flour, salt and pepper together. Coat fish with flour mixture; dip into eggs, then coat with bread crumbs. Fry in deep fat about 4 minutes or until golden brown. Or shallow- fry fish in 1½"-2" hot shortening in skillet about 4 minutes or until golden brown.

—Ms. Miriam Herschberger, Michigan

Breakfast Pie

1¼ c. milk
3 eggs
¾ c. flour
1 tsp. baking powder
½ tsp. salt
1 Tbsp. shortening
onions
ham
peppers

Double recipe for a 9x13 inch pan. Grease pan. Put in meat, onions, peppers, or whatever you like. Pour in mixture. Bake at 400° (medium hot oven) until knife in center comes out clean. About 20 minutes. When done, top with cheese. Place in oven until cheese is melted. A good breakfast that sticks to the ribs. One of the families favorites.

—Miss Phoebe T. Herschberger, Wisconsin

Breakfast Pizza

1 lb. sausage or beef
1 c. shredded potatoes
1 c. shredded cheddar cheese
5 eggs
½ c. milk
salt and pepper to taste

Line a pan with biscuit dough. Add browned meat, then potatoes and top with cheese. In a bowl, beat eggs, milk, salt, and pepper. Pour over all and bake for 25 to 30 minutes at 375°. One and one-half batch makes a 9x13 inch pan full.

—Mrs. Eddie (Ida) Borntrager, Wisconsin

Soups and Salads

Sweet Heart

- A few cloves added to vegetable soup will give it a delicious flavor.

- If the soup tastes very salty, a raw piece of potato placed in the pot will absorb the salt.

- Never put a lid on anything that is cooked with milk unless you want to spend hours cleaning up your stove.

- Before heating milk in a saucepan, rinse the pan with water and it will not scorch as quickly.

- Milk can be prevented from burning or sticking to the bottom of the kettle when boiling or scalding for any purpose by putting a small amount of water in the kettle to be used and heating it before adding the milk.

- Here is a great trick for peeling eggs the easy way. When they are finished boiling, turn off the heat and just let them sit in the pan with the lid on for about 5 minutes.

- When you cook hardboiled eggs, first use a knife handle and lightly crack each end of the egg, then boil them as usual. This helps make the eggs peel easier.

- Brush your metal grater with vegetable oil before grating cheese to keep it from sticking.

- Dip a tomato in boiling water for about 1 minute then into cold water, and it will peel easily.

- To beat eggs quickly, add a pinch of salt.

- When boiling eggs, add a few drops of vinegar to the water. It will help keep the shells from cracking.

- Fresh or hardboiled eggs? Spin the egg. If it wobbles, it is raw, but if it spins easily, it is hardboiled. A really fresh egg will sink and a rotten one will float.

Ham and Potato Soup

1½ c. butter, no substitutes
1 lg. onion, diced
1+ c. flour
12 qt. hot milk
6 qt. shredded, cooked potatoes
10 lb. turkey ham
1 box cheese
salt and pepper to taste

Brown butter, onion and flour in pan. Add milk, potatoes, ham, cheese, salt and pepper. Do not cook after ham and cheese are added.

—Mrs. Simon (Malinda) Yoder, Ohio

Creamy Potato Soup

2 Tbsp. butter
2 Tbsp. finely chopped onion
½ tsp. salt
¼ tsp. celery salt
⅛ tsp. pepper
3½ c. milk
1⅓ c. mashed potato puffs

Heat butter, onion, salt, celery salt, pepper and milk to scalding, stirring constantly. Add mashed potato puffs. Soup should be consistency of heavy cream. If desired, garnish each serving with paprika. Serves 4 people.

—Mrs. Emanuel (Esther) Herschberger, Michigan

You are never fully
dressed in the morning until
you put on a smile.

Chunky Beef Soups

- 3 qt. potatoes
- 3 qt. carrots
- 3 qt. peas
- 3 onions, chopped
- 1½ c. butter
- 3 c. flour
- 7 qt. water
- 1 c. beef bouillon
- 3 sm. cans beef broth
- 3 qt. tomato juice
- 1½ c. white sugar
- 3 Tbsp. salt
- 3 qt. crumbled hamburger

Cut potatoes and carrots in small cubes. Cook vegetables until almost soft. In a large stainless canner, brown the butter. Add flour like gravy. Slowly add water, bouillon, broth and tomato juice, stirring constantly. Add remaining ingredients. Cold pack for 2 hours. Makes 22-24 qt.

—Ms. Cassie H. Mast, Ohio

Cheddar Chowder

- 4 c. water
- 4 c. diced potatoes
- 1 c. diced celery
- ¼ c. chopped onions
- 2 tsp. salt
- ¼ tsp. pepper
- 1 c. diced carrots
- ¼ c. butter
- 6 c. milk, divided
- 1 c. flour
- ¼ c. powdered or grated cheese
- 2 c. diced meat

Boil first 7 ingredients together for 10-12 minutes or until ready. Brown butter and add 4 c. milk. Shake flour and 2 c. milk together. Add to boiling milk and boil until thick. Add cheese and meat. When sauce and vegetables are done, pour together. Very good! Yield: 15 servings.

—Mrs. John (Esther) Brock, Iowa

Russian Beet Soup Borsch

1 med. cabbage
4 or 5 med. potatoes
2 or 3 med. carrots
1 med. onion
5 or 6 whole beets
1 lb. beef ribs
1 lb. pork ribs
salt and pepper to taste
1 sm. can tomato sauce or 2 lg. very ripe tomatoes

Cut cabbage, potatoes, carrots and onions in small pieces. Leave beets whole for now. Boil everything except tomato sauce together in water for 30 minutes or so. Take the beets out and slice them thinly. Put back in. You may now add tomato sauce or tomatoes. Boil on low for 15 more minutes. Let stand for 1 hour or so. This soup tastes better the longer it stands. The Russians traditionally serve it with sour cream.

—Mrs. Uria (Sara) Miller, Michigan

Chili Soup

2 lb. ground beef
6 onions or less, diced
1 lb. kidney beans
½ tsp. chili powder or to taste
salt to taste
pinch of baking soda
1 gal. tomato juice
2 qt. water

Fry meat and onions together until brown. Cook kidney beans until soft. Mix all together and bring to a boil. Ready to serve or can.

—Mrs. Henry (Clara) Miller, Kentucky

If you are dog tired in the evening, maybe it's because you growled all day!

Vegetable Soup [1]

2 lb. ground beef
10 sm. onions, chopped
1 lb. butter
10 ribs celery, diced
10 med. carrots, diced
1 head cabbage, diced
½ gal. dry beans
1 lb. noodles
1 gal. tomato juice
1 qt. sweet corn
salt and pepper to taste
sugar to taste

Fry ground beef and chopped onions in butter. Dice celery, carrots and cabbage. Cook separately. Soak dry beans overnight then cook until soft. Cook noodles, then put all together in a stock pot with tomato juice, corn, salt, pepper and sugar. Some water may be added if not enough liquid.

—Mrs. Jake (Anna) Herschberger, Michigan

Vegetable Soup [2]

1 pt. carrots
1 pt. peas
1 pt. corn
1 onion, diced
¼ c. sugar
1 pt. potatoes
1 pt. cooked navy beans
1 pt. celery
1 c. noodles, cooked
2 lb. hamburger, browned
4 qt. tomato juice
salt and pepper to taste

Mix everything together. Put in jars and process in pressure cooker for 1 hour at 10 lb. pressure.

—Mrs. Rudy (Ella) Borntreger, Wisconsin

Sunshine Soup

1 c. chopped celery
3 c. cubed potatoes
1 med. onion, diced
1 qt. water
3 chicken bouillon cubes
1 lg. bag California blend vegetables
1 c. water
2 cans cream of chicken soup
1 can water
½ box Velveeta cheese

Simmer celery, potatoes and onion together in 1 qt. water and chicken bouillon for 20 minutes. Simmer California blend vegetables until barely tender in 1 c. water. Do not add salt. Add to soup pot with chicken soup, 1 can water and Velveeta cheese. Heat until cheese is melted. Do not boil.

—Mrs. Perry (Elizabeth) Weaver, Ohio

24-Hour Potato Salad

6 qt. potatoes, cooked and peeled
2 doz. hard-boiled eggs
½ c. minced onions
2 c. finely chopped celery
4 c. salad dressing
3 Tbsp. prepared mustard
1 Tbsp. salt
3 c. white sugar
½ c. vinegar

Put potatoes and eggs through a Salad Master when cooled. Mix with remaining ingredients. Makes 6 qt.

—Mrs. Elizabeth J. Yoder, Ohio

Even back in Grandpa's time they had something to make you sleep. It was called work.

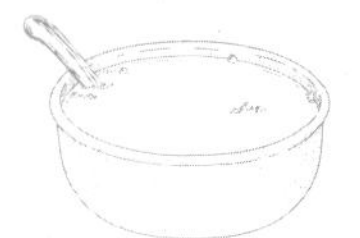

Overnight Potato Salad [1]

12 c. cooked unsalted potatoes
12 cooked eggs
1 sm. onion
1 c. diced celery
3 c. salad dressing
1 Tbsp. prepared mustard
2 c. sugar
2 tsp. salt
1 tsp. vinegar
½ c. milk

Put potatoes through Salad Master. Chop eggs and onion. Add celery. Mix remaining ingredients to make a dressing and add to potatoes, eggs, onion and celery. Let stand overnight. Will be good for 3-4 days.

Variation: The day you serve it, you can add 1½ c. chopped cheese.

—Mrs. John (Esther) Brock, Iowa
—Mrs. David (Barbara) Hershberger, Michigan

Overnight Potato Salad [2]

12 c. shredded, cooked potatoes
12 hard-boiled eggs, shredded
½ c. chopped onion
1½ c. celery

Do not cook potatoes too soft. This will keep up to a week if kept in a cool place.

Dressing:
3 c. salad dressing
2 Tbsp. vinegar
4 tsp. salt
2 c. sugar
½ c. milk

Combine and pour over potatoes, eggs, onion and celery.

—Mrs. Tobie (Ada) Miller, Michigan

Overnight Potato Salad [3]

12 c. shredded potatoes
12 hard-boiled eggs, chopped
1 c. chopped onions
1½ c. diced celery

Dressing:
3 c. salad dressing
1 Tbsp. vinegar
3 Tbsp. prepared mustard
4 tsp. salt
2 c. sugar
½ c. milk

Cook and shred potatoes. Mix dressing and pour over potatoes, eggs, onions and celery. Let stand overnight. It is important to shred the potatoes rather than cube them.

—Mrs. Elizabeth R. Borntreger, Wisconsin

Potato Salad [1]

3 c. salad dressing
¼ c. + 2 Tbsp. prepared mustard
2 tsp. salt
2½ c. sugar
¼ c. vinegar
12 c. shredded potatoes
12 hard-boiled eggs, mashed
½ c. onions
2 c. chopped celery

Mix salad dressing, mustard, salt, sugar and vinegar together. Add to remaining ingredients. Mix well. Will keep 4-5 days. Serves 30 people.

—Mrs. Atlee (Susan) Yoder, Ohio

To succeed you need three bones—a wishbone, a backbone and a funny bone.

Potato Salad [2]

6 qt. kettle potatoes, cooked and peeled
12 hard-boiled eggs, chopped
½ med. onion, chopped
1½ c. finely chopped celery

Shred potatoes. Add eggs, onion and celery. Combine dressing ingredients and mix with potato mixture. Fix and mix a few days ahead. Keep chilled.

Dressing:
3 c. salad dressing
4 c. white sugar
½ c. milk
2 Tbsp. vinegar
¼ c. mustard
2 tsp. salt

You may not need the milk.

—Mrs. Ida F. Yoder, Ohio

Sweet and Sour Dressing [1]

1 c. sugar
1 c. Mazola oil
⅓ c. vinegar
1 tsp. salt
1 tsp. celery seed
½ tsp. pepper
1 Tbsp. prepared mustard
2 Tbsp. Miracle Whip
1 sm. onion, finely chopped

Mix and beat slowly until smooth.

—Mrs. Fannie L. Raber, Ohio

Sweet and Sour Dressing [2]

2 c. salad dressing
1 c. vegetable oil
2 Tbsp. vinegar
1½ c. white sugar
½ tsp. celery seed
1 Tbsp. mustard
a pinch of salt

Whip together well.

—Mrs. Henry (Sarah) Yoder, Michigan

Sunset Salad

1 (3 oz.) pkg. lemon or orange gelatin
½ tsp. salt
1½ c. boiling water
1 (8 oz.) can crushed pineapple, undrained
1 Tbsp. lemon juice
1 c. coarsely grated carrots
⅓ c. chopped pecans, optional
whipped cream

Dissolve gelatin and salt in boiling water. Add undrained pineapple and lemon juice. Chill for 1½ hours or until very thick. Fold in carrots and pecans. Pour into individual molds or into a 1-qt. mold. Chill until firm. Unmold and garnish with pineapple if desired. Top with whipped cream.

—Mrs. Menno (Anna) Hershberger

If there's not enough left to save,
But a little too much to dump,
And you just can't help but eat it,
That's what makes the housewife plump.

Pineapple Cool Whip Salad

1 c. white sugar
1 (20 oz.) can crushed pineapple
6 Tbsp. water
2 Tbsp. Knox gelatin
2 c. whipping cream
2 med. carrots
1 c. chopped celery
1 c. cottage cheese
1 c. nuts
1½ c. mayonnaise

Mix white sugar and pineapple. In a saucepan, combine water and gelatin. Bring to a boil and pour over pineapple mixture and stir. Set in refrigerator. Whip cream and add carrots, celery, cottage cheese, nuts and mayonnaise or salad dressing. Mix with pineapple mixture and let set. Serves 12 people.

—Mrs. Noah (Susie) Gingerich, Ohio

Lime Cottage Cheese Salad

Crust:
1 c. flour
½ c. butter
1 c. graham cracker crumbs
½ c. nuts

Mix together and press into a 9" x 13" cake pan. Bake at 350° for 10-15 minutes.

1 (20 oz.) can crushed pineapple, drained
1 lg. box lime Jell-O
½ c. sugar
8 oz. cream cheese
1 c. Rich's topping
1 lg. box cottage cheese

Drain pineapple juice into a saucepan and add enough water to make 1 c. Heat to boiling. Add Jell-O and sugar. Dissolve and stir well. Cool until softly gelled. Beat cream cheese and Rich's topping separately and fold in pineapple and cottage cheese. Add to Jell-O mixture. Pour into crust.

—Mrs. Levi (Mattie) Yoder, Michigan

Summer Cool Salad

18 lg. marshmallows
1 c. milk
6 oz. lime gelatin
1 (#2) can crushed pineapple
1 c. shredded carrots
1 c. finely chopped celery
1 c. small curd cottage cheese
½ c. salad dressing
1 c. whipped cream
½ c. chopped nuts

Melt marshmallows and milk in top of a double boiler over boiling water. Pour over gelatin and stir until gelatin is dissolved. Cool. Add pineapple, carrots, celery, cottage cheese and salad dressing. Chill until mixture starts to gel. Fold in whipped cream and nuts. Pour into a bowl and chill.

—Ms. Rachel D. Mast, New York

Strawberry Pretzel Salad

¾ c. butter
2½ c. coarsely crushed pretzels
3 Tbsp. brown sugar
¾ c. white sugar
8 oz. whipped topping
8 oz. cream cheese
1 lg. pkg. strawberry Jell-O
2 c. boiling water
3 c. sliced fresh strawberries
whipped topping for garnish

Cream butter, pretzels and brown sugar together. Pat into a 9" x 13" cake pan and bake at 350° for 10 minutes. Cool. Cream sugar, whipped topping and cream cheese together. Spread over pretzel crust. Dissolve Jell-O and boiling water. Cool until slightly set. Fold in strawberries. Pour over cream cheese mixture. Let set. Top with whipped topping. Simple and delicious!

—Mrs. Floyd (Katie) Beechy, Michigan

Love is the only game two can play and both win.

Ribbon Salad [1]

3 c. miniature marshmallows
1 c. pineapple or orange Jell-O
2 c. water
2 tsp. salad dressing
12 oz. cream cheese
3 c. whipped cream
powdered sugar to taste

Melt marshmallows, Jell-O and water in double boiler. Mix salad dressing and cream cheese with wire whip. Gradually add whipped cream with wire whip. Add powdered sugar to taste. Pour a ¾" layer of Jell-O into 2 large 9" x 13" cake pans. Once hardened, top with cream cheese mixture. Chill again before adding top layer of Jell-O.

Variation: Pineapple may also be added.

—Mrs. David J. (Naomi) Herschberger, Michigan

Ribbon Salad [2]

1 pkg. lime Jell-O
crushed pineapple, optional
8 oz. cream cheese
1 c. Rich's topping, whipped
1 pkg. orange Jell-O
1 pkg. cherry Jell-O

Prepare lime Jell-O. Add pineapple if desired. Pour into a pan and chill until set. Combine cream cheese and whipped topping. Pour half over lime layer. Prepare orange Jell-O and cool until partially gelled. Top with remaining half of cream cheese. Prepare cherry Jell-O and pour over top. Chill until set.

—Mrs. John (Anna) Yoder, Michigan

You can talk about a
man all you please,
But when you do, please
do it on your knees.

Ribbon Salad [3]

½ c. lime Jell-O
5 c. boiling water, divided
4 c. cold water, divided
¼ c. pineapple or lemon Jell-O
¼ lb. marshmallows
8 oz. cream cheese
1 pt. crushed pineapple
1 c. cream, whipped
½ c. strawberry or cherry Jell-O

Dissolve lime Jell-O in 2 c. boiling water. Add 2 c. cold water. Pour into a pan and let set. Add 1 c. boiling water to pineapple or lemon Jell-O. Add marshmallows; melt. Dissolve cream cheese in hot Jell-O mixture. Add pineapple and cool. When starting to set add whipped cream and spread over first layer. Dissolve strawberry or cherry Jell-O in 2 c. boiling water. Add 2 c. cold water. Let it set until it is gelled a little before pouring over second layer. It is important to not put on your next layer on until it's gelled.

—Mrs. Ada J. Herschberger, Wisconsin

7-Up Fruit Salad

2 pkg. lemon Jell-O
2 c. hot water
2 c. 7-Up
1 can pineapples, drained
1 c. marshmallows
2 lg. bananas

Dissolve lemon Jell-O in hot water. When Jell-O is partially set, add remaining ingredients and pour into a 9" x 12" pan.

Topping:
½ c. sugar
2 Tbsp. flour
1 c. pineapple juice
1 egg, beaten
2 Tbsp. butter
1 c. whipped cream

Combine sugar and flour. Stir in juice and egg. Cook, stirring constantly. Add butter and cool. Fold in whipped cream and spread on Jell-O.

—Mrs. Emanuel (Esther) Herschberger, Michigan

Christmas Salad

½ c. Lime or Orange Jell-O
½ c. desired red Jell-O
1 can crushed pineapple
1 Tbsp. gelatin, soaked in ½ c. cold water
2 (8 oz.) pkg. cream cheese
3 c. whipping cream
1 c. nuts
white sugar to suit taste
vanilla
pinch of salt
1½ c. hot water
1½ c. cold water
2 Tbsp. pineapple Jell-O

Mix red Jell-O with 1½ c. hot water and 1½ c. cold. Add apples if desired. Mix in ½ of drained pineapple juice before hard. Put in pans. Bring pineapple juice to a boil; remove from heat and add 2 Tbsp. pineapple Jell-O. Put in gelatin. Add cream cheese; mix well, let cool, but not hard. Whip 3 cups cream and add sugar and vanilla; add to the above mixture. Put in rest of pineapple and nuts. Put lime or orange Jell-O on top.

—Mrs. Eddie (Ida) Borntrager, Wisconsin

Those who think revenge is sweet,
have never tasted LOVE.

Deviled Eggs

6 hard-boiled eggs
½ tsp. salt
½ tsp. dry mustard
¼ tsp. red pepper
3 Tbsp. salad dressing, vinegar or light cream

Cut peeled eggs in half lengthwise. Slip out yolks and mash with a fork. Mix in seasonings and salad dressing. Fill whites with egg yolk mixture, heaping it up lightly. Serves 6 people.

—*Mrs. Emanuel (Esther) Herschberger, Michigan*

Egg Salad Filling

6 hard-boiled eggs, chopped
½ c. finely chopped celery
1 Tbsp. minced onion
½ c. salad dressing
¼ tsp. salt
1 c. chopped bologna
chopped pickles
dash of pepper

Stir together until all ingredients are well mixed. Makes enough for 6 sandwiches.

—*Mrs. Emanuel (Esther) Herschberger, Michigan*

Mayonnaise

1 egg yolk
1 tsp. dry mustard
1 tsp. sugar
¼ tsp. salt
dash of red pepper
2 Tbsp. lemon juice or vinegar, divided
1 c. vegetable oil

In a small mixing bowl, beat egg yolk, mustard, sugar, salt, pepper and 1 Tbsp. lemon juice until blended. Continue beating, adding vegetable oil drop by drop. As mixture thickens, increase rate of addition. Stir in remaining 1 Tbsp. lemon juice. Beat thoroughly. Chill.

—*Mrs. Emanuel (Esther) Herschberger, Michigan*

Exploring Traditional Country Cooking

An additional,
Bit of looking ...
For Traditional
Country Cooking ...

A little yeast,
A little flour;
And we shall feast within,
Within the hour.

Slicing the bread,
Still steaming warm;
The butter we spread,
Melts up a storm.

"Goodness!" we utter,
As teeth sink in;
And all the butter,
Drips off our chin.

Let's thank the Lord,
As goodies unfold;
That we've explored,
From times of old.

Jonas A. Shrock

Candies and Snacks

- To crush individually wrapped candy, leave in wrappers and gently crush with a hammer.
- Before melting chocolate, rub the side of pan with butter. The chocolate will not stick to the pan.
- If you are melting chocolate and it is too thick, add a little vegetable oil to thin it.
- When corn does not pop satisfactorily, sprinkle a little water in the jar and shake up the popcorn so the moisture absorbs evenly.
- A pinch of baking soda added to any boiled syrup will keep it from crystallizing.

Taffy

2 c. white sugar
1 pkg. gelatin
1 pt. light corn syrup
1 pt. sweet cream
1 tsp. vanilla
paraffin the size of a walnut

In a 6-qt. saucepan over medium heat, cook all ingredients until soft ball stage. Remove from heat and pour into a buttered cake pan. When cool enough to handle, pull with buttered fingers until light-colored and cooled.

—*Mrs. Monroe (Mary) Hershberger, Wisconsin*

Toffee

1 c. pecans, chopped
¾ c. brown sugar
½ c. butter
6 oz. chocolate coating, melted

Butter a 9" x 9" x 2" pan. Spread pecans in pan. Heat sugar and butter to boiling, stirring constantly. Boil over medium heat for 7 minutes. Immediately spread mixture over nuts in pan. Spread melted chocolate over hot mixture. While still hot cut into 1½" squares. Chill until firm. Makes 3 doz. candies.

—*Mrs. Emanuel (Esther) Herschberger, Michigan*

Easter Candy

½ c. margarine
½ tsp. salt
1 lb. powdered sugar
⅓ c. light corn syrup
1 tsp. vanilla
½ c. coconut, optional

Shape like small eggs and dip in chocolate.

—*Mrs. Andy (Ada) Mast, New York*

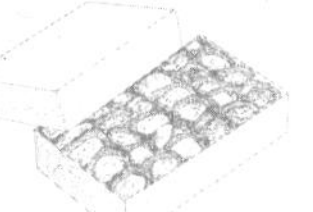

Goof Balls

1 lb. caramel candies
½ c. butter
1 (14 oz.) can sweetened condensed milk
large marshmallows
Rice Krispies

Melt caramels, butter and sweetened condensed milk. Roll large marshmallows 1 at a time in this syrup. Next roll marshmallow in Rice Krispies and cool.

—Ms. Sarah F. Brock, Iowa

Yum Yums [1]

1 (1 lb.) pkg. caramels
1 stick oleo
1 can Eagle Brand Milk
marshmallows
rice crispies

Melt caramels and butter. After mostly melted, add Eagel Brand Milk. Dip marshmallow in mixture, then dip in Rice Crispies.

—Mrs. Eddie (Ida) Borntrager, Wisconsin

Yum Yums [2]

2 c. peanut butter
2 c. powdered sugar
2 c. Rice Krispies
¼ c. butter
coating chocolate

Combine and mix first 4 ingredients and roll in balls. Dip in chocolate. Do not melt butter on stove.

—Mrs. Mahlon (Mary) Miller, Michigan

Best-Ever Caramels

6 c. white sugar
1 qt. sweet cream
3 c. corn syrup
1 lb. butter
2 tsp. vanilla

Combine all ingredients except vanilla in an 8-qt. saucepan. Cook slowly, stirring occasionally, until it reaches 245°. Remove from heat. Add vanilla and pour into a well-buttered pan. Cut and wrap each piece in waxed paper. You can use vegetable oil to make cutting and wrapping easier. Keep in a cool place. Makes 5½ lb. Elizabeth uses 2 Tbsp. vanilla.

—Ms. Emma J. Yoder, Michigan
—Mrs. Aaron (Elizabeth) Yoder, Wisconsin

Clark Bars

1 c. butter
2 c. crunchy peanut butter
2½ c. powdered sugar
1 lb. graham crackers, crushed
1 Tbsp. vanilla, optional
coating chocolate

Mix first 5 ingredients with your hands and roll in balls. Dip into chocolate. Delicious!

—Mrs. David (Lisbet) Mast, Wisconsin
—Ms. Fannie L. Raber, Ohio

"He is no fool who gives what he cannot keep to gain what he cannot lose."

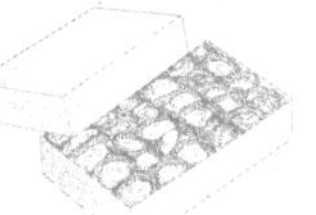

Kit-Kat Bars

4 c. graham cracker crumbs
1 c. white sugar
2 c. brown sugar
1 c. milk
1 lb. butter
2 tsp. vanilla

Combine everything except crackers in a pan and bring to a boil. Reduce heat and cook for 5-6 minutes, stirring constantly. Put a layer of crackers in a 9" x 13" buttered pan. Pour half of cooked mixture over the crackers. Add another layer of crackers and top with remaining mixture. Add another layer of crackers. Spread frosting over top and cool.

Frosting:
2 c. chocolate chips
2 c. butterscotch chips
1⅓ c. peanut butter

Melt and spread over top.

—Ms. Dora M. Herschberger, Ohio

Baby Ruth Bars

1 c. sugar
1 c. syrup
1½ c. peanut butter
1 Tbsp. marshmallow creme
1 c. peanuts
4 c. Rice Krispies
coating chocolate

Bring sugar and syrup to a boil. Add remaining ingredients except coating chocolate. Pour into a greased 9" x 13" pan and cool. Cut into 1" x 3" squares or desired size and dip into chocolate. Delicious!

—Mrs. Daniel (Katie) Mast, Wisconsin

Milky Way Bars

2 lb. sugar
8 oz. light corn syrup
1 c. cold water
4 egg whites
1 Tbsp. vanilla
1 Tbsp. cocoa
coating chocolate

Cook sugar, corn syrup and water to hard ball stage. Beat egg whites until stiff. Pour syrup over egg whites, beating until it holds shape. Add vanilla and cocoa. Press into a greased pan. Cut in bars. Chill, then dip in melted chocolate.

—Mrs. Daniel (Katie) Mast, Wisconsin

Peanut Butter Logs

1 c. peanut butter
¼ c. butter
1½ c. powdered sugar
¾ c. Rice Krispies
1 c. chopped peanuts
1 pkg. chocolate chips
2 Tbsp. shortening

Mix peanut butter, butter and powdered sugar. Mix in cereal by hand and shape into small logs. Roll into nuts and place on cookie pans. Melt chocolate chips and shortening in a double boiler and drizzle over logs. Chill. Makes around 40 logs.

—Ms. Lovina A. Mast, New York

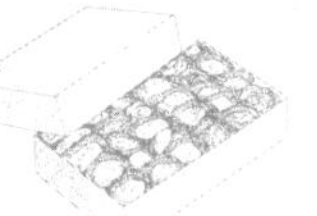

Napoleon Cremes

½ c. butter
¼ c. white sugar
¼ c. cocoa
1 tsp. vanilla
1 egg, slightly beaten
2 c. finely crushed graham crackers
1 c. flaked coconut
½ c. butter
3 Tbsp. milk
1 (3¾ oz.) pkg. instant vanilla pudding
2 c. powdered sugar
2 Tbsp. butter
6 oz. semi-sweet or white chocolate

Combine butter, sugar, cocoa and vanilla in top of double boiler. Cook over simmering water until butter melts. Stir in egg. Continue cooking and stirring for 3 minutes or until mixture is thick. Blend in cracker crumbs and coconut. Press into a buttered 9" square pan. Cream ½ c. butter well. Stir in milk, pudding mix and sugar. Beat until fluffy. Spread evenly over crust and chill until firm. Melt chocolate and 2 Tbsp. butter over simmering water in top of double boiler. Cool. Spread over pudding layer. Chill. Cut into bars.

—Mrs. Alvin (Elizabeth) Mast, New York
—Mrs. Levi (Fannie) Mast, Ohio

Yummy Chocolate Squares

1 lb. marshmallows
1 pkg. vanilla or chocolate chips
3 Tbsp. butter
1 tsp. vanilla
½ tsp. salt
1 c. chopped walnuts
1 c. Rice Krispies

Melt marshmallows, chocolate and butter over low heat until melted, stirring constantly. Mix in remaining ingredients. Spread in a well-buttered pan and cut in squares.

—Mrs. Samuel (Malinda) Mast, Pennsylvania

No-Bake Cookies

2 c. sugar
¼ c. butter
½ c. milk
3 Tbsp. cocoa
2-3 c. oatmeal
½ c. peanut butter
1 tsp. vanilla
nuts, optional

Mix sugar, butter, milk and cocoa in a saucepan. Boil together for just 1 minute. Remove from heat and add oatmeal, peanut butter and vanilla. Add nuts if desired. Drop quickly onto waxed paper by teaspoonsful.

—Ms. Esther S. Herschberger, Michigan
—Ms. Sarah M. Hershberger, Wisconsin

White Chocolate Peppermint Fudge

1½ tsp. + ¼ c. butter, softened, divided
2 c. sugar
½ c. sour cream
12 (1 oz.) sq. white baking chocolate, chopped
1 (7 oz.) jar marshmallow creme
½ c. crushed peppermint candy
½ tsp. peppermint extract

Line a 9" square pan with foil. Grease the foil with 1½ tsp. butter and set aside. In a heavy saucepan, combine sugar, sour cream and remaining butter. Cook and stir over medium heat until sugar is dissolved. Bring to a rapid boil. Cook and stir until a candy thermometer reads 234° (soft ball stage) for about 5 minutes. Remove from heat and stir in white chocolate and marshmallow creme until melted. Fold in peppermint candy and extract. Pour into prepared pan. Chill until firm. Using foil, lift fudge out of pan. Gently peel off foil and cut fudge into 1" squares. Store in the refrigerator. Makes 2 lb.

Variation: Any flavor hard candy can be used. Omit peppermint extract and use flavoring according to candy.

—Mrs. Enos (Ada) Mast, New York

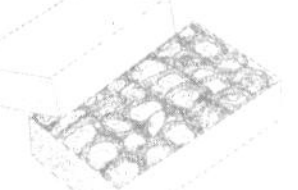

Easy and Delicious Fudge

10 oz. marshmallows
2 Tbsp. butter
2 c. chocolate chips
2 c. coconut
2 c. nuts
2 c. Rice Krispies
1 tsp. vanilla

Partially melt marshmallows, butter and chocolate chips. Add remaining ingredients. Pat into a greased pan. Cut when cool.

—Mrs. Jacob (Sadie) Hershberger, Wisconsin

Peanut Butter Fudge

2 c. white sugar
⅔ c. milk
1 c. marshmallow creme or
  16 marshmallows
1 c. peanut butter
1 tsp. vanilla

Cook sugar and milk to soft ball stage (235°). Stir while cooking. Remove from heat and add marshmallows, peanut butter and vanilla. Cool and cut into squares.

—Ms. Miriam D. Herschberger, Michigan

Words from the head
are heard, words from
the heart are felt.

Popcorn Candy Cake

1 (16 oz.) pkg. miniature marshmallows
¾ c. vegetable oil
½ c. butter
5 qt. popped corn
1 (24 oz.) pkg. gumdrops
1 c. peanuts

In a large saucepan, melt marshmallows, oil and butter until smooth. In a large bowl, combine popcorn, gumdrops and peanuts. Add marshmallow mixture and mix well. Press into a well-greased pan. Cover and refrigerate for 5 hours or overnight. Dip in hot water for 5-10 seconds to unmold. Slice cake and serve. Serves 18 people.

—Mrs. Emanuel (Esther) Herschberger, Michigan

Chocolate Popcorn Balls

1½ c. sugar
⅔ c. water
4 qt. well-salted popcorn
3 sq. chocolate
⅓ c. corn syrup
⅓ c. molasses
1 Tbsp. butter
1 tsp. vanilla

—Ms. Saloma E. Mast, New York

Baked Caramel Corn

1 c. butter
2 c. brown sugar
½ c. light corn syrup
1 tsp. salt
1 tsp. vanilla
½-1 tsp. baking soda
6-8 qt. popped popcorn

Melt butter. Stir in brown sugar, corn syrup and salt. Bring to a boil, stirring constantly. Boil without stirring for 5 minutes. Remove from heat and stir in vanilla and baking soda. Pour over warm popcorn. Mix well and bake at 225° for 1 hour, stirring with a fork every 15 minutes.

—Ms. Amelia A. Slabaugh, Wisconsin
—Ms. Edna B. Yoder, Ohio
—Mrs. Floyd (Katie) Beechy, Michigan

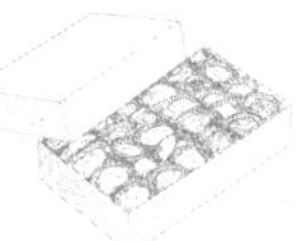

—Mrs. Noah (Edna) Brenneman, Michigan
—Ms. Amanda J. Mast, New York

Favorite Party Mix

2 c. Cheerios
2 c. Kix
2 c. small pretzals
2 c. Rice Chex
2 c. Corn Chex
2 c. Wheat Chex
2 c. mixed nuts
½ c. melted butter
2 Tbsp. Worcestershire sauce
1½ tsp. Lawry's seasoning
¾ tsp. garlic powder
½ tsp. onion powder

Mix cereals well. Melt butter and add seasonings. Pour over mixed cereals. Stir until evenly coated. Bake one hour, stirring every 15 minutes in a 250° oven. Cool and store in an airtight container. Makes 14 cups snack.

—Mrs. Eddie (Ida) Borntrager, Wisconsin

Party Mix

3 c. Wheat Chex
6 c. Corn Chex
3 c. Rice Chex
5 c. pretzels
4 c. peanuts
4 c. Cheerios
1 c. butter
4 tsp. Worcestershire sauce
1 tsp. garlic salt
1 tsp. seasoned salt
1 tsp. celery salt
1 tsp. onion salt
1 pkg. Bugles
1 box Cheese crackers

Mix Chex, pretzels, nuts and Cheerios in a large bowl. Melt butter and add seasonings. Pour over mixture in bowl. Toss until well coated. Toast at 250° for 1 hour, stirring every 10-15 minutes. Do not add Bugles and cheese crackers until finished toasting since they scorch easily.

—Ms. Miriam D. Herschberger, Michigan

Original Ranch Snack Mix

8 c. Crispix cereal
2½ c. small pretzels
2½ c. bite-sized cheddar cheese crackers, optional
3 Tbsp. vegetable oil
1 (1 oz.) env. Hidden Valley Ranch seasoning mix

Combine cereal, pretzels and crackers in a gallon-size bag. Pour oil over mixture. Seal bag and toss to coat. Add seasoning mix. Seal bag and toss again until well coated. This is my mom's favorite!

—Mrs. Perry (Rebecca) Herschberger, Wisconsin

Seasoned Ritz Crackers

1 lb. Ritz or saltine crackers or pretzels
1 c. vegetable oil
3-4 Tbsp. sour cream and onion powder
3 Tbsp. cheese powder

Put crackers in a large bowl with cover. Mix oil and powders together and pour over crackers. Cover and shake well. Put in a pan and bake at 250° for 20 minutes, stirring occasionally.

—Mrs. Samuel (Dora) Mast, New York
—Mrs. Aden (Mary) Mast, New York

Very Good Crackers

2 pkg. snack crackers
1 c. vegetable oil
5 Tbsp. sour cream and onion powder

Put crackers in a large bowl with a lid. Mix vegetable oil and powder. Pour over crackers and shake together. Put into a cake pan and bake at 250°, stirring every few minutes. Cool and enjoy. Good with dip.

—Ms. Sarah M. Hershberger, Wisconsin

White Trash

1¼ lb. white chocolate
6 c. Fruit Loops, Cheerios or cereal of your choice
4 c. small pretzels
2 c. dry roasted peanuts
1 lb. M&M's

Melt chocolate over medium heat in a double boiler. Mix remaining ingredients. Pour chocolate over snack mixture and mix to coat. Spread on waxed paper or trays to cool.

—Mrs. John (Anna) Yoder, Michigan

Trash Candy

2 lb. white chocolate
10 c. Cheerios
5 c. broken pretzels
2 c. M&M's
10 c. Kix
10 c. Rice Chex
2 c. pecan halves

Melt chocolate in a double boiler. In a large bowl, mix remaining ingredients. Pour chocolate over dry ingredients and toss to coat. Makes approx. 2½ gal.

—Ms. Sarah J. Brock, Iowa

White Chocolate Chex Mix

1 c. Cheerios
1 c. Crispix
1 c. Fruit Loops
1 c. Cocoa Krispies
1 c. Rice Chex
1 c. chow mein noodles
1½ c. unsalted mixed nuts
2 Tbsp. vegetable oil
20 oz. white chocolate

Combine all cereals, noodles and nuts. Pour vegetable oil over white chocolate and melt in a heavy saucepan over low heat or in a double boiler. Pour over cereal mixture, mixing with a wooden spoon. Press into a greased pan. Cool to room temperature and cut into squares. Any combination of cereals or regular chocolate may be used.

—Ms. Emma J. Yoder, Michigan

Graham Crackers [1]

2 c. white flour
2 c. brown sugar
1 c. sweet milk
1 c. butter
4 c. graham flour
1 tsp. (heaping) baking soda
1 tsp. salt

This is a stiff dough but crisp if you add the milk the recipe calls for. Knead dough a bit. Roll out very thinly and cut in squares. Prick with a fork to give the graham cracker look. Bake in a hot oven until slightly brown.

—Mrs. Ephraim (Amanda) Mast, Michigan

Graham Crackers [2]

2 c. white bread flour
2 c. fine graham flour
2 c. brown sugar
1 tsp. (heaping) baking powder
1 tsp. (heaping) baking soda
pinch of salt
1 c. sweet milk
1 c. butter or lard

Mix dry ingredients and butter. Add milk and roll out thinly. Bake at 350°-400°.

—Ms. Mary L. Hershberger, Ohio

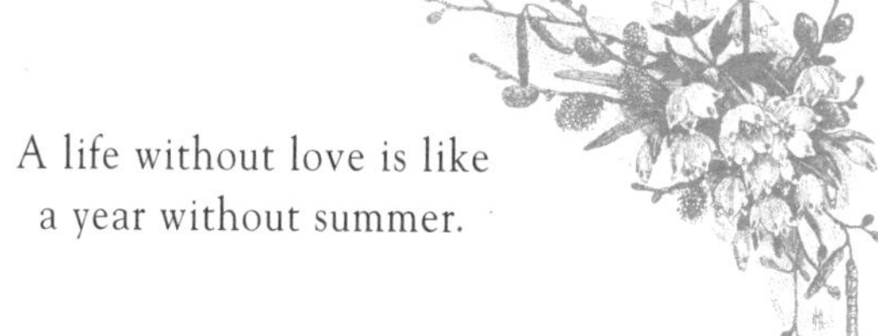

A life without love is like
a year without summer.

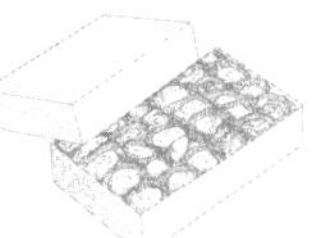

Finger Jell-O [1]

3 Tbsp. unflavored gelatin
3 pkg. flavored Jell-O
4 c. boiling water

Mix unflavored gelatin with Jell-O, then add boiling water and stir until dissolved. This works best if it can set overnight. Do not freeze!

—*Ms. Esther S. Herschberger, Michigan*

Finger Jell-O [2]

1 c. lime Jell-O
8 c. boiling water, divided
¼ c. Knox gelatin
½ c. cold water
1 (14 oz.) can sweetened condensed milk
1 c. strawberry Jell-O

Dissolve lime Jell-O in 3 c. boiling water. Pour into pans ¼" thick and chill until firm. For second layer, soak gelatin in cold water for 10 minutes. Add to 2 c. boiling water and sweetened condensed milk. Stir until dissolved. Chill but do not thicken and pour on top of first layer. After second layer has set, dissolve strawberry Jell-O in 3 c. boiling water. Cool until slightly thick and pour over second layer. Chill until firm and cut into squares. A nice holiday treat!

—*Mrs. Eli (Mattie) Yoder, Ohio*

Finger Jell-O [3]

1 Tbsp. unflavored gelatin
½ c. cold water
⅔c. flavored Jell-O
2 c. hot water

Dissolve gelatin in cold water. Dissolve Jell-O in hot water separately. Add some of hot Jell-O mixture to gelatin before adding the remainder. Chill and cut into small squares. Very healthy treat for children.

—*Mrs. Ora (Rachel) Beechy, Michigan*

Eagle Brand Finger Jell-O

Jell-O Layers:
4 sm. pkg. Jell-O
4 c. boiling water, divided
4 pkg. gelatin
1 1/3 c. cold water, divided

Use 4 different flavors of Jell-O. Dissolve each package in 1 c. boiling water. Add 1 pkg. gelatin dissolved in 1/3 c. cold water to each flavor of Jell-O.

White Layer:
4 pkg. gelatin
3/4 c. cold water
2 c. boiling water
1 can sweetened condensed milk

Dissolve gelatin in cold water. Combine boiling water and sweetened condensed milk. Add to the dissolved gelatin. Layer 1 flavor Jell-O in pan. Chill until set, then cover with 1 1/3 c. white layer. Chill again. Repeat until you have 7 layers ending with Jell-O. If white layer sets before last layer is ready, set in a dish of hot water.

—Mrs. Perry (Elizabeth) Weaver, Ohio

Soft Pretzels

1/2 c. brown sugar
1 Tbsp. yeast
1 1/2 c. warm water
may add 1/2 tsp. salt and 1 tsp. vanilla
5 c. flour
3 c. boiling water
3 tsp. soda

Stir until dough no longer sticks to bowl. Put out on floured surface and knead until elastic. Leave on counter for at least 1/2 hr. Shape pretzels. Dip in boiling water mixed with baking soda. Then put on buttered and salted cookie sheets. Bake at 475° for 8 minutes until done. Dip in butter and salt on top. (not oleo)

—Miss Phoebe T. Herschberger, Wisconsin

When Christmastime
Again rolls around
Many girls and women
In the kitchen will be found!

Making all kinds of goodies
Both candy and snacks.
Everywhere you look
There are stacks and stacks.

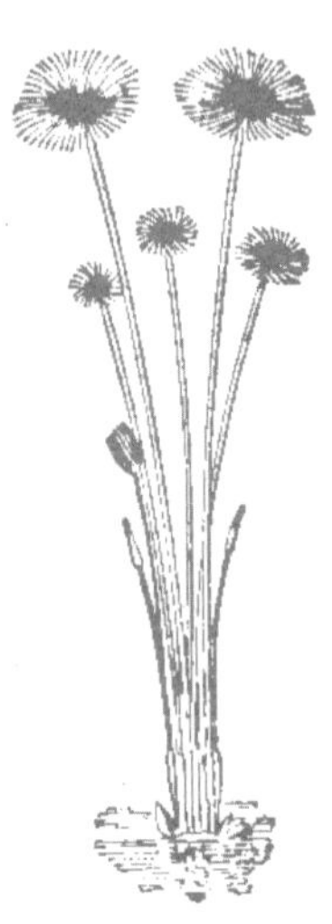

There's mint patties, caramels,
Peanut brittle and fudge too,
Bonbons and sugar plums,
I've only named a few.

There's muddy buddies
And granola bars,
Cracker jack and party mix.
Be sure and fill all your jars.

Canning
Sweet Heart

- Add a squirt of dish soap to the water in canner when canning meats to prevent grease from settling on your jars. Makes cleaning the canner easier too. Add vinegar to water to prevent lime buildup on jars.

- When cooking red beets leave an inch of the stem on to retain color. They peel easily if dipped in cold water.

- When canning pears, add 1 Tbsp. any flavor Jell-O to your filled jars. Pineapple and lime make great-tasting pears.

- A little salt added to your applesauce takes less sugar and brings out the flavor.

- Sprinkle apple with baking soda, and it won't turn brown.

- If cold packing bologna, cold pack for 2-3 hours instead of pressure cooking. It won't be so dry.

Cold Packing

Item	Time	Item	Time
Beef Chunks	3 hours	Peas	3 hours
Steak	2 hours	Beans	3 hours
Steak if fried	1½ hours	Carrots, chopped	2 hours
Meatballs	1½ hours	Corn	3 hours
Hamburger pressed in jars	2 hours	Peaches	10 minutes
Sausage	2 hours	Pears	10 minutes
Pork Chops	2½ hours	Applesauce	10-15 minutes
Pork Roll	1 hour	Cherries	10 minutes
		Raspberries	10 minutes

—Mrs. Merle (Emma) Coblentz, Ohio

Peach Fruit Thickening to Can

10 c. water
1½ c. instant clear jel
6 c. white sugar
3 Tbsp. lemon juice
1 tsp. salt

Mix in a large bowl and fill with fresh peaches. Cold pack for 15-20 minutes. This makes peaches a little more special for lunches. Can also add fresh fruit when opened.

—Mrs. Amos (Mattie) Garber, Ohio

Apple Pie Filling

4½ c. sugar
1⅓ c. cornstarch
2 tsp. (heaping) cinnamon
¼ tsp. nutmeg
1 tsp. salt
10 c. boiling water
3 Tbsp. lemon juice
approx. 7 qt. apples, sliced, chopped or shredded

Mix sugar, cornstarch, cinnamon, nutmeg and salt. Add enough water to make a paste. Pour slowly into boiling water while stirring. Stir until it boils. Add lemon juice. Mix with apples. Fill jars, leaving a good 3" headspace. Hot water bath for 20 minutes.

—Mrs. Levi (Mary) Shetler, Michigan

Strawberry Pie Filling

6 c. sugar
6 sm. pkg. strawberry Jell-O
1 c. + 2 Tbsp. instant clear jel
6 c. water
5 qt. strawberries

Combine sugar, Jell-O and clear jel. Mix well. Then add water, mixing well. Let set for 10 minutes. Add berries and cold pack for 10 minutes.

—Mrs. Joe (Martha) Yoder, New York

Pie Filling to Can

24 c. water, divided
9 c. sugar
1½ c. Jell-O
3½-4 c. Therma-flo
approx. 8-10 qt. fruit

Heat 20 c. water, sugar and Jell-O. Mix remaining 4 c. water and Therma-flo together. Stir into sugar/water mixture and boil 1 minute. Add fruit and ladle into jars. Coldpack in hot water bath for 10 minutes. Makes 16 qt. You can use any fresh fruit. Use flavor of Jell-O according to kind of fruit you're using.

—Mrs. John (Anna) Yoder, Michigan

Canned Strawberries [1]

approx. 4 c. sugar
4 c. water
pinch of salt
⅛ tsp. red pepper
2 c. water
1½ c. Perma-flo
½ c. strawberry Jell-O
approx. 10 qt. whole or chopped strawberries

Combine sugar, water, salt and red pepper and bring to a boil. Mix water and Perma-flo and add to boiling sugar water, stirring until it boils. Cook for 5 minutes.
Add strawberry Jell-O. Stir well. Pour over strawberries and mix until strawberries are well coated. Fill jars and cold pack for 5 minutes.

—Mrs. Levi (Mary) Shetler, Michigan

Canned Strawberries [2]

9 qt. strawberries
4 c. sugar
1¾ c. instant clear jel
2 pk. strawberry Kool-Aid
5 c. water

Crush berries a little. Mix sugar, clear jel and Kool-Aid. Add water. Mix into berries. Cold pack for 10 minutes. If it is too thick with berries, use fewer berries. You can also use this recipe for sour cherries, blueberries, peaches and more fruits. Only use the matching Kool-Aid. This is handy to fix quick desserts.

—Mrs. Levi (Sadie) Yoder, Michigan

Canned Strawberries [3]

9 qt. strawberries
5 c. white sugar
1 c. instant clear jel
2 pk. strawberry Kool-Aid

Crush strawberries coarsely. Mix sugar and clear jel together. Stir into strawberries. Add Kool-Aid and mix well. Put in jars and cold pack for 10 minutes.

—Mrs. Simon (Malinda) Yoder, Michigan

Zucchini Brownies to Can

4 eggs, beaten
2 c. white sugar
2 c. flour
1 tsp. salt
2 tsp. cinnamon
¼ c. cocoa
1¼ c. vegetable oil
1 tsp. vanilla
3 c. shredded zucchini
2 tsp. baking soda
1 c. raisins and/or nuts

Mix. Put in dry, hot jars. Fill only half full and bake slowly at 300°-350° for 1-1½ hours. Set jars on cookie sheet or in cake pan to put in oven. Have lids and rings hot to put on and seal as soon as you remove from the oven. Good to open for a quick dessert for lunch buckets or company. Fix as a pudding with whipped cream and thickened fruit.

—Mrs. David (Naomi) Herschberger, Michigan

Before you flare up at others' faults, take time to count ten—of your own!

Chili Soup to Can

8 lb. hamburger
3½ c. chopped onion
4 c. brown sugar
2 c. flour
1¼ c. clear jel
¾ c. chili powder
⅓ c. salt
½ c. seasoned salt
2 Tbsp. oregano
2 Tbsp. black pepper
2 qt. water
14 qt. tomato juice
6 cans chili beans
6 cans pork-n-beans

Fry hamburger and onion together. Put into a large container. Combine all dry ingredients and add water, then add to hamburger. Add tomato juice and beans. Mix well. Put in jars and cold pack for 2 hours or pressure cook for 45 minutes. This is very good. Makes 28 qt.

—Mrs. Amos (Mattie) Garber, Ohio

Chunky Beef Soup

16 lb. hamburger or venison
salt and pepper to taste
4 qt. carrots
2 qt. green beans
3 qt. peas
4 qt. potatoes
3 qt. onions
6 qt. tomato juice
2½ gal. water
1 c. beef bouillon
2 lg. cans beef broth, optional
1¾ c. sugar
¼ c. salt
4 c. Perma-flo or flour
water

Fry hamburger in butter. Add salt and pepper to taste. Cut vegetables in small cubes. Heat tomato juice, water, beef bouillon, broth, sugar and salt together until boiling. Mix Perma-flo with a little water at a time, enough to make a smooth paste. Add to mixture and bring to a boil. Mix hamburger, vegetables and boiled mixture together. Put in cans and pressure cook for 40 minutes at 10 lb. pressure. Makes about 30 qt.

—Mrs. Jonas (Anna) Miller, Michigan

Pork-n-Beans

8 lb. navy beans
1/3 c. salt
4 qt. tomato juice
1/2 tsp. black pepper
1 tsp. cinnamon
1 lg. onion, diced
3 lb. wieners, sliced
9 c. white sugar
4 c. brown sugar
26 oz. ketchup
1/4 c. cornstarch

Soak beans overnight. Cook beans until soft. Mix remaining ingredients together and cook a few minutes, then add to beans and mix well. Cold pack for 1 1/2 hours. Makes 15 qt.

—Mrs. Albert (Lizzie) Miller, New York

Hot Pepper Butter

42 hot peppers
1 pt. prepared mustard
6 c. sugar
1 Tbsp. salt
1 qt. vinegar
1 c. flour
1 1/2 c. water

Grind peppers. Add mustard, sugar, salt and vinegar. Bring to a boil. Make a paste of flour and water. Add to mixture and cook for 5 minutes. Put in jars and seal. You can also use some sweet peppers and fewer hot peppers if you wish.

—Mrs. Atlee (Fannie) Miller, New York
—Mrs. Noah (Malinda) Miller, New York

Frosting makes a loving cake,
Whether decorated or plain,
But the children's greatest joy is—
To lick the spoon and pan.

Sandwich Spread [1]

3-4 qt. green tomatoes
1 qt. onion
12 lg. peppers
2 lg. celery ribs
1 c. salt
1 qt. vinegar
6 c. sugar
1 qt. mayonnaise (more if desired)
½ sm. jar mustard

Measure green tomatoes, onions, peppers and celery before grinding and add salt. Drain overnight in a cloth bag. Press remaining juice out in the morning. Add vinegar and sugar and boil for 25-30 minutes. When cooled, add mayonnaise and mustard.

—Mrs. Eli (Rachel) Mast, New York

Sandwich Spread [2]

6 ripe red peppers
6 green peppers
6 cucumbers
6 onions
6 tomatoes
1 pt. chopped celery
½ c. salt
1 qt. vinegar
3 c. sugar
1 c. flour
1 pt. prepared mustard
1 pt. vinegar

Finely chop or grind peppers, cucumbers, onions and tomatoes. Add celery. Add water until vegetables are covered. Add salt and mix well. Let soak for 2 hours. Drain as dry as possible. Mix 1 qt. vinegar, sugar, flour and mustard. Bring to a boil. Stir in 1 pt. vinegar. Add to vegetables. Mix well. Fill jars and hot water bath for 10 minutes. To use, open jar of spread and mix with equal amount of salad dressing or mayonnaise. Use on eggs, meat, etc. Very good!

—Mrs. Levi (Mary) Stutzman, Michigan

When you feel like criticizing the younger generation, just remember who raised them.

Aunt Rachel's Sandwich Spread

1 doz. red peppers
1 doz. green peppers
2 lg. onions
2 med. green tomatoes
4 med. carrots
1 c. vinegar
3 c. sugar
1 Tbsp. salt
7 Tbsp. flour
water
1 pt. prepared mustard
1 qt. salad dressing

Grind peppers, onions, tomatoes and carrots all together and drain. Add vinegar, sugar and salt. Boil for 10 minutes. Thicken with flour stirred to a thin consistency with water. When done, add mustard and salad dressing. Put in jars and cold pack for 5-10 minutes.

—Ms. Elizabeth J. Herschberger, Michigan

Hot Dog Relish

1 gal. cucumbers, ground
1 pt. onions, ground
¼ c. salt
3 c. sugar
1 Tbsp. mustard seed
1 Tbsp. celery seed
3 c. vinegar
green food coloring, optional

Soak cucumbers, onions and salt for 2 hours, then drain. Mix sugar, mustard seed, celery seed and vinegar together. Add food coloring if desired. Heat to boiling point. Mix with cucumbers and bring to a boil again. Put in jars and seal.

—Mrs. Jonas (Anna) Miller, Michigan

More people are killed by worry, because more people worry than work.

Corn Relish

12 ears corn
2 onions
1 head cabbage
4 med. carrots
1 bunch celery
1 c. prepared mustard
3 c. sugar
1 tsp. tumeric
1 Tbsp. salt
½ tsp. black pepper
10 oz. vinegar
6 oz. water
2 Tbsp. cornstarch
½ c. water

Cut corn off ears. Finely chop or shred onions, cabbage, carrots and celery. Mix mustard, sugar, tumeric, salt and pepper. Slowly add vinegar and 6 oz. water, stirring well to prevent lumps. Mix liquid into vegetables and bring to a boil. Mix cornstarch and ½ c. water and add to boiling vegetables. Fill jars and cold pack for 30 minutes. Makes 5 qt.

—Mrs. Levi (Mary) Shetler, Michigan

Pickled Peppers for Sandwiches

1 gal. hot peppers
1 gal. sweet peppers
2 gal. chopped hotdogs (16 pkg.)
2 c. vegetable oil
½ c. vinegar
1 Tbsp. salt
2 c. sugar
3 reg. bottles ketchup
2 qt. pizza sauce

Cop ingredients as needed. Mix all together, then pack in jars. Cold pack for 20 minutes. You can use fewer hot peppers and more sweet peppers or add your favorite vegetables in the sauce. Homemade bologna can be used instead of hotdogs.

—Mrs. Lewis (Elizabeth) Yoder, New York
—Mrs. Harvey (Katieann) Raber, New York

Pickled Red Beets

beets
4 c. white sugar
1 qt. beet juice
2 Tbsp. mixed pickling spice or 2 tsp. cinnamon
2 c. vinegar
1 Tbsp. salt

Wash and boil beets until tender. Peel, slice and fill cans. Put pickling spice in a cloth and hang into juice. Bring juice to a boil. Pour juice into cans. Boil cans for 10 minutes.

—Mrs. Rudy (Ella) Borntreger, Wisconsin

Kosher Dill Pickles

cucumbers
3 qt. water
1 qt. vinegar
3/4 c. (scant) salt
1/4 tsp. powdered alum
1 clove garlic
2 heads dill
1/4 tsp. chopped red pepper

Cut up cucumbers and put in jars. Heat remaining ingredients to boiling. While this is heating, set jars with cucumbers (without lids) in canner with water and bring water to boiling. When both are boiling, pour vinegar mixture in jars. Put lids on and remove immediately from canner. Set them upside down, so they seal better. Makes 7-8 qt. pickles.

—Ms. Clara M. Herschberger, Wisconsin

My kitchen not too modern
Guess it has that lived-in look,
And likely paint is flaking off,
Inside my breakfast nook.
But "Welcome" holds out both her hands
In hopes of being shook.
So come you in and sit you down,
And sample what I cook!

Cinnamon Pickles

2 gal. lg. cucumbers, peeled, seeded and cut up
8½ qt. cold water
2 c. lime
3 c. vinegar, divided
1 Tbsp. alum
1 bottle red food coloring, optional
2 c. water
10 c. sugar
1 pkg. cinnamon red hots

Let cucumbers stand 24 hours. Drain and wash in clear water. Soak 3 hours in cold water and lime, then drain off. Simmer for 2 hours in 1 c. vinegar, alum, red food coloring and water to cover. Drain off. Make syrup out of remaining 2 c. vinegar, 2 c. water and sugar. Pour over pickles and let stand overnight. Drain and reheat 3 days. Pack in jars and seal. The last day, heat and add red hots.

—Mrs. Ephraim (Amanda) Mast, Michigan

Hamburger Pickles

3 c. vinegar
3 c. sugar
1 Tbsp. mustard seed
2 Tbsp. salt
2 tsp. celery seed
1 tsp. tumeric
2 onions, sliced
1 gal. sliced cucumbers
heads of dill
garlic cloves

Boil first 7 ingredients and pour over cucumbers. Put 1 head of dill and 2 cloves garlic in each jar before adding pickles. Allow pickles to come to a boil before canning and sealing.

—Mrs. John (Edna) Herschberger, Wisconsin

Keep a fair-sized cemetery in your backyard to bury the faults of your friends.

Pizza Sauce [1]

- ½ bu. tomatoes
- 3 lb. onions, sliced
- 4 garlic cloves
- 1½ green peppers
- 5 hot peppers
- 1 pt. vegetable oil
- 12 cans tomato paste
- 1½ c. white sugar
- 1 Tbsp. sweet basil
- 2 Tbsp. Italian seasoning
- 1 c. salt
- 1 Tbsp. oregano
- black pepper

Cook tomatoes, onions, garlic and peppers until soft. Put through a strainer. Add vegetable oil and cook for 30 minutes. Add next 6 ingredients and simmer until it boils. Add black pepper to taste. Makes 24 pt.

—Mrs. Joseph (Martha) Miller, Ohio

Pizza Sauce [2]

- ½ bu. tomatoes
- 4 jalapeño peppers
- 3 lb. onions
- 10-12 garlic buds
- 1½ c. sugar
- ½ c. salt
- 1 Tbsp. oregano
- 2 Tbsp. parsley flakes
- 6 bay leaves
- 2 Tbsp. basil
- 2 c. vegetable oil
- 2 c. Perma-flo
- 2½ c. water

Chunk tomatoes and boil until soft and put through food mill. Remove seeds from jalapeños, wearing plastic gloves. Grind or finely chop jalapeños, onions and garlic. Boil tomato juice, peppers, onions and garlic for 1 hour. Mix sugar, salt, oregano, parsley flakes, bay leaves, basil and vegetable oil. Add to tomato mixture and boil for 2 more hours. Mix Perma-flo and water. Add to boiling pizza sauce, stirring until desired consistency is reached. Fill jars. Hot water bath for 10 minutes.

—Mrs. Levi (Mary) Shetler, Michigan

Pizza Sauce [3]

4 qt. tomato juice
1 lg. or 2 sm. onions, diced
1 clove garlic, diced
¼ c. brown sugar
1 Tbsp. salt
1 tsp. oregano
1 tsp. Italian seasoning
½ tsp. chili powder
½ tsp. cinnamon
3 Tbsp. clear jel

Boil everything except clear jel for 1½-2 hours. Thicken with clear jel and cold pack for 20 minutes. This is also good to make spaghetti and sloppy joes.

—Mrs. Ephraim (Amanda) Mast, Michigan

Beef Barbecue Sauce

10 lb. ground beef
5 c. chopped onions
1½ c. brown sugar
¼ c. salt
½ c. vinegar
2 Tbsp. liquid smoke
1¼ Tbsp. pepper
½ c. prepared mustard
⅔ c. Worcestershire sauce
4 c. cooked oatmeal
4 c. ketchup
4 c. beef broth or water

Brown hamburger and onions. Add remaining ingredients. Add more liquid if necessary. Steam for 10 minutes. Pack in jars and pressure cook for 1 hour at 10 lb. pressure. Makes 9-10 qt.

—Mrs. John (Esther) Brock, Iowa

The recipe for a happy family includes
a heaping cup of patience.

Ketchups

7 c. sugar
1 Tbsp. cinnamon
½ tsp. pepper
3 lg. onions, diced
6 Tbsp. salt
2 tsp. allspice
½ tsp. cloves
1 Tbsp. dry mustard
2 gal. tomato juice or purée
2 c. vinegar
1½ c. vinegar
1-2 c. Perma-flo

Combine spices with juice and 2 c. vinegar and cook for 35 minutes uncovered. Make a paste with 1½ c. vinegar and Perma-flo. If paste is too thick, add water until right consistency. Cook well before canning.

—Mrs. Atlee (Edna) Yoder, Wisconsin
—Mrs. Reuben (Irene) Brock, Wisconsin

Hamburger Patties to Can

15 lb. hamburger
4 eggs
4 slices bread
2 c. rolled oats
72 soda crackers, crushed
6 c. milk
½ c. salt
2 tsp. pepper

Sauce:
1½ qt. ketchup
3 med. onions, diced
2 Tbsp. Worcestershire sauce
2 Tbsp. prepared mustard
½ c. brown sugar
1 Tbsp. seasoned salt

Make your patties and put on a cookie sheet. Bake at 400° for about 5 minutes. Turn over and bake other side almost 3 minutes or until brown. Put in jars. Add sauce and fill jars ¾ full. Cold pack for 2 hours. They are very good. Makes 14 qt.

—Mrs. Menno (Anna) Hershberger, Kentucky

Meatballs to Can [1]

meatballs
2 c. ketchup
1 c. brown sugar
3 Tbsp. barbecue sauce
1 Tbsp. prepared mustard
½ tsp. liquid smoke

Form balls, put on cookie sheet and bake until brown. Put in jars and top with 1 c. sauce. Cold pack for 1 hour.

—Mrs. Lewis (Elizabeth) Yoder, New York

Meatballs to Can [2]

40 lb. hamburger or venison
16 eggs
6 c. milk
3 qt. tomato juice
12 c. oatmeal
½ c. salt to salted meat
1 c. brown sugar
1 lg. bottle ketchup, optional
6 Tbsp. liquid smoke, optional

Weigh ground meat into a large container. Add all ingredients and mix well. Form into small balls and bake well. I like to let set a while before making balls but have often started right after mixing. After balls are baked, put in jars and fill with water or barbecue sauce. Also makes good meatloaf. A favorite with our family!

—Mrs. Paul (Edna) Brenneman, Michigan

Canned Meatloaf

15 lb. ground beef
½ c. salt
4 slices bread
36 soda crackers, crushed
1 c. oatmeal
3 c. tomato juice
4 eggs
pepper
chopped onions

Mix well and pack in jars. Boil for 3 hours or pressure cook for 1½ hours at 10 lb. pressure.

—Mrs. Amos (Ella) Beechy, Ohio

To Can Beef Steaks

Layer **beef steaks** in a stainless steel canner. **Salt** each layer, then cover with foil. Let stand for 10-14 days in the basement. Then rinse in water until water in almost clear. Put in jars. Do not squeeze in. Just lay it in until the jar is full. This makes it easier to get out again without falling apart. This recipe makes that they are not ready to eat. Can at 10 lb. pressure for 1 hour.

1 gal. water
1 c. brown sugar
2 tsp. salt
3 Tbsp. black pepper

Mix and put 1 c. in jars, then add steaks. If jar does not have enough syrup, add some more.

—Mrs. Levi (Sadie) Yoder, Ohio

Sausage

1⅔ c. salt
2½ Tbsp. black pepper
1 tsp. red pepper
2 Tbsp. (heaping) sage
1 tsp. nutmeg
1 c. flour
1 c. brown sugar
50 lb. sausage
3 c. water

Mix all ingredients together except water. Mix with sausage before grinding. Add water as you grind it.

—Mrs. Noah (Lovina) Miller, Wisconsin

Be patient with the faults of others.
They have to be patient with yours.

Pork Sausage

50 lb. pork sausage
1½ c. salt
3 Tbsp. black pepper
5 Tbsp. dry mustard
2 Tbsp. ginger
2 Tbsp. sage
a little brown sugar

Mix well.

—Mrs. Neil (Esther) Kauffman, Wisconsin

Lydia's Canned Ham

1 pt. Tender Quick
1 gal. water
1 pt. brown sugar
2 Tbsp. liquid smoke

Divide this into 14 qt. jars. Fill with raw sliced ham. Cold pack for 1 hour. This also works for deer meat.

—Mrs. Aden (Mary) Mast, New York

Turkey for a King

1 c. Tender Quick
¾ c. salt
¼ c. liquid smoke
2 Tbsp. brown sugar
¾ Tbsp. black pepper
½ Tbsp. red pepper
1½ gal. water

Soak a 12 lb. turkey in this brine for 3 days, then roast as usual on the fourth day. Very good!

—Mrs. Alvin (Elizabeth) Mast, New York

Quick and Easy Bologna

40 lb. beef
10 lb. pork
18 oz. salt
2 oz. Pink Curing Salt
2 lb. nonfat dry milk
2 oz. coriander seed
3 oz. black pepper
6 oz. brown sugar
½ oz. garlic powder
1 oz. phosphite
10 lb. water (may vary)

Grind beef and pork with salt and Pink Curing Salt 3 or 4 times. Mix dry milk, coriander seed, pepper, sugar, garlic, phosphite, and water in a mixing bowl. Add to meat. Mix really well. Stuff in casing and smoke or stuff in jars bulk and can.

—Mrs. Lewis (Elizabeth) Yoder, New York

Bologna – 100 lb. meat

100 lb. meat
2 lb. Tender Quick
24-28 oz. salt
2 tsp. saltpetre
2 oz. pepper
2 lb. cornstarch
1½ oz. ground coriander seed
4 tsp. mace
1 tsp. garlic
4½ qt. water

For chicken, use 85 lb. chicken and 15 lb. beef. For beef, use 50 lb. beef and 50 lb. pork. Mix meat, Tender Quick, salt and saltpetre. Grind and let stand for 2-4 days. Grind again and mix with remaining ingredients. Stuff and smoke for 4 hours at 125°-150° for 30 minutes for 2" casings and for 90 minutes for 4" casings. Put in hot water at the same temperature and same amount of time. Then put in cold water for a few minutes.

—Ms. Mary L. Hershberger, Ohio

Character is what you know you are not what others think you are.

Our Bologna

40 lb. beef
10 lb. pork
1 lb. Tender Quick
1 tsp. saltpetre
¼ lb. salt
2 oz. coriander seed
1 Tbsp. black pepper
1 Tbsp. garlic
1 tsp. mace
5 Tbsp. liquid smoke
8 lb. water
couple boxes fine white crackers, crushed

Grind meat, Tender Quick, saltpetre and salt. Let cure for 24 hours. Grind twice. Mix in remaining ingredients. Put in jars and pressure cook at 10 lb. pressure for 45 minutes.

—Mrs. Samuel (Katie) Hershberger, Michigan

Bologna

40 lb. beef or venison
10 lb. pork
1 lb. Tender Quick
¾ c. salt
6 pk. soda crackers
2 qt. warm water
1½ lb. brown sugar
3 Tbsp. coriander seed
1½ Tbsp. mace
2 Tbsp. black pepper
2 Tbsp. garlic powder
2 Tbsp. paprika or extra pepper
6 Tbsp. Worcestershire sauce
6 Tbsp. soy sauce, optional
2 qt. cold water

Mix meats, Tender Quick and salt together and grind finely. Let set for 2-3 days, then grind again. Soak crackers in warm water and add remaining ingredients except for cold water. Pour meat into a tub to mix and add cracker mixture. Mix with hands for 20 minutes, adding the cold water as you need it to keep it moist. Stuff into casings and smoke for 4 hours at 120°-125°. Then float in hot water at 150°-160° for 30 minutes as soon as you remove it from the smokehouse. Put in cold water for a few minute when you remove it from hot water.

—Mrs. Harvey (Lisbet) Mast, Pennsylvania

Trail Bologna

½ lb. salt
1 lb. Tender Quick
20 lb. pork
30 lb. venison or beef, coarsely ground
1½ lb. dry milk
2 gal. warm water, divided
¾ oz. mace
½ oz. garlic
1 oz. saltpetre
2 oz. black pepper

Mix salt and Tender Quick into meat and let set 48 hours, then grind twice through a fine plate. Mix dry milk and 1 gal. water. Add remaining gallon warm water and mix in spice. Now put in casing and smoke for 2-3 hours at 120°-140°. From there place in hot water at 160° for 30 minutes. From there put in cold water for 3-5 minutes. Important: Mix for 30 minutes. We got this recipe from someone who butchers for people, and it's their all-time favorite as well as ours.

—Mrs. Danny (Edna) Borntrager, Wisconsin

Improved Chicken Bologna

30 lb. meat
1 lb. Tender Quick
1 oz. black pepper
½ c. sugar
2 tsp. saltpetre
2 tsp. garlic powder
2 lb. cracker crumbs
1 Tbsp. liquid smoke
1 gal. water

Cut raw meat from chickens. Add Tender Quick to meat and grind twice—first through coarse then through fine blade. Let set for 24 hours. Add pepper, sugar, saltpetre and garlic powder. Mix into cracker crumbs. Add liquid smoke and water. Mix well and cold pack for 2 hours.

—Mrs. Simon (Clara) Miller, Michigan

The reason people blame things on previous generations is that there's only one other choice.

Cure for Meat

4 gal. water
2 lb. brown sugar
5 lb. salt
1 oz. saltpetre
2 oz. pepper
1 c. liquid smoke

Heat water, sugar, salt, saltpetre, pepper and liquid smoke until salt is dissolved. Cool, then pour over hams and bacons. Put a weight on top to keep meat under water. Soak bacon 3 days and hams 3-4 weeks.

—Mrs. Reuben (Irene) Brock, Wisconsin

Brine for Curing Turkey

1 c. Tender Quick
10 c. water
1 tsp. saltpetre
3 Tbsp. liquid smoke
3 Tbsp. brown sugar

Make sure the meat is all covered with brine. Cover and let set for 2-3 days, depending on how big your turkey is. For chicken leave in 24 hours.

—Mrs. Albert (Lizzie) Miller, New York

T-Bone Cure

9 c. water
1 c. Tender Quick
5 Tbsp. liquid smoke

Slice or make chunks with ham and soak for 3 days. Can.

—Mrs. Neil (Esther) Kauffman, Wisconsin

Cure for Ham

ham
Tender Quick
brown sugar
liquid smoke

Slice ham. Mix equal parts of Tender Quick and brown sugar. Sprinkle over meat slices. Sprinkle with liquid smoke. Repeat in layers. Let set for 3-4 days. Fry and serve. To can, put in cans after curing and cold pack for 3 hours.

—Mrs. Levi (Esther) Nisley, Ohio

Product	Preparation before Canning	Steam Pressure Cooker	Hot Water Bath
Asparagus	wash, grade, keep tips above water, boil 3 minutes, pack	10 lb. for 40 min	3 hours
Beans	tip, top them, wash	10 lb. for 40-55 min.	3 hours
Beets	wash, keep 1" stem, boil 15-20 min. slip skins, pack	10 lb. for 40 min.	2 hours
Cabbage	wash, boil 10 min., add salt, pack	10 lb. for 40 min.	1½ hours
Cauliflower	soak in cold brine, boil 3 min., pack	10 lb. for 40 min.	1½ hours
Carrots	wash, scrape, boil 5 min., pack	10 lb. for 40 min.	2 hours
Corn (on cob)	boil on cob 5 min., pack	10 lb. for 70 min.	3½ hours
Corn	boil on cob 5 min., cut from cob, pack loosely	10 lb. for 70 min.	3½ hours
Eggplant	peel, cut into ¼"-½" slices, boil 3 min., pack, don't add salt	10 lb. for 60 min.	2½ hours
Kohlrabi & Turnips	wash, boil 15 min., slice, pack	10 lb. for 45 min.	2 hours
Mushrooms & Okra	wash, skin if necessary, boil 3 min.	10 lb. for 40 min.	3 hours
Parsnips	wash, scrub, boil 15 min., pack	10 lb. for 45 min.	2 hours
Peas	shell, grade, boil 3-5 min. loosely pack	10 lb. for 1 hour	3 hours
Pumpkins & Squash	wash, cut into pieces, cook until tender, mash, pack	15 lb. for 75 min.	3½ hours
Sweet Potato	wash, boil or steam 15 min., peel, pack	10 lb. for 2 hours	3½ hours
Tomatoes	scald and peel, pack whole or cut into pieces, pack	5 lb. for 15 min.	½ hour

Thank God for dirty dishes—
They have a tale to tell.
While others may go hungry
We are eating well.
With home and health and happiness,
I shouldn't want to fuss
By this stack of evidence
God's been very good to us.

Seven-year-old Ellen was punished one night by not being allowed to eat with the rest of her family. Instead she was made to eat her supper alone at a little table in the corner of the kitchen. The rest of the family set about ignoring her completely until they heard her saying grace over her solitary supper in these words, "I thank thee Lord, for preparing a table before me in the presence of mine enemies..."

Large Quantities

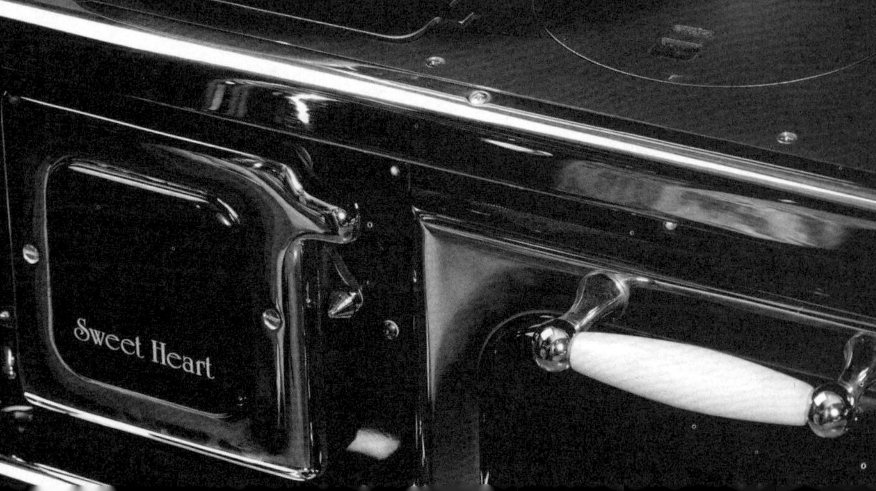

Food for a Barnraising

5 gal. pork-n-beans with
3 lb. wieners
24 qt. salad
150 lb. chicken meat
12 qt. gravy
24 qt. dressing
30 qt. mashed potatoes
12-15 pails ice cream
20 pies
10 cakes

This was for 110 men and 70 women and children.

—Mrs. Reuben (Irene) Brock, Wisconsin

Elephant Stew

1 elephant
2 rabbits, optional
seasoned brown gravy

Cut elephant into bite-sized pieces. This will take about 2 months. Cover with brown gravy and cook over a kerosene fire about 4 weeks at 465°. This should serve 3,800 people. If more people are expected, add rabbits. Do this only if necessary as most people do not like to find a hare in their stew.

—Ms. Cassie H. Mast

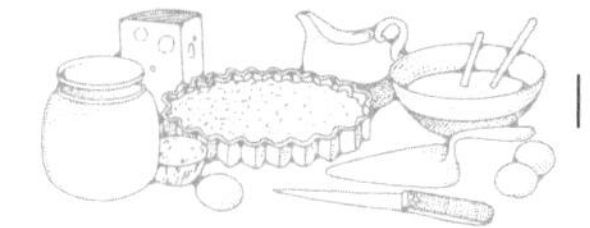

Noodles

4 qt. potatoes
4 qt. (or more) chicken
16 sm. cans chicken broth
1 bottle minced onion
8 cans cream of chicken soup
2 (3 lb.) boxes Velveeta cheese
10 pkg. noodles
water as needed
2 qt. carrots
parsley

Serves 500 people.

—Mrs. Rebecca O. Mast, Ohio

Noodles for a Large Crowd

4 lg. cans chicken broth or
 6 qt. canned chicken broth
 plus 6-7 c. water
5 lb. noodles
3 sm. cans cream of chicken soup
chicken bouillon to taste
1 lb. butter, browned

Cook everything except butter 5 minutes, then cover and let set for 1 hour. Add browned butter. Serves 100 people.

—Mrs. John (Anna) Yoder, Michigan

Too many of us think it's a hardship to do without things our grandparents never heard of.

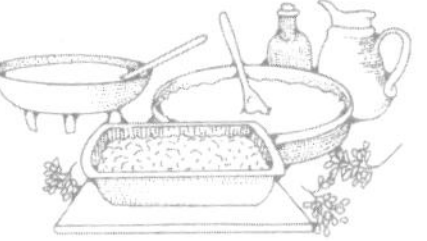

Chicken Noodle Soup

2 qt. rich chicken broth with lots of meat
20 qt. stockpot half full boiling water
1 c. (or more) diced onions
2 qt. diced, cooked potatoes
1 qt. diced, cooked carrots
1 pt. diced, cooked celery
5 oz. chicken bouillon
salt and pepper to taste
2½ gal. fine noodles, packed

Add chicken broth to boiling water, then add onions, potatoes, carrots, celery, chicken bouillon and salt. Bring to a boil and add noodles. Cover and remove from heat. Have hot water on hand, in case you need to add some to the soup. Serves 50 people.

—Mrs. Aaron (Elizabeth) Yoder, Readstown, Wisconsin

Garden Slaw

16 heads cabbage, finely shredded
12 green peppers, finely diced
12 c. finely diced celery
4 red peppers, finely diced
4 c. finely shredded carrots
⅔ c. salt
⅓ c. mustard seed
24 c. sugar
8 c. white vinegar

Combine and mix well. Serves 400 people.

—Mrs. Rebecca O. Mast, Ohio

You can pray, believe
and receive...or you can pray,
doubt and do without.

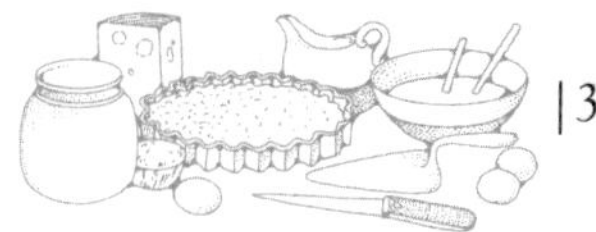

Dressing for a Wedding

1 wash tub full bread crumbs (about 25 homemade loaves)
3 lb. butter
3 qt. finely diced potatoes
4 qt. finely chopped celery
2 c. chopped onions
2 qt. finely grated raw carrots
1½ gal. finely chopped chicken
lots of parsley
3 doz. eggs, beaten
salt and pepper to taste
⅓ c. chicken broth
⅓ c. water
⅓ c. milk

Brown crumbs in butter. Cook next 4 ingredients. Add crumbs and remaining ingredients. Fry or bake.

—Mrs. Harvey (Katieann) Raber, New York

Mock Steak for a Wedding

60 lb. ground beef
40 c. cracker crumbs
40 c. milk
salt and pepper
5 cans mushroom soup
5 cans milk
2 lb. Velveeta cheese

Mix ground beef, cracker crumbs, milk, salt and pepper together. Let set overnight. Fry meat in patties. Melt remaining ingredients to make sauce and put in layers in roasters. Heat in oven until bubbly and hot. One batch sauce is plenty for 1 large roaster. Serves 300-350 people.

—Mrs. John (Esther) Shrock, Iowa

Gravy for a Wedding

4 gal. broth
6 c. cornstarch and flour
2 doz. egg yolks (1 qt.)
1 lb. butter
1 c. chicken bouillon

Heat broth until almost boiling. Mix cornstarch and flour with beaten yolks and water until smooth. Add to broth and stir until boiling. Brown butter lightly in skillet and add to gravy. Add chicken bouillon.

—Mrs. John (Anna) Yoder, Michigan
—Mrs. David (Naomi) Herschberger, Michigan

Pork-n-Beans

8½ lb. beans, soaked overnight
1½ lb. finely cut pork
⅓ c. salt

Cook beans, pork and salt slowly until nearly done. Fill cans ¾ full with beans and sauce. Cold pack for 2½ hours or pressure cook at 10 lb. pressure for ¾ hours.

Sauce:
4 qt. tomato juice
2 qt. water
1 lb. white sugar
½ c. baking molasses
⅔ c. brown sugar
½ tsp. prepared mustard
1 tsp. cinnamon and/or ginger
1 c. flour

Combine and mix with beans before putting in jars.

—Mrs. David (Naomi) Herschberger, Michigan

There is only one thing worse than a wife who can cook but won't. That's one who can't cook but will!

Miscellaneous

Farm House Cheese

½ tsp. liquid rennet
4 gal. warm milk
¼ c. salt

Stir rennet into warm milk for 1 minute. You do not even have to cool the milk, since it is usually the right temperature right after it's milked. Let stand until thick, then set in warm water. Heat and stir until 120°. Do not overheat. Drain off most of whey. Add salt. Mix and put in a cheese bag. Let drain a few hours.

—Ms. Ada J. Herschberger, Wisconsin

Cheese Spread for a Large Group

10 lb. aged Monterey Jack and 4 lb. Velveeta cheese or all American cheese or 3 lb. aged Colby and 12 lb. Velveeta cheese
4⅔ c. milk
1 c. butter
8 c. cream

Use a big dishpan with hot water. Set another dishpan in hot water in which to make the cheese. Heat milk, butter and cream first until nice and warm. Add cheese, reserving Velveeta to add after other cheese is melted. If Colby or Monterey Jack are shredded first, they will melt faster. Cool off some on a small plate and check if it needs more milk. Store in an airtight container and stir 3 or 4 times until set.

—Mrs. David (Naomi) Herschberger, Michigan

Cheez Whiz

3 pkg. Velveeta cheese
3¼ c. cream
2 c. milk
½ c. butter

Melt cheese in a bowl with a bowl of water beneath it similar to a double boiler. Add cream, milk and butter and make soft. Add a little more milk if you want it thinner.

—Mrs. Henry (Sarah) Mast, Ohio

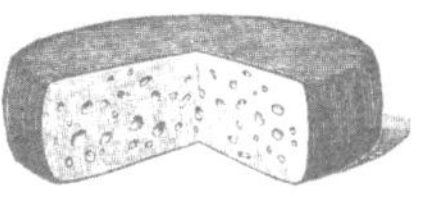

Velveeta Cheese [1]

2½ gal. milk
2 tsp. baking soda
½ c. butter
½ c. cream
1 Tbsp. salt
3 Tbsp. cheddar cheese powder

Let milk sour until thick. When thickened, scald until too hot to touch. Let set for several hours, then drain through a cheese cloth or strainer. Drain well! Crumble curds to make fine crumbs. Add baking soda and mix well. Let set for 2 hours. Place butter in a double boiler and melt. Add curds, cream and salt. Melt until smooth, stirring often. Add cheese powder and pour into buttered containers. Let set until completely cooled. Slice.

—Mrs. Harvey (Lisbet) Mast, Pennsylvania
—Ms. Rachel D. Mast, New York

Velveeta Cheese [2]

1½ lb. dry curd cottage cheese
3 or 4 eggs
2 tsp. salt
salt to taste
¼ c. butter

Mix everything except butter together. Brown butter in a heavy saucepan. Add cheese mixture and cook over low heat until curds are melted.

—Mrs. Noah (Susie) Gingerich, Ohio

Give others a piece of your heart
not a piece of your mind.

Mozzarella Cheese

4 gal. whole milk
5 tsp. citric acid, optional
1 c. cold water, divided
1 tsp. liquid rennet
¾ c. salt
1 gal. water

Pour whole milk into a large stockpot. Dissolve citric acid in ½ c. cold water and add to cold milk. Mix well. Heat to 90°-95°. Remove from heat. Add liquid rennet to ½ c. cold water and add to warm milk. Mix well. Let set for 30 minutes. Cut into 1" square cubes with a long-bladed knife. Do not stir. Let set 5-10 minutes. Heat to 110°, stirring constantly to prevent curds from sticking together. Remove from heat. Let set for 20 minutes, stirring occasionally. Meanwhile mix salt into 1 gal. water and heat to 170°. Drain cheese curds in colander for 15 minutes. Cut or pull apart into small cubes and put in a large bowl. Add hot salt water. Use a wooden spoon and stretch and lift in an upward motion until soft and stretchy. Drain in a colander. Knead a bit and put in container to cool. A bread pan works well. Delicious for pizza or toasted cheese sandwiches or just to snack on.

—Mrs. Levi (Mary) Beller, Michigan

Kraft Cheese

5 c. dry cheese curds
1 Tbsp. baking soda
2 tsp. salt
½ c. butter
½ c. hot cream or milk
¼ c. cheddar cheese powder

Mix curds and baking soda and let stand for 20 minutes. Add butter. Put in double boiler, stirring occasionally while cooking. Cook until curds are melted, then add remaining ingredients. If you want to slice it, omit cream or milk.

—Mrs. Menno (Anna) Hershberger, Kentucky

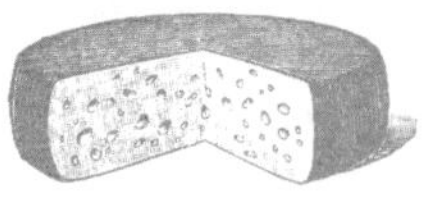

Cooked Cheese

2 tsp. baking soda
5 c. really dry cheese curds, made from sour milk
½ c. butter
1 c. hot cream
2½ tsp. salt
flavorings

Work baking soda into the curds. Let stand a while. Melt butter in a saucepan. Add curds. Stir constantly until melted and smooth. Heat cream and add a little at a time. Add salt and whatever flavoring you wish. I add cheese powder, chicken bouillon and some seasoned salt. This is for a slicing cheese. Add more cream for a spreading cheese.

—Mrs. David (Naomi) Herschberger, Michigan

Marshmallow Creme

2 c. white sugar
2½ c. light corn syrup, divided
1 c. water
⅞ c. egg whites (6)
1 tsp. vanilla
Jell-O, optional

Mix sugar, 2 c. corn syrup and water. Cook to 250°. Cool for 5 minutes. Beat egg whites until fluffy. Add remaining ½ c. warmed corn syrup. Beat again until fluffy. Add first mixture in a fine stream, beating constantly. When mixed, add vanilla. Jell-O may be added if desired. Beat hard. Makes about 3 qt.

—Mrs. Enos (Ada) Mast, New York
—Ms. Esther S. Herschberger, Michigan

Whipped Topping

½ tsp. cream of tartar
¾ c. white sugar
1 egg white
¼ c. boiling water
1 tsp. vanilla

Beat until it stands in peaks. Make sure you start beating soon after the boiling water is added. Add vanilla after you beat it.

—Mrs. Simon (Clara) Miller, Michigan

Church Spread

3 c. brown sugar
2 c. cream
½ gal. light corn syrup
½ tsp. maple flavoring

Boil brown sugar and cream to 260°. Add corn syrup and maple flavoring. Bring to a boil to 230°. Makes 3 qt. It is very good to spread on bread or to use on ice cream.

—Mrs. Emanuel (Esther) Herschberger, Michigan

Spring Jam

5 c. finely chopped rhubarb
3 c. white sugar
½ c. flavored Jell-O

Combine rhubarb and sugar and let stand overnight. The next day mix well. Bring to a boil and cook for 12-15 minutes. Stir in Jell-O. Seal at once.

—Ms. Ada J. Herschberger, Wisconsin

Grape Surprise

1 qt. grapes
1 qt. sugar
½ c. water
5 lb. grapes
5 lb. sugar
½ lb. water

Boil for 25 minutes. Put through a sieve and then can. Makes a delicious jelly that's quickly and easily made.

—Mrs. John (Gertie) Kurtz, Wisconsin

Beet Gel

6 c. beet juice
2 pkg. Sure Jel
1½ c. lemon juice
8 c. sugar
1 sm. pkg. raspberry Jell-O

Boil for 6 minutes. Add Jell-O. Put in jars and seal.

—Mrs. Samuel (Katie) Herschberger, Michigan

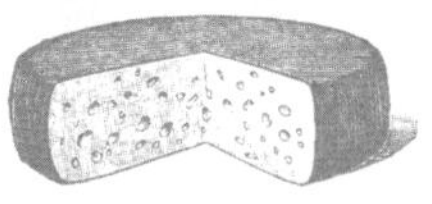

Grandma's Zucchini Jam

6 c. zucchini
¼ c. water
1 pkg. Sure Jel
1¼ c. lemon juice
6 c. sugar
1 c. pineapple
½ c. apricot Jell-O

Peel and shred zucchini. Cook zucchini in water for 10 minutes. Drain and add Sure Jel, lemon juice, sugar and pineapple. Cook 6 more minutes. Now add Jell-O and bring to a boil. Put in jars and seal.

—Ms. Elizabeth J. Herschberger, Michigan

Honey Peach Butter

18 med. peaches, peeled
¼ c. water
2¼ c. sugar
¾ c. honey

Chop peaches coarsely. Cook in water until soft. Press through a sieve or food mill. Measure 6 c. pulp into a large saucepan. Stir in sugar and honey. Heat to boiling point, stirring frequently. Boil gently for 40-50 minutes or until mixture thickens.

—Mrs. Emanuel (Esther) Herschberger, Michigan

Noodles

3 doz. eggs, separated
1 doz. eggs, whole
2 Tbsp. vegetable oil
2 c. water
yellow coloring, optional
flour

Beat all together with egg beater. Add flour until too stiff to stir, then knead until right consistency to cut.

—Mrs. David (Naomi) Herschberger, Michigan

Hot Water Noodles

1 c. hot water
2½ c. egg yolks
salt, optional
10½ c. pastry flour

Mix water with egg yolks. Beat well. Quickly add salt and flour all at once.

—Mrs. Ephraim (Amanda) Mast, Michigan

Homemade Noodles

pastry flour
3 doz. egg yolks
1 Tbsp. salt
1½ c. boiling water

Measure pastry flour in a Fix-and-Mix bowl to weigh 4 lb. including bowl. Beat egg yolks with salt and boiling water until foamy. Make sure water is boiling hot and then beat quickly. Pour into the flour and stir with a large fork. Shape into a ball with hands and cover with lid. Let set for 30 minutes. Knead a bit before rolling them. Work a little lard or butter in them when you shape them into a ball. Makes them easier to roll.

—Mrs. Enos (Ada) Mast, New York

Quick Homemade Noodles

2½ c. egg yolks, beaten
1 c. boiling water
⅓ c. vegetable oil
10 c. pastry flour

Beat egg yolks. Add boiling water. Be sure to keep stirring while adding water. This recipe is easier to work the flour in, than it is the old-fashioned way.

—Mrs. Levi (Sadie) Yoder, Ohio

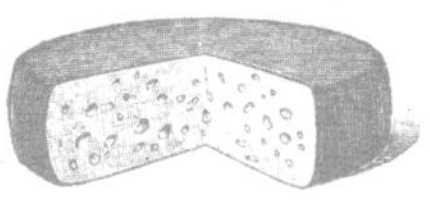

Granulated Soap [1]

1 can lye
4 lb. grease
3 qt. water
2 c. borax
1¼ c. ammonia
½ c. Wisk
2-3 c. granulated detergent

Big Batch:
60 oz. lye
15 qt. water
40 c. grease
10 c. borax
7 c. ammonia
4 c. Wisk
1 box granulated detergent

Sprinkle lye over grease to dissolve. Add cool water. Add borax and ammonia. More borax may be added especially since it makes the soap nice and white. Add Wisk and granulated detergent and stir really well. Then stir occasionally until too thick. Rub through a screen or crumble with hands. Dry for 2-3 weeks, then store in 5 gal. pails with lids.

—Mrs. David (Naomi) Herschberger, Michigan

Granulated Soap [2]

1 can lye (2 c.)
3 qt. cold water
¾ c. borax
4½ lb. lard, melted

Dissolve lye in water and add borax. When dissolved, slowly add lard. You want your lye water and lard the same temperature when you mix it together. Stir slowly and constantly for 10-15 minutes. Stir occasionally for the next 24-36 hours. The soap will be white and granular and easy to handle for all household uses. Will not be in cakes but almost like Tide or Cheer.

—Mrs. Harvey (Lisbet) Mast, Pennsylvania

Homemade Soap [1]

1 box lye
3 qt. cold water
3/4 c. borax
4 1/2 lb. lard, melted
1 box granulated soap

Mix lye in cold water. Add borax and melted lard. Add soap, then stir off and on until cold. To keep softer, add 5 qt. water instead of 3 qt.

—Mrs. David (Naomi) Herschberger, Michigan

Homemade Soap [2]

40 lb. lard
5 c. borax
9 lb. lye
7 1/2 gal. water
10 c. ammonia
1 box Arm & Hammer soap

Heat lard until melted. Add borax and stir until creamy. Pour lye over lard mixture. Keep stirring for 15 minutes. Add water and ammonia. Stir occasionally after it is mixed, 1/2-1 hour is often enough. Add other soap when it is set a little. You may also use any soap you prefer. It doesn't have to be Arm & Hammer. I also use more borax. Makes approx. 15 gal.

—Mrs. Samuel (Naomi) Miller, Wisconsin

Soft Laundry Soap

1 can lye
3 1/2 c. tallow, melted
3 1/2 c. lard, melted
1 c. ammonia
2 c. borax
3 c. Wisk

Use a 5-gal. pail. Fill half full with soft water. Add lye and grease and stir. Add borax, ammonia and Wisk. Mix all together, then add enough water to fill the pail. Stir a few times a day for a week. Use for dishes, grease, hands, laundry, etc. Can also put in extra 3 c. powdered detergent.

—Mrs. David (Naomi) Herschberger, Wisconsin

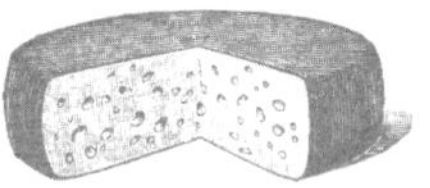

Edible Play Dough

1 c. honey
1 c. creamy peanut butter
2 c. powdered milk

Mix all ingredients together thoroughly. Add more or less powdered milk to achieve preferred consistency. Use chocolate chips, M&M's or raisins for decorations.

—Mrs. John (Esther) Miller, Ohio

Easy Play Dough

food coloring
1 c. water
2 c. flour
1 c. salt

Put a few drops of food coloring in water. Mix flour and salt together, adding water a little at a time. Knead well.

—Ms. Lovina D. Herschberger, Michigan

Play Dough

2½ c. flour
½ c. salt
3 Tbsp. cooking oil
1 Tbsp. powdered alum
2 c. boiling water
food coloring

Mix flour, salt, oil and alum together in a bowl. Add water and food coloring. Stir with a wooden spoon until cool enough to knead. Knead very well until no longer sticky. If kept in an airtight container, this will stay very soft. Fun to make and fun to play with!

—Mrs. Samuel (Naomi) Miller, Wisconsin

No man ever injured his eyesight by looking on the bright side of things.

Rainy Day Play Clay

1 c. flour
½ c. salt
2 tsp. cream of tartar
1 c. water
1 tsp. vegetable oil
food coloring

Mix all ingredients together and stir over low heat until it clings to a spoon. Mixture should form a ball. Remove from saucepan and place on a smooth, dry surface to cool. Knead until smooth. Store in an airtight container. Happy playing!

—Ms. Esther S. Herschberger, Michigan

Clay

2 c. boiling water
2 Tbsp. powdered alum
1 Tbsp. vegetable oil
½ c. salt
food coloring

Stir together. Put on a warm burner until it feels like clay. Place on counter top and knead until smooth. Add food coloring. Store in an airtight container in a cool place.

—Mrs. Neil (Esther) Kauffman, Wisconsin

Kool-Aid Play Dough

4 c. bread flour
1 c. salt
4 c. water
¼ c. vegetable oil
½ c. cream of tartar or
  ¼ c. baking powder and
  ¼ c. baking soda
1 pkg. unsweetened Kool-Aid

Mix all ingredients in a saucepan. Cook and stir over low-medium heat until play dough is formed and no longer looks sticky. Allow to cool slightly before storing in an airtight container. Not edible!

—Mrs. John (Esther) Miller, Ohio

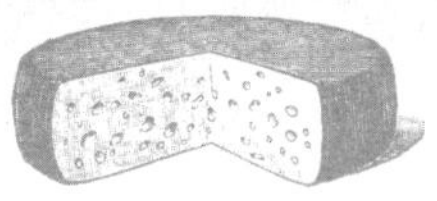

Magic Garden

6 Tbsp. liquid blueing
6 Tbsp. water
6 Tbsp. salt
1 Tbsp. ammonia
coal, rock or clinkers
4 colors food coloring

Mix liquid blueing, water, salt and ammonia together and pour over a lump of coal, piece of rock or clinkers in a deep dish or fish bowl. Add 4 different colors of food coloring at various places. Set aside and watch it grow.

—Ms. Lovina D. Herschberger, Michigan
—Mrs. Henry (Sarah) Mast, Ohio

Bubbles

½ c. Joy liquid dishwashing soap
2 c. water
2 tsp. sugar
food coloring

Mix the solution in a shallow pan. Add food coloring for pretty bubbles. Make bubble wands out of wire clothes hangers, etc. Dip and wave to create bubbles or blow into the wand.

—Mrs. John (Esther) Miller, Ohio

Paint and Varnish Remover

1 can lye
1 qt. cold water
4 Tbsp. (heaping) cornstarch
2 qt. water

1 part vinegar
1 part water

In a pail (not aluminum) add lye to cold water, pouring lye in slowly a little at a time and stirring until dissolved. In second pail, stir cornstarch into water, stirring constantly. Next pour lye mixture into cornstarch mixture, stirring to form a thick paste. Apply to surfaces with an old brush. Use rubber gloves to protect hands. Keep wet for 5 minutes. Flush loosened paint with water. Rinse with solution of 1 part vinegar and 1 part water. Not recommended for oak flours or aluminum surfaces.

—Mrs. David (Naomi) Herschberger, Michigan

Health Advice

Pneumonia Salve

1 (13 oz.) jar Vaseline
½ block camphor
1 tsp. turpentine, no substitutes

Put all ingredients in a saucepan and heat until camphor is completely melted. When cool, pour back into Vaseline jar and use as needed. Rub on chest and back and over lungs. Cover with a warm cloth, and then with plastic to make it sweat. Make sure the plastic is fastened, so the child can't get it in the mouth or nose. Always wear a T-shirt or pajamas over the plastic. Wash off chest and back before taking child outside. Note: You can get camphor in most drugstores or pharmacies.

—Mrs. Enos (Ada) Mast, New York

Homemade Pedialyte

4 tsp. sugar
½ tsp. baking soda
½ tsp. salt or
¼ tsp. salt substitute
3-4 c. boiling water
¼ c. orange Jell-O, optional

Mix well and chill enough to put in baby bottle or drinking cup. Give this to children with diarrhea or for vomiting to prevent dehydration. Jell-O is only for flavor, so they drink it better. Tang or Kool-Aid may also be used. Offer this to them every time they want something to drink.

—Mrs. John (Susan) Miller, New York
—Mrs. Dannie (Lizzie) Yoder, Michigan

A good memory is fine, but the ability to forget is the true test of greatness.

Pedialyte

2 Tbsp. white sugar
1 Tbsp. orange Jell-O
½ tsp. salt
1 qt. boiled water

This is very good to give for flu in bowels and upset stomach. Helps to prevent dehydration when they can't keep anything down.
Note: Try ¼-½ tsp. dry Jell-O if they can't keep anything down.

—*Mrs. Samuel (Malinda) Mast, Pennsylvania*

For Dehydration

4 c. water
1 tsp. salt
8 tsp. sugar

Mix water, salt and sugar. Give the sick child as much of this mixture as they need in small frequent doses. If the child vomits, wait 10-15 minutes and start in again with small frequent doses. Continue until the child starts to void.

This mixture does not contain potassium, so a mashed banana may be given to the child. It is not helpful to make the mixture stronger. Too much salt may cause convulsions in severely dehydrated children. More sugar can aggravate the diarrhea. Raw sugar or sorghum may be used instead of refined sugar but no honey. You may wish to boil the water beforehand but do not add sugar to boiling water as that may decompose the sugar. Dehydrated children should never be given plain water as this may make their condition worse. If the child's condition improves, bananas, rice, applesauce and toast can be given. If the child's condition does not improve or gets worse, seek medical attention because it can be dangerous. You may wish to speed recovery by giving probiotics.

—*Mrs. Enos (Ada) Mast, New York*

A Hot Flu Tonic

1 c. ginger
1 c. diced hot peppers
1 c. garlic
1 c. minced onions
1 c. horseradish
vinegar

Put in a gal. jar and fill up with vinegar. Can start using within 24 hours.

—Mrs. Melvin (Emma) Herschberger, Ohio

Whooping Cough Syrup

½ pt. flaxseed oil
1 qt. water
1 lemon, thinly sliced
pinch of red pepper
2 oz. honey

Simmer everything except honey for 4 hours. Do not boil! Strain while hot. Add honey. If this is less than 1 pt., add enough water to make 1 pt.

—Mrs. David J. (Naomi) Herschberger, Michigan

Favorite Cough Syrup

½ gal. pink clover blossoms
1 qt. water
1 c. white sugar or honey

Simmer clover and water for 1 hour which makes a very dark syrup. Strain and add sugar or honey. Cook until a little syrupy. Give this to child freely. The best cough syrup on the market! We really found this helpful for whooping cough. It really wanted to crystallize for me. Maybe if a little baking soda or vinegar would be added, it wouldn't do that. Makes about 1 c.

—Mrs. Paul (Edna) Brenneman, Michigan

Cough Remedy

1 tsp. cinnamon
1 tsp. nutmeg
½ tsp. ginger
1 tsp. cloves
1 tsp. allspice
½ tsp. dry mustard
lard to make a paste

Make a plaster and put on chest or throat.

—Mrs. Jacob (Sadie) Hershberger, Wisconsin

Pneumonia

a few onions
2-3 Tbsp. lard
1-2 Tbsp. vinegar
cornmeal

Chop onions up or slice and put in a pan with lard. Use more lard depending on how big a poultice you want to make. Fry them until half brown. Remove from heat and add vinegar and enough cornmeal to make a poultice. Don't make it too dry but good and moist. Put between 2 rags and cover up the sides as it crumbles up and falls out when the infection is drawn out. This is good for chest colds and pain in chest and back from pneumonia.

—Mrs Eli (Sarah) Mast, New York

Cough Syrup

handful flat-cedar leaves
2 lbs. raisins
11/2 qt. water (add more if necessary)
1 c. honey

Cook until raisins are mushy, just a slow boil. Press through cloth and add honey. Simmer until syrupy. This should make about one pint. The flat-cedar might be growing in your yard.

—Miss Phoebe T. Hershberger, Wisconsin

- A great relief for arthritis is to drink lots of lemonade made with honey. Drink it every day. It helps!

- For high blood pressure, eat apples, grapes, cranberries or drink their juice. Eat a small amount of honey at each meal.

- Pneumonia Salve—Mix 3 parts starting fluid, capsicum and witch hazel.

- For pneumonia, mix equal parts of ammonia, turpentine and olive oil. Rub on chest and back.

- Liniment—Combine 3 eggs, ½ pt. turpentine and 1 pt. vinegar.

- Spring Tonic—mix sulfur, cream of tartar and Epsom salt in a jar of water. Take 2-3 swallows each morning.

- Dandelion roots are a very good remedy for cancer. You can make a tea with it.

- For appendicitis, take 1 Tbsp. flaxseed in some water.

- For appendicitis, mix equal amounts of turpentine and olive oil. Rub it on the affected area and eat flaxseed.

- Never put warm towels on a child that is croupy. Instead wrap child in a blanket and apply cold, wet towels to neck and chest. Hold and rock child to calm them down as this will help release the swelling of the glands.

- For croup, mix equal amount of ammonia, turpentine and baby oil. Rub on chest. This can be used on babies.

- For croup in babies, rub chest and back with Melaleucca T36 oil or a good grade of tea tree oil.

- When a child has a chest cold or is croupy, hang a cold, wet bed sheet over the child's crib, shutting off all other air. This also helps for asthma and pneumonia victims.

- For diarrhea, eat dried persimmons or raw cucumbers with lots of sugar, vinegar and salt. Also dry strawberry Jell-O helps.

- Mix 1 tsp. flour, 1 tsp. brown sugar, 1 tsp. nutmeg and pinch of salt. Add a little hot water, then drink as soon as you can. Repeat every 4 hours. This is a good remedy for diarrhea.

- Remedy for severe diarrhea in babies—1 c. raw quick oats and 3 c. warm tap water. Mix this together and soak for a few minutes. Strain off water and give to child instead of milk. I barely gave them anything else until it cleared up. Also very good on diaper rash and eczema.

- For diarrhea, heat 1 c. milk but do not boil. Dissolve 1 Tbsp. gelatin in ¼ c. cold water. Let stand a few minutes, then add warm milk and drink as warm as you can. Flavored Jell-O may be added, since children will like it better that way.

- Fry a few onions in 2 Tbsp. lard until half brown. Remove from heat and add 3 Tbsp. apple cider vinegar and enough cornmeal to make a paste and put between cloths and put on chest. This is good for flu, colds, etc.

- Put honey in a double boiler and add onions. Cook until onions are soft. Take this for colds and coughs.

- Dice ½ onion into a pint jar. Add 1 tsp. brown sugar. Let stand for an hour or so. Give 2-3 tsp. of juice every hour for colds.

- If you have a bothersome tickling cough, try chewing on a whole clove. It also sweetens the breath.

- For a cough, rub chest and back with peppermint oil. This will often help.

- Pedialyte Pep—Bring 4 c. water to a boil, then add 1 Tbsp. sugar, ½ tsp. salt and 2 Tbsp. orange Jell-O or mix in Tang. Let cool. Give to drink whenever they want. If a child is sick and doesn't want to eat, this will keep them from dehydrating. Can also be used for adults.

- Drinking warm Jell-O water will oftentimes settle an upset stomach.

- For fever, take egg white and beat it with spoon until foamy. Add a little sugar and a little hot water and drink it.

- To reduce fever in children, soak a washcloth in a little alcohol and place on chest.

- Try using vanilla on cuts, bruises or burns. This works as a pain killer.

- For burns, wet area with cold water and sprinkle table salt on the spot. It will stop the burn and will not blister. Do this immediately.

- To rid yourself of poison ivy, stir some alum into Vaseline. Put this mixture on affected area until it's gone.

- For headache relief, place a wet, hot vinegar cloth over the forehead.

- For car sickness, place a few cotton balls in a tight plastic bag. Squirt in 2 drops lavender oil. When you get sick, take a whiff.

- For bed wetting, give the child 1 tsp. honey before going to bed. Also let the child eat lots of raisins. Parsley tea made of 1 tsp. (heaping) parsley per 2 c. water is also good to drink 3 times a day.

- For bedwetting, try B-complex with iron or a good multivitamin.

- For earache, dip cotton swab in olive oil. Sprinkle with black pepper and apply to ear.

- For earache, dip cotton in molasses and put in ear. Pain will cease.

- For mad dog bites, wash the bitten part in vinegar water 2-3 times daily. Give a teaspoon vinegar and water every morning for 2-3 days.

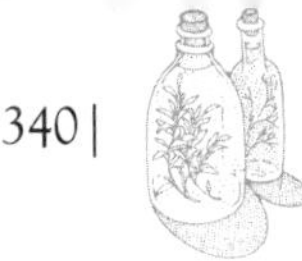

- Rub a bee sting with an onion slice for relief.
- Put some baking soda on a knife. Put a few drops of vinegar on it—just enough to make a paste, and put on bee sting.
- For bee sting or any kind of sting, use a stainless steel knife to hold on stings. It will pull out the poison.
- For bee stings, wet the injured area and apply meat tenderizer. It stops the pain immediately.
- If a person is allergic to bee stings, put a little Tender Quick on sting and give allergy medicine.
- Vinegar in your rinse water when you wash your hair will mean no more dandruff.
- Mix equal parts of baking soda and salt. Use occasionally to brush teeth. It will make them feel very clean.
- Wild cherry bark is a very good remedy for toothache. You can make a tea with it. Put some in your mouth and hold it, then swallow it. In a couple minutes, your toothache will disappear.
- To get gum out of hair, soak with baby oil, and it will easily comb out.
- If you burn your tongue, try sprinkling a few grains of sugar on it for instant relief.
- If chickens have a cold, use 2 oz. red pepper, 4 oz. allspice and 6 oz. ginger. Mix in pail with feed and give 2-3 times a week.
- Of all the home remedies, a good wife is best.

Home Remedies for Horses

- Salve for wire scratches (grease heal)—mix equal parts of sulfur, alum and fat. Heat and stir until mixed. Stir until it cools without separating. Store in a cool place.

- Mix 2 parts 7% iodine and 1 part castor oil. Pour in a spray bottle. Put lime on the cut in the morning and the castor oil mix in the evening. Use this right away, and it seldom gives infection or proud flesh. It also works when a flap of skin is hanging loose. No stitching required. The flap will dry up and heal off. It is very important to use lime to keep it dry. Treat daily.

- For proud flesh, peel the inner white lining from an egg shell. Apply the wet side of the lining to the proud flesh. It will thump for 30 minutes. After a few days the proud flesh should be gone. This treatment might fail if the proud flesh is a couple months old.

- Another treatment for proud flesh is to take some wood ashes. Pour boiling water over it and let set a little. Soak the proud flesh in this water as hot as the victim can take it. Repeat every day or so until the proud flesh is gone. Both of these proud flesh treatments work for man and beast.

—Mrs. Enos (Ada) Mast, New York

Tips and Hints

- Never bleach your laundry. It shortens the life of your laundry by half. Instead use 1 c. baking soda and a good soap. Use good hot water.
- Glue can be loosened by soaking spot with a cloth soaked in vinegar.
- Ink can be removed from clothes if you spray with hair spray. Allow to dry and spray again until it's all off or spray several times before putting in wash machine.
- To remove ink from cloth, use peroxide.
- Hairspray takes out ink marks on clothing.
- For whiter socks, boil them in water to which a lemon slice has been added.
- To remove blood from clothes, use rubbing alcohol.
- To remove blood stains from clothing, use peroxide. It will bubble right out.
- To remove blood stains, dampen the spot with cold water then rub in salt. Let set about a half hour, then rinse in cool water.
- As the mother of small children who get their share of boo-boos, I have found that shampoo works well to remove blood stains from clothing. Any brand of plain shampoo works. Use with cool water, and it will take the blood out quickly.
- To make your own Spray-n-Wash, mix 1 c. ammonia, 1 c. water and 1 c. Wisk or liquid soap together. Spray on soiled spots or dirty laundry.
- For window cleaner, mix 1 qt. alcohol and 1 Tbsp. detergent. Add enough water to make 1 gal. Put in spray bottle.
- Hot water sets a stain and cold water does too. Tepid water often takes out a stain without any soap.

- Put a dab of vinegar in your rinse water when doing laundry. It's a natural water softener, and it takes the soap out of clothes.
- To remove rust from clothes, soak the material in lemon juice, then cover it with table salt. Lay it in the sun, like inside a window. When really dry, wash the material. If it doesn't come out, try it again. It should work on white Sunday clothes too.
- Make a paste of water and cream of tartar to remove rust.
- If your baby is bothered with diaper rash, try adding ⅔ c. vinegar to the last rinse water when doing laundry.
- When ironing starched whites and brown spots appear, try cleaning with peroxide. They usually disappear.
- Soak white handkerchiefs in a pan of cold water along with ⅓ tsp. cream of tartar. Soak for 30 minutes, and then wash as usual. This keeps them snowy white.
- For a bleach for fine organdy, try salt mixed with lemon juice. Smear on spot and lay in bright sunshine for several hours. Wash in soap and water.
- Add 1 tsp. Epsom salts to each gallon of water, and colored garments will neither fade nor run.
- To keep your laundry from freezing so hard, add a cup of vinegar to your rinse water. This will also soften your wash.
- To prevent clothes from sticking to the washline on a cold day, wipe the line with a cloth dampened with vinegar.
- Rub vinegar and alcohol over hands just before hanging out wash when weather is cold. Dry hands thoroughly before going out. This keeps them from getting so cold.
- Put tinfoil under your ironing board to make ironing easier.

Cleaning

- Use fabric softener sheets for removing dust, etc. from window screens. This way they don't always need to be washed.

- Amazing Cleaner—Mix 1 c. ammonia, 1 c. vinegar, 1/4 c. baking soda and 1 gal. water. This works well for cleaning walls and for taking off extra varnish.

- Use baking soda to clean your stove top, kitchen counters and stainless steel.

- To give copper-bottom pans that shiny look, just sprinkle salt on the bottom and wipe with a vinegar cloth.

- Add a little baking soda to your dishwater. This will help clean dishes. It also helps clean meat jars more easily.

- To take lime out of tea kettle, put marbles in or set outside in 0° weather to freeze. Have kettle wet to set out. Repeat if necessary. Also putting a few drops of vinegar in tea kettle with water every time you fill it helps keep lime loose.

- Corningware can be cleaned by dropping in water with 2 denture cleaning tablets. Let stand for 30-45 minutes.

- Cold Weather Window Cleaner—Mix 1/2 c. ammonia, 2 Tbsp. cornstarch, 1 c. white vinegar and 1/2 c. rubbing alcohol. Put in a bucket of warm water and use to prevent ice from forming on your windows while washing.

- Want a sparkling clean thermos? Fill with water and add 1 or 2 tables of Efferdent denture cleaner. Let stand overnight.

- Always rinse your dishrag in cold water and you'll have a sparkling clean, fresh smelling dishrag.

- To wash dirty combs, soak in hot baking soda water.

- Baking powder will remove tea or coffee stains from china pots or cups.

- Dish cleaner—Fill a stainless steel canner 3/4 full of cold

water. Pour in 1 c. bleach, 1 c. lye and 1 c. Cheer or Tide. Keep heated. This cleans your Tupperware, plastic cookware, silverware, etc. Just dip in this water. Remove and wash thoroughly. Be sure to remove all handles of your cookware beforehand. Wear rubber gloves.

- A splash of rubbing alcohol in your window washing water will make them sparkle and dry easily.

- Toothpaste removes lead pencil marks from most painted surfaces.

- If your hands smell from handling onions or fish, rub toothpaste on them and wash with soap. The smell is gone.

- To clean a narrow-necked milk bottle, fill it up with water and a few drops of ammonia. Within a few minutes the bottle will be sparkling clean. This also works for meat jars.

- Yellow bathtubs or sinks will return to their original whiteness if washed in turpentine and salt.

- Fill blender partways with water. Add a drop of detergent. Cover and turn on for a few seconds. Rinse, drain and dry.

- Don't panic if you accidently scorch the inside of your favorite saucepan. Just fill the pan halfway with water and add 1/4 c. baking soda. Boil a while until the burned portions loosen and float on top.

- Before washing fine china or crystal, place a towel in the bottom of the sink as a cushion.

- To remove lime deposits from tea kettles, fill with equal parts of vinegar and water. Bring to a boil and allow to stand overnight.

- Use a wet kerosene cloth to clean window screens. This way they don't always need to be washed.

- Following a spill on the oven, sprinkle immediately with salt. When oven is cool, brush off burnt food and wipe with a damp sponge.

Gardening

- Plant Food—Mix 1 tsp. baking powder, 1 tsp. saltpetre, 1 tsp. Epsom salts and ½ tsp. ammonia in 1 gal. tepid rain water. Store in a glass jug. Water houseplants every 6 days.
  —*Mrs. David (Barbara) Herschberger*
- Here is a garden tonic that works well to boost plants. Mix 1 Tbsp. Epsom salts, 1 Tbsp. ammonia, 1 Tbsp. baking powder, 1 Tbsp. saltpetre and 1 gal. rainwater. Apply every 2 weeks or less. This is also works for tomato blight, etc.
- For beautiful houseplants, give them a little of this mixture once a week: 1 tsp. cream of tartar, 1 tsp. ammonia, 2 tsp. saltpetre, 1 tsp. Epsom salts and 1 gal. water.
- For little mites or bugs on your impatients, mix 1 tsp. red pepper, 1 Tbsp. ammonia and 2 Tbsp. dish soap. Mix in a pint of water and spray your flowers.
- Save the water when you boil eggs. When cool, use it to water seedlings or houseplants.
- Ferns and other houseplants like leftover coffee or coffee grounds.
- A few drops of ammonia added to each quart of water for watering houseplants will improve the color of plants.
- Your African violet will bloom longer and more abundantly if you stick a few rusty nails in the soil beside them.
- After watering African violets, pour hot water on tray and let the roots absorb it. Never let the leaves get wet. Coffee also works fine. Add fertilizer every other week.
- Give your flowers and vegetable plants dry oatmeal. This gives them a meal to live on. When planting, put 1 Tbsp. in hole.
- For carrot and radish pests, add a little salt when planting and the worms will keep away.
- Worms won't bother tomatoes if you plant dill nearby.
- When planting radishes, sprinkle plenty of wood ashes in the row to deter worms.

- Tomato Blight—Mix 1 gal. water, 1 Tbsp. saltpetre, 1 Tbsp. Epsom salts, 1 Tbsp. baking powder and 1 tsp. ammonia. Give 1 pt. of this mixture to each plant for 2 weeks.
  —*Mrs. Noah (Malinda) Raber*

- Blight in tomatoes is often a lack of calcium. Push 2 Tums in the soil beside the plant soon after planting to help.

- Epsom salts are really good for tomatoes. Combine 1 Tbsp. Epsom salts and 1 gallon water. Give to each tomato plant every week while they're blooming. This helps with blight, and it will also help produce more tomatoes. It also helps if you mulch your tomato plants with straw, newspaper or old hay to keep the tomatoes from rotting in summer.

- For spray for blight on tomatoes and celery, dissolve 1 cake Ivory soap in 1 qt. water. When dissolved remove from stove and add 4 oz. saltpetre, 4 oz. borax, 3 qt. rain water and 1 pt. ammonia. Store in a glass container and keep covered tightly. To spray, use 1 Tbsp. of this to 1 qt. water to spray plants.

- For blight in raspberries, spray throughout summer with lime and sulfur water.

- You can hardly pile too much manure on rhubarb. For thick, long juicy rhubarb stalks, cover the bed thickly with up to 1 ft. horse manure in the fall and leave on through the growing season.

- For tasty melons, mix 6½ Tbsp. Epsom salts and 3½ Tbsp. borax with 5 gal. water. Apply when vines start to run again and when fruit is about 2" in diameter. Melons do not cross with cucumbers or pumpkins, so you can't blame flat taste on cross pollination. We really like this recipe, and they seem to taste sweeter. When they started to give fruit, I gave them some every 4 weeks or however needed.

- Booster for sweet melons: mix 1 Tbsp. ammonia, 1 Tbsp. saltpetre, 1 Tbsp. Epsom salts and 1 Tbsp. baking soda well in 1 gal. water. Divide between 6 melon plants every 2 weeks. Also works well on other plants.

- To kill dandelions, apply vinegar.
- Round-up Solution—Dissolve 1 gal. vinegar, 1 bottle Palmolive soap and 1 c. salt before putting in sprayer. For best results apply on a sunny day. Works well! No more trimming.
- For weed killer, mix 1 gal. white vinegar, 3 c. salt and 1 bottle detergent and spray.
- Pour the hot water from your cold packer along the sidewalk to kill weeds.
- To keep potato bugs under control, pick the bugs off the potato plants and drown them in kerosene. During the first part of the season, do this daily. Later in the season, go over the patch once or twice a week. It's important to get the bugs before they grow up to adults but still get the tiny ones and the eggs if they are found. If this is done regularly, it probably won't take longer than dusting them would to keep them controlled.
- We like to wait until after hard rains to plant our main garden. It seems things do better, and there are a lot fewer weeds to deal with.
- For easy rooting of rose cuttings, stick the end into a potato and plant, potato and all.
- If you have a small strawberry patch and would like to have more and bigger berries, take your extra milk and spread it on the patch. You can start in fall and put it on until after the ground is frozen.
- When putting away carrots, potatoes, onions, cabbage, apples, squash or anything else that you put up in the fall, wait until it's new moon, and it will keep a lot better.
- Do not peel pumpkins or squash. Wash them, remove seeds and put them into a pressure cooker with very little water (½-1 c.). Cook them for 10 minutes, timing after cooking starts. The shells will then come off easily and they are ready to use.
- For your worms on cabbage, mix 1 c. flour and 2 Tbsp. cayenne pepper. Mix and sprinkle over cabbage.

Miscellaneous

- Sharpen sewing machine needles by stitching through sandpaper.
- Keep patterns from tearing and wrinkle-free by spraying with spray starch.
- When doing hand sewing with double thread, tie a knot in each thread instead of tying them together.
- Your thread will never knot or kink when sewing if you always knot the end of thread that first leaves the spool.
- Dip broken shoelace tip into clear nail polish and allow tip to harden. The new tip will last a long time.
- Fresh cut flowers will last longer in a vase if ¼ Tbsp. or 20 drops of Clorox bleach is added to each quart of water.
- Scratches on light stained furniture can be hidden by using tan shoe polish. However, only use on shiny finishes.
- To make your own room air freshener, cut an orange in half, remove pulp and fill peel with salt. This has proven effective in absorbing strong orders all around the house.
- To thread needles, apply some hairspray to your finger and to the end of the thread, stiffening the thread enough to be easily threaded.
- For homemade fly paper, simmer equal amounts of sugar, corn syrup and water until granules dissolve. Brush onto narrow strips cut from paper bags.
- To stop ants in your pantry, seal off cracks with putty and petroleum jelly. Also try sprinkling red pepper on floors and counter tops.
- Sharpen scissors by cutting through steel wool.

- For chimney fires, pour a good amount of baking soda or salt in the stove. Never use flour.

- For plucking chickens, add 2 Tbsp. baking soda to 4 gal. water.

- To increase the life of flashlight batteries, take some sandpaper and sand the ends of the batteries after they are dim and they'll brighten up again.

- To get rid of flies at an upstairs or attic window, set a small amount of kerosene on the windowsill. For some reason, the flies just tumble in.

- If your bottom cellar step is painted white, it may help prevent many a fall in the dark.

- Place sulfur where rats and mice run. They won't go through sulfur.

- To sharpen noodle maker cutting knives, try running a piece of Emery cloth through the cutting apparatus 1 forward and 1 backward. We did this for ours and now it works like a charm.

- When making homemade noodles, a quick and easy way to dry and cut them is clean your stove top. Heat it to where you can hardly stand having your hand on it. Make a few noodles hot by laying them on the stove top. Cut them immediately while they are still warm.

- A small crack in chinaware disappears if boiled in milk.

- Before pouring hot water into a glass, put a spoon in it. This will prevent cracking.

- A rule to remember is "Left is loose and right is tight."

- To keep your stove from clogging up with tar, throw 1 c. rock salt in stove each day.

- Keep several moth balls in your mailbox or swing set to keep wasps from building nests in it.

- To get rid of starlings, feed them beef tallow until you draw in thousands from your whole area. Mix a batch with a lot of salt, maybe 1/4 salt. In about a day your whole area will be rid of them. They carry disease from lot to lot.

- A jar lid or a couple of marbles in the bottom of a double boiler will rattle when the water gets low or warn you to add more water before the pan scorches or burns.

- Instead of using commercial waxes, shine with rubbing alcohol.

- Spray furniture polish on your iron, so it will iron smoothly.

- Try a drop of vinegar on a tissue. It is the best thing yet to clean your eyeglasses but don't use on plastic.

- For hardened brown sugar, place the sugar in a big kettle. Set a saucer on top and put a wet sponge on the saucer. Cover tightly with a lid for several days and your sugar will be soft again.

Meanie and Moe's Bakery

Eenie, Meanie, Miney, and Moe,
Tied their aprons with a bow;
Measured the yeast and stirred the dough;
And in the pans the globs they throw.
They watched the ovens, their eyes aglow;
Browning the loaves, just like a pro;
And off to the market - there they go!
Eenie, Meanie, Miney, and Moe.

Jonas A. Shrock

Index

Appetizers, Beverages and Dips

Pancakes and Cereals

Breads and Rolls

Cakes and Frostings

Cookies and Bars

Pies

Desserts

Meats and Main Dishes

Soups and Salads

Candies and Snacks

Canning

Large Quantities

Miscellaneous

Health Advice

Give Mom a gift she will cherish and enjoy. Give her

Traditional Country Cooking.

'YOU'LL FIND TRADITIONAL COUNTRY COOKING THE PERFECT COOKBOOK TO USE AROUND THE HOUSE. SO TAKE IT AND START ENJOYING TODAY … THE TRADITIONAL WAY!'

Traditional Country Cooking

o Order Traditional Country ooking, check your local ookstore or contact:

Emanuel Herschberger
Post Office Box 93
Jasper, NY 14855

ONLY $14.95!

Do you know a young bride who would benefit for the tasty recipes and tips found in Traditional Country Cooking? Help her achieve delicious cooking skills by presenting her with

Traditional Country Cooking.

'YOU'LL FIND TRADITIONAL COUNTRY COOKING THE PERFECT COOKBOOK TO USE AROUND THE HOUSE. SO TAKE IT AND START ENJOYING TODAY … THE TRADITIONAL WAY!'

To Order Traditional Country Cooking, check your local bookstore or contact:

Emanuel Herschberger
Post Office Box 93
Jasper, NY 14855